Complete Guide for Horse Business Success

The Complete Guide for Horse Business Success, 2nd Edition

ID# 2456
ISBN: 1-59247-300-8

Printed in The United States of America

Scholargy Publishing
17855 N. Black Canyon Hwy.
Phoenix AZ 85023
www.scholargy.com

Author
Janet E. English, CPA

Disclaimer

Every effort has been made in the writing of this book to present accurate and up-to-date information based on the best available and most reliable sources. The use and results of this information depend upon a variety of factors not under the control of the author or publisher of this book. The author and publisher of this book also recognize that the information is subject to change from year to year. Therefore, neither the author nor the publisher assumes any responsibility for, nor makes any warranty with respect to, results that may be obtained from the information contained herein. Neither the publisher nor the author shall be liable to anyone for damages resulting from reliance on any information contained in this book whether with respect to taxation, liability, contractual agreements, or by reason of any misstatement or inadvertent error contained herein.

The reader is encouraged to procure the services of a CPA and an attorney for specific advice on taxation and legal issues, according to the short-term and long-term goals of the individual horse business.

Table of Contents

6

Dedication

To Gene, who gave me horses.

Preface

This book was originally written as an outgrowth of a class called Equine Business Principles that I developed as part of the curriculum for the Equine Science Department of Scottsdale Community College in Scottsdale, Arizona. At that time there were many good business books to be found and much had been written about horses, but a book on equine business was not available.

The purpose of this book was, and remains, to address what I call the "real world" of horses as a business. It was written for those who want to have a business involving horses but do not know where to begin; and for those who may not be aware that they already have a valid business, and are in need of some business guidance. And no less important, it was written for the classroom as a practical hands-on textbook.

This second edition retains all of the original material which has been revised and enlarged to include much more in the way of useful information.

Janet E. English, CPA

Troy, Missouri

Introduction

People who rely on their horse activities for part or all of their income frequently find themselves needing good business advice. The most important advice I can give is to start off with a sound business plan.

Record keeping is a must for any business. Keeping adequate and accurate records may not sound very appealing, but it is one of the primary factors that the Internal Revenue Service considers in determining whether a horse operation is a legitimate business. Most activities of an equine operation need to be recorded. Detailed records should be kept on activities like breeding, boarding, health care, and registration. Financial records should document income and expense, buying and selling horses, employee payrolls, contracts, installment sales, and depreciation.

Accounting and taxation are perhaps the most difficult subjects to understand when applied to the horse industry. These topics are covered in a fashion to provide the present or future business owner with a basic understanding, but it would also be wise to consult a tax advisor.

This book will also help equine entrepreneurs develop effective marketing strategies, find insurance policies to fit their needs, and use computer programs specifically designed to help them manage their operations more efficiently.

Every horse owner can benefit from reading this book, but it should be especially helpful for those who wish to succeed in the horse business.

ECONOMIC & BUSINESS ESSENTIALS

Fig. 1–1.

Getting started in the horse business is no longer a simple agricultural undertaking. In fact, the horse industry has evolved into a complex and dynamic part of the economy. Consequently, it has become necessary that horse business owners operate in a knowledgeable, professional manner. Understanding basic business principles, keeping adequate business records, and planning for the future are essential to the success of any horse business. By seeking knowledge and advice from experts, owners can keep informed of industry trends and can make educated financial forecasts their businesses.

HORSE INDUSTRY TRENDS IN THE 1990'S

The horse industry was experiencing a boom time in 1985. At that time racetracks were flourishing, unhampered by competition from casinos and lotteries. This was also a time when horses were considered a very good investment because of the advantages in tax laws and very high prices horses were commanding. Beginning in 1986 that would change.

More than a few people were caught up in the schemes and dreams of immense financial rewards in the 1980s. Hopefully we have learned that horses are not works of art to be marketed as speculative investments, but are rather to be used for work or recreation in partnership with people.

The desire for partnership with horses that is shared by so many people is what has carried the horse industry back to a period of growth. This is in spite of the cost of equestrian hobbies, harsh regulations, loss of open areas for riding, and things like liability insurance expense. The horse industry has become more realistic because of the excesses in the past. The number of people involved in the horse industry continues to grow as does the need for pleasure and performance horses.

In spite of the increasing competition from casinos, lotteries and dog racing tracks, as well as other forms of entertainment, racing devotees take comfort in the statistics showing increases in wagering totals, foal crops, purse money, and other critical aspects of the sport. Most racing trends these days indicate longed-for stability and incremental growth.

MONETARY RISK & PROFITABILITY

Investing money in any business is a gamble—the greater the investment, the greater the risk. The most obvious example is horseracing, where high profit is attainable, but with it comes substantial investment and some risk. However, being educated on the characteristics of the industry greatly reduces the risk and increases the profit potential. Personal experience, education, and willingness to seek input from experts in the field greatly enhance the likelihood of profitability.

Racing Operation

Just as in other businesses, the owner of a racing operation must have a good plan and know just what the goals of the business are. Choosing the right horses and matching them to the tracks where they will be raced is the foundation of a racing operation. Then the owner needs to put in place a system of buying and keeping horses to maintain the racing business until that super horse is found.

One safe and simple way to run a profitable operation may be to work from the viewpoint of stalls, not horses. Instead of looking at the horses purchased as long term assets and making plans and setting goals around these horses, a more profitable strategy is to decide how many stalls the operation can maintain year around.

The plan is to keep a set number of stalls filled with winning horses. This would mean constantly purchasing, selling, trading, upgrading, and culling instead of having a fixed group of horses. It would also mean selling horses at a profit when the market is right and constantly culling the unprofitable ones. This allows the owner the opportunity to keep a set number of stalls filled with winning horses. And the more horses that are run through the operation, the better chance of finding or developing a major stakes winner.

The idea is to buy right and to sell when a profit can be made, thus maximizing the yield on each horse. To do this it is necessary not to hold on to horses for any reason other than to profit the business, in other words not to "fall in love" with certain horses. This does not mean that the horses receive any less care or that time is not allowed for development of a good horse. Some good runners may stay for many years. But to maintain the number of stalls, every horse in the barn needs to be for sale, always. That way the profit can be used to purchase new horses that may make more money for the operation.

Using this method, the owner is more able to correctly compute the costs involved in running the operation. It is a simple matter to total the costs for trainer, veterinarian, and farrier along with trailering and other miscellaneous items. For example these could total to around $50 per day or about $18,000 per year per stall. If three stalls were kept full at the racetrack, the operation would actually need to have four or five horses. This is because there will always be some horses that are not old enough to race, or are laid up because of injury or for R&R. It is generally calculated that one and a half horses are needed per stall. Of course, every situation if different. If dealing in mostly unraced young stock the percentage will be even higher and could be lower with actively racing older horses.

In any new business venture it is wise to have an amount equal to six months' expenses held in reserve and racing operations are no exception. The three stalls will require cash reserves of approximately $34,000. This would include the one or two inactive horses. Expenses for these horses can be calculated at one half the cost of the racing horses. The cash reserve will allow for a number of unprofitable months without causing the business to be in dire straights or having to resort to panic measures. The owner who cannot manage to have this amount in reserve should not attempt any kind of business venture.

The best plan is to begin with three or four stalls and endeavor to keep them filled with active, profitable horses, little by little increasing the numbers. It is all to easy to acquire too many horses, too hastily. But at the same time, movement of horses is also very important in order to have a chance at coming up with a really great horse. For that reason more than one or two stalls are needed in the beginning. In time, the number of stalls can be doubled and then even tripled as long as a carefully controlled operation is maintained with a constantly higher quality of horse being acquired.

The next step is to find a way to buy racehorses at a moderate price. A price that will allow for the development of the horse's potential and the possibility of earning enough in race winnings to cover the original purchase amount, or perhaps a selling price of that amount or more.

These young unraced horses are not a wise choice for a small stable with a limited amount of capital. In order to become markedly successful at buying and developing yearlings and two-year-olds, the owner would need to have an especially well run operation with large amounts of cash to invest. Proven and predictable racehorses are a much better choice for investment. These horses can be acquired through private purchase and claiming races. It is possible to develop a good racehorse stable in this manner, as it will allow for less risk more action and earlier returns.

It is possible that a $10,000 to $50,000 claim could turn out to be a profitable asset; and it is even possible that such a horse will develop into a Graded stakes winner.

A wise alternative to claiming is to buy active horses privately, from breeders or owners. This way the horse can have a prepurchase exam, can be observed in training, and can be carefully evaluated. None of which is possible when claiming a horse. A really good horse that is sound in every way will not be low-priced, but it is far better to pay the price for a horse with a proven record and years of racing life left. And this makes more sense than paying an equal amount on a yearling that has never been on a racetrack.

In order to procure quality racehorses, it is best to work with a trainer who knows this element of racing business and to seek out the horse operations who have a reputation for selling successful horses.

Although the foundation of the business should be proven, active racers, it is good to mingle in an occasional younger, less expensive and unproven horse.

Begin with a limited number of stalls, provide expert care, concentrate on active racehorses, don't become enamored with certain horses, and move as many horses as feasible - this is a formula for success in the racing business.

The Business of Breeding

In every breed there are those who consistently produce outstanding horses—for racing, three-day eventing, show and performance, rodeo, and competitive trail riding. The breeding business is a vital and necessary aspect of the horse industry.

Some have entered the business in search of that one special horse and have stayed to produce many quality specimens for the sales market. A large number of horse owners have entered the Thoroughbred breeding business because they have outstanding racehorses that can no longer race due to injuries or age. Lately, however, there have been more newcomers to the breeding business who have done so strictly as a business venture.

Whatever the reasons for entering into the business of breeding horses, the considerations are the same. Of foremost importance is the quality of breeding stock and goals of the breeding operation.

The business may be breeding for the sales market, or for private treaty sales or may be involved in raising and training of horses for the show or rodeo circuit, or the racing sector. In any event, the business of breeding horses is not a seasonal endeavor, but requires year-round management, planning, and work.

During November, a breeding preparation program will be started for the open and barren mares and replacement fillies. In December and January, the stallions are prepared for breeding season, which usually begins around the middle of February and lasts until the middle of June. During this time the mares will be foaling and being rebred for the next year. June can be a very hectic month with all the foals on the ground and they require a lot of attention over and above the ordinary mare care. As soon as the breeding season is over and the herd health needs attended to, attention turns to the preparation of yearlings for their various sales. And then there are registration papers to be filed. In the fall months foals will be weaned from their dams and the process begins all over.

Breeding horses can be quite expensive because of the length of time it takes to produce a live foal and all the variables involved in that undertaking. The gestation period for horses is 11 months and every mare bred does not produce a live foal every year (the national average is less than 75% conception rate), so there is unproductive time. In addition to the cost of acquiring the mares, there is the cost of stud fees or the purchase price and cost of maintenance for a stallion, in addition to the cost of daily keep for the mares, veterinary care, farrier, insurance, and other costs. For those reasons careful planning of each mating is a must.

Careful consideration should be given to the goals of the breeding business. Are the mares of the quality needed to produce foals that will fulfill these goals? Has she been bred to the very best stallion for this purpose? Has the mare had problems with being barren in the past?

It is very important to make the proper arrangement for the mare at a farm that is satisfactory prior to sending the mare there. A good reputation takes time to build and a farm with a good reputation may well be worth a higher rate.

Standing a stallion is a separate and distinct business from boarding mares. It requires specialized facilities, plus a qualified, experienced crew. Whether a farm stands one stallion or ten, a competent stallion handler is vital. Standing a stallion includes not only the physical breeding operation but requires personal contacts, advertising, and public relations on the part of the stallion manager and the farm.

Whatever the goals of the breeding business remember that quality is the best investment.

Other Horse Business Concepts

Not everyone who is in the horse business is involved in breeding, raising, and training horses. There are many other business ventures that include horses. Riding instruction, horse care, horse vacations, horse sales, and horse product creations and repairs are a few of the horse business undertakings to be considered. Each of these business concepts has its profit potential and its demands on the owners.

Riding Instruction

Riding instruction includes private or group lessons using the owner's horses or those belonging to the students. This concept might also include activities such as clinics and day camps for children and adults. The principle of the business should have special teaching skills and a good education in various types of riding at many levels. It is helpful (though not absolutely necessary) to have instructor certification from the equine department of a college or university.

In creating a successful business giving riding lessons, there are fundamental areas that require special consideration. First of all, the horses chosen must be suitable for the riders. The teacher/owner must be able to communicate well, and goals of the lessons must be practical.

Horses chosen for a lesson program must be safe, sound, and gentle and have smooth gaits. Because they will be carrying

8

inexperienced riders, they cannot be nervous or high strung, and must have a forgiving nature. Geldings tend to be the best choice for lessons. Mares can be quite good for lessons also, although some may not be consistent enough for beginning riders. Whether gelding or mare, the horse should not be less than six years old.

Because riding instructors must be able to see something from the ground and communicate it to the student, there is a great need for communication skills. It is not enough to be a good trainer and rider, good teachers must genuinely like people and be able to make their instruction understood by the students.

Lessons will need to be tailored to the needs, abilities, and desires of the students. Adults quite often want to learn to ride for relaxation or exercise, while young children usually just want to learn to ride. And both adults and children may want to prepare for competition. The teacher must recognize those differences in the students and have realistic goals for the lessons.

A riding instruction business also requires appropriate facilities, tack and other equipment, and proximity to an adequate consumer base.

The profit potential of riding instruction can be low or high, depending upon the instructor's training and skills and the way the business is set up. Holding clinics for a large number of persons could be quite profitable, while individual private lessons may not generate a lot of income. Most likely there would be a combination of these factors.

Insurance costs for this type of business can be quite high, especially where there is no certified instructor. And the hours of instruction will need to vary to meet the time frame of the students. For the person who loves to teach, this business can be rewarding and enjoyable.

Boarding and Horse Care

Some people are happiest with a hands-on business of horse care. This concept could include short- or long-term boarding, foaling out or lay up boarding, and equine retirement. It could also include horse-sitting where the care is provided at the customer's barn.

This business requires thorough horse-care knowledge, safe structures for the horses, access to trails, adequate area for customers to ride and school their horses, and the ability to get along well with people and horses.

The profit potential for a horse care business will most likely not be very high, unless there is a large volume of horses involved. Repairs and maintenance to the horse property will be an ongoing issue as horses are known to be quite hard on fences and stalls. In addition, there will be a need for liability insurance and perhaps care, custody, and control insurance as well. *(See Chapter 7 for more information about insurance.)*

Horse Vacations

For those who love to entertain, a horse vacation business could be quite appealing. It could be a bed-and-breakfast, guest ranch, group retreats, and seminars or adventure travel.

This business requires highly attractive and well-maintained facility and grounds, a scenic or otherwise appealing location, opportunities for recreation, and horses even a beginner can ride. Business ventures of this nature must be licensed, and open to inspection by various agencies. This is a business for people who do not require a lot of privacy.

The profit potential depends on the facility, the fee that could be charged, and the amount of time open for business.

Horse Sales

The business of horse sales could include acting as an agent of horses for sale (brokering), selling horses that are purchased for resale (trading), and the sale of young stock raised by the business.

This type of business requires an extensive network of horse world contacts, a well-developed eye for horse flesh, up-to-date knowledge of the horse market, the ability to fit out and train horses, good breeding stock, horse care and breeding expertise, and an attractive and accessible location.

The profit potential of horse sales could be quite high, depending upon how well costs are controlled and the horses involved.

Horse sales is the ideal business venture for people who love to sell. There could be some drawbacks where the horses are housed and sold on the business property. In such a case there would be a need for liability insurance. And maintaining an inventory of horses can have a risk factor.

Horse Products and Product Repairs

There are many variations to horse product creation and/or repair businesses. The business could be tack making and leather repair, or trailer painting and repair, truck lettering and detailing, woodworking or forged items, parade outfits or other costumes, design and sewing of custom show clothes, and any number of horse-themed home decor items.

This business would require a method of getting the creations or services to the public and would involve connections with retail outlets or craft shows. A workshop or studio would be needed along with appropriate tools and equipment. The owner must have creative ability and artistic talent, be able to concentrate and work alone, and be able to deliver goods when promised.

Depending upon the volume produced, the cost of raw

materials, and the markup, this type of venture could have a low to high profit potential. This can be an excellent venture for a person who wants to start small and grow with time.

Financial Investment

In any business undertaking, the first couple of years require the greatest financial outlay. In addition to horses and equipment, start-up costs for a horse venture will most likely include investment in some type of horse property.

Horse Property

In obtaining horse property there are several factors to keep in mind. These factors are location, zoning and covenants, and physical aspects of the property.

Location

The location of any horse property is a very important feature. To a certain extent, location depends on the intentions for its use. For example, breeding farms do not need regular access by customers, and can be fairly remote. But livery stables and riding schools must be within easy reach of the paying customers. There are negative factors to being too close to town. One is that the price of land is usually higher closer to residentially developed areas. Another factor is that people who live in urban areas are usually not horse fans and would be less likely to put up with things like horse manure and flies. And then, there is the factor of not having an adequate place to ride. It is unwise to purchase property without first analyzing the location.

There are legal restrictions on the use of property in the form of zoning laws. These zoning laws have been put in place by local governments to protect the use of the property. Because some property is not zoned for horse operations, it is wise to contact the local government to determine the zoning regulations for the desired location. Agricultural zoning is usually the best for a horse operation as it allows a wide range of livestock, and the use of horses would not be questioned. Land that has been zoned agricultural is usually established as farming or ranching land and the size of the properties is quite large.

Another type of zoning that may be attractive for a horse operation is rural residential. These tracts are of a smaller size (usually no more than 40 acres) and the zoning is more restrictive as to the kind and number of livestock permitted, the size and placement of buildings, distance from neighbors, and issues like manure disposal. It is important to realize that the zoning on a piece of property is not necessarily permanent, and may be changed for a variety of reasons. It is likely, as more and more land is being developed, we will be seeing fewer and fewer open pastures.

In addition to zoning, covenants need to be investigated before purchasing a piece of property. Covenants can limit the number of horses allowed, restrict the use of stallions entirely and even prevent grazing on the land.

The physical layout of the horse property is vitally important. It can be divided into three parts: site, building improvements, and site improvements.

Site

The site should be the largest that can be handled from the standpoint of both actual labor and financial outlay required. It will need enough pasture to at least partially sustain the horses, and a reliable water source. Easy access to a good public road and appropriate topography are other desirable features. Also the improvements ought to be arranged to meet the requirements of the intended use.

Building Improvements

Building improvements include housing, barns, and other outbuildings. Knowledge of basic construction is helpful in recognizing good and bad design and construction. If the property includes an existing home or other buildings, they must be inspected to ensure they meet building codes, and to determine whether there are any repairs to be made. The inspector hired should be a licensed building contractor.

An adequate watering system that is in working order is of utmost importance. Another feature to be considered is hay storage, which must be convenient and protected. Other buildings would include loafing sheds, equipment buildings and indoor riding arenas.

If the property has no building improvements, then it is necessary to erect a barn on the property. The key is to plan the barn as the center of a functional horse facility. While planning for the barn, consider all the machinery, equipment, tools, and supplies that come with barns. And remember to include things like a building for receiving and storing hay and feed, tractor and equipment storage, and a location to deposit manure.

When selecting the site for the barn, keep the horses' well-being in mind. Build from the perspective of what is best for the horse rather than what best suites the owner. Horses need fresh air and also must be out of drafts to remain healthy. So the barn should shelter the horses from cold winds and at the same time provide constant fresh air.

When planning the location for the barn on the property, think of the prevailing wind patterns. Then place the barn to gain the most benefit: insulating from winds in cooler climates and using the winds for cooling in warmer climates.

Moisture is something else that needs careful consideration. It is best to view a potential location during or after a heavy rain to get an idea of the affect precipitation will have on the property.

Many local governments have identified areas that are subject to flooding. A visit to the local planning department will help determine if the property is in a floodplain. If the land is not in a floodplain and yet tends to be soggy after a rainstorm, it may be necessary to have the property assessed and graded to keep it dry. It is best if the horse barns are located on ground that is somewhat above the area that surrounds them. To make sure that extra strain is not placed on the horses legs, be sure that the ground they will be standing on is level.

When it comes to selecting the style of barn, there is much to choose from. It is a matter of deciding which is the best for the horses, most suitable for the property, and the amount of money is to be spent.

Wooden Barns

Wooden barns are fairly inexpensive to build. A budget of $10,000 – $15,000 will buy a four to six stall barn with a wooden frame. This includes the outer shell of the barn with a tack room and hay storage area. Stalls and any exterior finish chosen would be extra.

Wood is the first choice in building material for horse barns, and has remained so for hundreds of years. This is true largely because of the availability of wood, and the excellence of air circulation in the wooden barn. Also it is a safe environment for horses, where the walls absorb kicks without hurting the horse. Wooden barns are also flexible and can easily be enlarged by additions when needed.

For example, one of the most common type of wooden barn structures is a pole barn. This barn has been around for many years and the simplicity of structure and ease of construction has kept this a very popular wooden barn. It is built by placing treated poles into the ground in concrete. Walls are then raised over a wooden frame, with trusses spanning the roof.

Another reason wood is a good choice for horse barns is the

fact plans for wooden barns are easily obtained. Another plus is that very little help is needed to build a barn from available plans because they are so detailed that even an inexperienced owner can handle the construction. Once the exterior is in place, the interior features can be purchased ready-made and easily assembled. When the barn is built by a professional contractor, the construction time is generally less than a week.

Although a wooden barn adds value to property, there are a couple of drawbacks to the wooden barn, the primary one being risk of fire. And barns built today are not of the same quality lumber as used in older barns. The fact that we have very old barns still standing is evidence that they were built of a heavier, better grade of wood than today's barns. To compensate for this lesser quality wood, treatments to wood has been developed to prevent rot. Fire should not be a great danger if the barn is properly cared for and where alarm and smoke detector systems are in place. Wood is still a smart choice today.

Prefabricated Barns

The cost of prefabricated barns varies widely because of the number of options available, and depending upon how much work the owner provides. Price for a four to six stall barn can vary from $12,000 to $25,000, including the exterior framework and interior stalls.

Prefabricated barns may be a wise choice for the smaller horse operation. They can easily be adapted to any conditions or surroundings. They are built using steel frames which are set into concrete piers. The roof and walls are constructed of steel also. An option may be to have the steel walls covered with wood, sided to match the house and other buildings. These barns can easily be insulated and are equipped with plumbing and heating as needed. The stalls come with sliding doors with grates at the top. Other options include wash racks, feed rooms, tack rooms and complete ventilation systems. The options are included in price and most even carry warranties to protect the buyer.

Companies that manufacture prefabricated barns are prepared to erect the complete barn, and some give owners the choice of building the barn themselves. In either case, construction does not take a lot of time. These barns come in four foot panels that snap together. After the concrete foundation is laid, the rest of the barn can be completed in short order. Of course having the supplier construct the barn would be the quickest and easiest as they can accomplish this in just a few days.

There are many advantages to the prefabricated barn. Some have been constructed to be fully portable. This would be important where the property was being leased. In this case the barn could be disassembled, carted to a new location, and reassembled without too much trouble. In addition to being portable, they are essentially fire proof. The wood faced metal walls and doors are built in such a way that horses are unable to chew off pieces as they can when the walls and doors are made completely of wood. All of the doors, both interior and exterior are of the sliding types, for ease of entrance and exit. And the stalls come with grates that allow for the movement of air through each stall. Some suppliers even make a sanitary stall for medical use or foaling that has a unique plastic surface that can be disinfected.

Ventilation in these barns is ordinarily very good, as is the insulation. One thing to be watchful of is having the barn too heavily insulated. Some people like this because it keeps the horses' coats slick in the cold winter months, and so that they themselves will keep warm. However, this is not the best from the aspect of ventilation for the horses and must be compensated for by the use of fans to provide movement of air inside the barn.

Block Barns

Block barns have been around for a very long time and at one time were where the vegetables were stored. The barns were buried midway in the ground to keep crops safe from insects and moisture, and to provide a cool temperature. Block barns of today are usually found on large horse operations and are sometimes used for indoor arenas.

All block barns are built of cement blocks and are sealed with mortar. The surface can be made to blend in with other buildings by overlaying blocks with wood, bricks, stucco, or other types of finish.

Block barns have the benefit of being made of durable material that will last and not need much upkeep. Another great benefit is the coolness of the barn, especially in the hot months of the year. These barns are virtually fireproof.

Block barns do have some disadvantages. They are not good for horses with respiratory problems, as the blocks tend to hold moisture and develop mold spores. Ventilation is not good and although they are great in the summer heat, they can be cold in winter months especially in the colder climates. Another concern is the safety of the horses. Unless the block walls of the stalls are properly lined, a horse could conceivably injure himself from kicking the wall.

It may not be practical to build a block barn of a small size because of the cost of construction. However, building a larger barn of block construction will run more in the same price range of other types of comparable size. This most likely would not be the type of barn an owner would take part in building because a mason is needed to lay the block. When this cost is added to the interior stalls and the exterior finish the total for a small six stall barn could be $22,000 – $30,000.

Horses and Equipment

The investment in horses and horse equipment, of course, varies depending on the type of horse operation. *(Chapter 5 covers the purchase of horses in detail.)*

Every horse operation must have equipment to manage the upkeep of the property. At the very least horse property owners need a conveyance for heavy or bulky materials. Managing horse manure is probably the number one reason horse people own tractors. Unless haymaking or crop farming is taken up, the equipment needed to manage the land is limited to a few simple items. A cart, for hauling manure; a mower, for pasture mowing; a flexible harrow or chain-link drag, for riding areas and pasture; scraper blades for leveling and snow removal; front-end loader, for manure; and a post hole digger, for fence building. The purchase of property-upkeep equipment requires the same care and consideration as purchasing the property itself.

Operating Expenses

In addition to the initial investment, operating expenses should be considered. The following items are examples that would fall under the category of operating expenses:

- advertising and promotion
- building and vehicle repair, operation, and maintenance
- exercise riders, hot walkers, and jockeys/drivers
- farrier and veterinary services
- feed, bedding, and waste removal
- rent or mortgage payments
- taxes and insurance
- training fees
- telephone and utilities

Due to the time involved in breeding, raising, and training horses, most horse businesses operate on long-term rather than short-term profits. It could be a few years before there is a return on the initial investment. Therefore, it is good to conduct extensive market research and have adequate financial backing.

Investment of Time and Effort

The amount of time and effort owners are personally able to devote to the business can affect their profits. Before starting any venture—whether it is launching a new business, purchasing an existing one, or even changing concentrations within the industry—it is wise to count not only financial cost, but the investment of time and effort.

FORM OF DOING BUSINESS

All horse businesses fall under one of the following classifications based on the type of ownership:

- sole proprietorship

- partnership (general or limited)

- corporation (regular or subchapter S)

Syndication, which deals with ownership interests, is popular in the horse industry, particularly in horseracing, and will also be discussed. Each of these business entities may have advantages and disadvantages.

Sole Proprietorships

The least complicated and perhaps most popular form of horse business is the sole proprietorship. A sole proprietorship is simply a person doing business for and by him/herself. As the sole proprietor, the individual has full responsibility for the income or losses, and assumes all risks and liabilities for the business operation. The income or losses of this type of business are included in the total income of the owner for tax purposes. In other words, any income from the horse operation is added to other income earned by the individual and any losses from the horse operation are deducted from the total income received by that individual.

Despite this combination of income, it is essential that business records be kept separate from all other records.

Because the sole proprietor form of doing business allows for this direct deduction of losses from other income, it is probably the most widespread form of business in the horse industry. However, there are limitations on deductibility when the individual does not materially participate in the operation of the business.

Material Participation

Material participation means the individual must be involved in the operations of the activity on a "regular, continuous, and substantial basis." The IRS has seven tests to determine this type of participation; the business owner must meet one of them to qualify as having materially participated during that tax year. The tests are listed in Figure 1–2.

If a business owner does not materially participate in the business, then any losses incurred by the business are considered "passive losses." *Passive losses are deductible only to the extent of passive income.* If passive losses exceed passive income (from any source), as may happen in the start-up phase of a new business, the remaining losses are not deductible from the business owner's total income. However, passive losses may be carried forward an unlimited number of years until there is enough passive income to offset them. Expert tax advice should be sought in cases where the business owner is merely investing in the business without materially participating.

Most horse business owners have no difficulty meeting the test for material participation because they routinely spend more than 500 hours per year actively involved in their operation on a "regular, continuous and substantial basis."

When the involvement in a horse business is through an investment in a limited partnership, difficulties arise in meeting the material participation test. Unless limited partners work more than

500 hours during the year in the business or meet the criteria for either Test #3 or Test #5, they have not met the requirements for material participation. Considering that the 500 hours would average about 10 hours per week, it is difficult for investors to meet this regulation unless they are spending time at the site of the business operation on a regular basis. And businesses that have limited partners generally are run by an on-site manager or trainer.

It is possible that some people may qualify their horse activity because they have participated for more than 100 hours during the year and they have spent more time than anyone else (Test #3). The "anyone else" would include non-owners like employees and trainers. This could include management time, but spending more time than anyone else may prove very difficult.

Test #5 is an exception that should apply where the limited partner's previous participation in the business during five of the past ten years was considered material. This could happen when the partner has retired from previous regular involvement with the horse operation.

Plans should be made in advance to be in compliance with the material participation test. The taxpayer may establish participation in an activity by any logical means. This should include a report of hours spent and services rendered. Keeping a journal, using an appointment book or calendar are all appropriate.

There are many activities involved in racing, breeding, or showing horses that should be documented to meet the annual hourly requirements for material participation. They include:

- Time spent making decisions concerning the training of horses.

- Time spent selecting managers, trainers and/or other employees.

- Time spent at racetracks or horse shows (not recreational time), evaluating potential purchase and claiming prospects, talking with trainers, jockeys, checking out the conditions of the barns and horses, and visiting the race office.

- Time spent pursuing additional education related to the horse industry.

- Time spent consulting with experts and advisers.

- Time spent attending auctions and horse sales, and visiting horse farms to purchase horses.

- Time spent consulting with financial professionals and attorneys about the horse operation.

- Time spent making decisions about veterinary treatment of horses.

- Time spent developing breeding strategy, pedigree research, booking mares for breeding, visiting breeding farms, and viewing stallion prospects.

Other kinds of activities that could be documented are: day-to-day care of horses, including grooming and cleaning stalls and checking on horses being worked, paying bills, making cost projections and inspecting financial records, examining business plans and making necessary revisions, communicating with potential customers and suppliers.

Partnerships

A partnership is when two or more individuals join in a business venture. These individuals may each contribute money, property, or business expertise and effort, and also share the operation's profits or losses. Partnerships have developed in the horse industry primarily because of the high price of doing business alone.

It has been said that "one should exercise as much care in

Tests for Material Participation

1. You participated in the activity for more than 500 hours during the tax year.

2. Your participation was substantially all of the participation in the activity of all individuals (including individuals who did not own any interest in the activity) for the tax year.

3. You participated in the activity for more than 100 hours during the tax year, and participated at least as much as any other person (including individuals who did not own any interest in the activity) for the tax year.

4. The activity is a significant participation activity for the tax year, and you participated in all significant participation activities for more than 500 hours during the year. An activity is a "significant participation activity" if it involves the conduct of a trade or business, you participated in the activity for more than 100 hours during the tax year, and you did not materially participate under any of the material participation tests (other than this test 4).

5. You have materially participated in the business activity for 5 of the 10 prior tax years.

6. The activity is a personal service activity in which you have materially participated for any 3 prior tax years. A personal service activity is an activity that involves performing personal services in the fields of health, law, engineering, architecture, accounting, actuarial science, performing arts, consulting, or any other trade or business in which capital is not a material income-producing factor.

7. Based on all the facts and circumstances, you participated in the activity on a regular, continuous, and substantial basis during the tax year. But you do not meet this test if you participated in the activity for 100 hours or less during the tax year. Your participation in managing the activity does not count in determining if you meet this test if any person (except you)—
   a. received compensation for performing management services in connection with the activity, or
   b. spent more hours during the tax year than you spent performing management services in connection with the activity (regardless of whether that person was compensated for the services).

Fig. 1–2. If a business owner does not meet at least one of these tests, the activity will be considered "passive."

choosing a business partner as in choosing a spouse." Although it is possible to form a partnership without a formal written partnership agreement, it is not advisable to do so. It is important to have in writing all the rights and duties of each partner. *(Appendix A contains a sample partnership agreement.)*

There are two types of partnerships—general and limited.

General Partnership

In the general partnership, each partner has a say in the management of the business and each has unlimited liability for it. Each partner is responsible for all of the liabilities of the business. A partnership must also file a separate tax return (in addition to each partner's return) and the profits and/or losses flow through to the individual partners. Any profit or loss of the partnership is reported on the individual's personal income tax return—the partnership is not taxed.

Limited Partnership

Unlike general partners, limited partners have little say in management and only limited liability to the partnership. This reduced responsibility for management and liability can be an advantage.

The down side of having a "limited" interest in a partnership is that the IRS may consider the limited partner's involvement as a "passive" or "non-participatory" activity, discussed previously in the section called "Material Participation."

A limited partnership must also file a separate tax return, in addition to each limited partner's return, and the profits and/or losses again flow through to each partner.

Regulation of Partnerships

When entering into a limited partnership, it is necessary to meet the requirements of the Uniform Limited Partnership Act.

Because these and other business requirements vary slightly by state, it is best to seek counsel from a tax advisor and an attorney before entering into either type of partnership agreement.

Other entities may also have rules concerning partnerships. The Jockey Club, which registers Thoroughbred racehorses and regulates racing, has drawn up *The American Racing Manual Rules of Racing*. Most State Racing Commissions base their rules of racing on The Jockey Club's regulations, with slight variations. Under The Jockey Club's *Rules of Racing*, a partnership must be registered annually with the Office of The Jockey Club or with the Clerk of the Course, which will forward its registration to The Jockey Club. The Jockey Club must approve the application for registration and the partnership must pay a fee (per horse) before a horse may be entered by that partnership. The application includes such information as the names and addresses of each partner and the amount of their respective interests in the partnership.

No horse may be entered and run by a partnership with more than four members, or by a partnership in which one partner has less than 25% interest. The Jockey Club does allow that horse to be leased from the partnership, either by one (or more) of the partners or by another person, and entered by the lessee. (A lessee may also be required to obtain an owner's license.)

Corporations

A corporation is a separate legal entity and is generally more complicated than operating as a sole proprietor or a partnership. Incorporating usually requires legal assistance, because of certain legal requirements that must be met. One of these requirements is the filing of a Certificate of Disclosure, which lets the incorporating body of the state know if any of the incorporators have been convicted of felonies or involved in bankruptcies. Incorporators are the people who organize, promote, raise funds, and file the forms for the corporation. All corporations must have incorporators and a statutory agent (legal agent of the corporation).

Once a corporation is formed and chartered in accordance with state statutes, the incorporators transfer money or property to the corporation for the issuance of shares of stock. As employees/ shareholders of the corporation, they must treat the corporation as a distinct and separate entity. This is sometimes confusing to the individual who has been operating as a sole proprietor and expects to treat the corporation as an extension of the sole proprietorship. The rights and duties of the shareholders and the corporation should be outlined in the Articles of Incorporation. *(Appendix A contains a sample of Articles of Incorporation.)*

Management of corporations should be clearly defined. The corporation must appoint officers to carry out the daily operations of the business. If the operation is other than an individual affair, the matter of how and by whom the business is to be managed can be critical. For any corporation, large or small, bylaws and minutes are very important. The bylaws spell out how the corporation is to be run, and the minutes document the meetings where major decisions affecting the corporation are made. Especially for shareholders of smaller corporations, who may tend to treat the corporation as an extension of themselves, having clearly defined areas of accountability and control will help the activity to operate in a proper business manner.

There are two types of corporations—regular and subchapter S.

Regular Corporation

A regular corporation is taxed directly and pays taxes on its profits just as an individual does. And when these profits are distributed to the shareholders, the shareholders are also taxed on the distributions. When this type of corporation has losses instead of profit, the losses cannot be deducted by the individual shareholders of the corporation on their individual tax returns.

Subchapter S Corporation

It is possible for the shareholders to elect to be treated as a Subchapter S corporation. A Subchapter S corporation is treated much the same as a partnership regarding taxation. The income or loss from the business flows through to the individual shareholders, who then report this income or loss on their individual tax returns. As far as accounting and tax laws are concerned, a Subchapter S corporation is a little more complicated form of business, but may be the most practical choice during the start-up phase of a business.

Advantages of Incorporation

In addition to the tax aspects of incorporating, carefully consider the liability factor. Forming a corporation limits the individual's liability for business debts, losses, and negligence, thus protecting personal assets. It may be just as prudent to purchase liability insurance to protect these assets and satisfy the liability consideration. This matter is one that should be discussed with legal counsel and an insurance agent to determine the best approach for the operation, as costs and risks of liability vary. The more assets involved, the greater the need for (and cost of) protection.

Another advantage of the corporate form of doing business is the ability to raise capital by the issuance of shares.

Syndicates

Syndication, another form of group ownership, has been used in the horse industry for many years. The most common type has been the stallion breeding syndicate, where ownership interests (referred to as shares or units) are sold. These shares, which are different from corporation shares, entitle the holder to a breeding each year during the lifetime of the stallion. The shareholders may sell onetime breeding rights or may sell their share outright.

Syndicates have also been formed for racing and showing, and broodmare syndicates have become more commonplace. *(Appendix A contains a sample syndicate agreement.)*

Because the sale of interests in a horse (for profit) is considered a "security," having an attorney arrange terms for the syndicate is a must. Regardless of what form the syndicate takes, the shareholders are bound by state and federal regulations. Failure to abide by these regulations could result in strict penalties from the Securities and Exchange Commission. Most stallion syndicates are excepted, because a breeding right is considered co-ownership, not a security.

Treatment of Syndicates

A syndicate may be treated as co-ownership of property for tax purposes, or it may be considered a partnership (this classification should be clarified in the syndicate agreement). The determining factor is whether the syndicate engages in any business activities, such as buying and selling property.

For instance, the stallion syndicate mentioned above would be treated as co-ownership of property because each member can either retain the breeding right or sell the share. Money received from the sale of the share belongs to that member only and is not shared with other members.

Generally, in a broodmare syndicate, a broodmare is purchased, bred each year to a selected stallion, and her foals are sold as weanlings or yearlings. Because collective property is being bought and sold, broodmare syndicates are most often treated as general or limited partnerships.

When a syndicate is considered to be co-ownership of property, the co-owners each regard their shares as part of their horse businesses. Income and expenses are reported on their individual tax returns with all other income and expenses. If the syndicate is a partnership, the income and expenses would be reported on a partnership tax return, and then flow through to the individual partners. Because of the complexity of the partnership tax return and the time and expense involved in filing, it is usually more desirable to treat a syndicate as co-ownership of property.

BUSINESS ADVISORS

The decision whether to use the services of an advisor depends on the extent of the owner's experience, the size of the investment, and the extent of the owner's personal involvement. An advisor can be any one of a number of people: a general advisor, a bloodstock agent, a horse trainer, a farm operator, a lawyer, or an accountant.

As discussed in Chapter 3 under "What the IRS Looks For," the Internal Revenue Service places considerable emphasis on the choice of advisors and experts when determining whether a horse operation qualifies as a business. Also, banks and lending institutions place similar emphasis when determining whether to lend money to the horse operation.

In addition to consulting an advisor, keep current with developments in the equine industry. Quite a few colleges now offer short courses on equine topics. Extension agencies offer seminars on a variety of subjects. Also, self-instruction is popular among busy horse business people, who use videos and the Internet to keep abreast of the latest developments in the horse world.

BUSINESS NAMES

When choosing a name for the business, sole proprietors, partners, and corporations have the option of using an individual business owner's name or a fictitious business name. A fictitious business name is any name other than the owner's legal name. If any part of the owner's legal name is included in the business name, it is not considered fictitious.

If the business entity chooses to have a fictitious name, it should be professional sounding, and give a good indication of what services are offered. For instance, calling a horse business "Berkshire Stud Farm" would indicate a breeding establishment, whereas calling it "Berkshire Training Stable" would indicate a training facility.

It is important that the owner register the fictitious business name with the county or state in which the business is located. (State regulations dictate whether the business owner registers with the county or state.) An application for registration should be available from the office of the County Clerk or the Secretary of State. The name may be registered on or after the first date of use in some states, but that does not necessarily mean the state has awarded or will protect the name. It is suggested that before choosing a name, a check be made of similar businesses. If a similar name is found already in use, the name may not be accepted for registration.

Also, the fictitious name should be published in a newspaper of general circulation. Then, if it is discovered that another business is using the same name, the business which first published the name has prior rights to it (under common law).

Failure to register and publish the fictitious business name could be detrimental. Not only could it prevent the owner from setting up a bank account under that name, but it could also keep the owner from filing a lawsuit under it. Many banks will not open a checking account for a business without seeing proof of filing and publication of the business name.

In some states, the fictitious name must be both registered and published to be considered legal. In other states, it is not necessary to register or publish a business name. Again, the owner should check with the County Clerk or Secretary of State for a particular state's requirements.

The Jockey Club also has formulated regulations regarding

FORM OF BUSINESS	TAXATION
SOLE PROPRIETORSHIP	• Individual files tax return and is taxed on income from all sources, including income from horse business.
GENERAL/ LIMITED PARTNERSHIP	• Partnership files tax return, but is not taxed on income. • Partners file individual tax returns and are taxed on total income, including income from partnership.
REGULAR CORPORATION	• Corporation files tax return and is taxed on income. • Shareholders file individual tax returns and are taxed on total income, including distributed corporation profits. • Shareholders may not deduct corporate losses.
SUBCHAPTER S CORPORATION	• Corporation files tax return, but is not taxed on income. • Shareholders file individual tax returns and are taxed on total income, including income from corporation. • Shareholders may deduct corporate losses.
SYNDICATE	• When treated as co-ownership of property, each owner files tax return as a sole proprietor. • When treated as a general partnership, same rules apply as for a general partnership that is not a syndicate. • When treated as a limited partnership, same rules apply as for a limited partnership that is not a syndicate.

Fig. 1–3. Tax rules for different business entities.

FORM OF BUSINESS	ADVANTAGES	DISADVANTAGES
SOLE PROPRIETORSHIP	• Least complicated form • Losses may be deducted from personal income • Least expensive to form and maintain	• Owner has unlimited liability—no legal separation between individual and business • Raising capital
GENERAL PARTNERSHIP	• Expenses are shared • Each partner has equal say in management decisions • Losses may be deducted from personal income	• Each partner has unlimited liability for the partnership • Partnership must file a separate tax return • Partners must contribute or borrow to raise capital
LIMITED PARTNERSHIP	• Expenses are shared • Limited partners have limited liability for the partnership • Losses may be deducted from personal income	• Passive loss limitations • Limited partners have no management control • Partnership must file a separate tax return • Partners must contribute or borrow to raise capital
REGULAR CORPORATION	• Lower income tax rates • Ability to raise capital through issuance of shares • Shareholders have limited personal liability	• Losses may not be deducted from personal income • Corporation must file a separate tax return
SUBCHAPTER S CORPORATION	• Losses may be deducted from personal income • Ability to raise capital through issuance of shares • Shareholders have limited personal liability	• Most complicated form • Corporation must file a separate tax return
SYNDICATE	• Risks/expenses are shared	• Complex tax methods

Fig. 1–4. Advantages and disadvantages for different business entities.

business names. An individual can register a "stable name," which is the same as a fictitious name, with The Jockey Club. He or she must renew the registration annually and must also pay a fee each year. The name is subject to the approval of The Jockey Club.

However, a person cannot register more than one name at a time, and cannot also race a horse under his or her legal name. A member of a partnership may also register a stable name and race all horses owned by that partnership under the stable name. Racehorse trainers may not use stable names, but they may be a member of a partnership that uses another member's stable name.

BUSINESS LICENSES

Certain licenses for different types of horse businesses or trainers may be required by the state or locality. The American Horse Shows Association registers farms, corporations, syndicates, and partnerships (for a fee) and provides a certificate. A certificate or license, whether voluntary or required, lends legitimacy to a new horse business and should be displayed in the business office and used in promotional materials.

In the horseracing industry, each state's Racing Commission has formulated detailed regulations and licensing procedures which must be followed. Nearly everyone associated with a racetrack must be licensed. This list of people includes grooms, hot walkers, exercise riders, jockeys, veterinarians, racehorse owners, and even the president of the racetrack.

The State Racing Commission often maintains an office at the local racetrack. There, the applicant fills out a form, has fingerprints and a photograph taken, and pays a fee, which ranges from $10 to over $200, depending on the license. A copy of the rules and regulations of racing for that state is also available at this office. Some licenses must first be approved by the racing stewards and/or the State Racing Commission before they are issued. For example, a racehorse owner's license is only sent after approval is granted. Then a badge is issued with the photograph on it, which allows the owner free access to the backstretch.

These licenses are not valid in all states. If, for example, a racehorse owner wishes to race horses in both Maryland and New York, he or she must obtain an owner's license from both states. Racehorse trainers must pass both a written and practical exam for licensing. Although the trainer's test is only required once, all licenses must be renewed annually.

Some states require a sales tax license if horse sales are taxable in that state. Other states do not tax agricultural sales, and sales of horses may be considered agricultural. When beginning a new horse activity (or a new aspect of an existing one), the business owner should contact the city, county, and state of residence to determine what, if any, licenses are required by those entities.

SUCCESSFUL HORSE BUSINESS GUIDELINES

Business Plan—A good business plan is a necessity, regardless of the type of business activity. It takes time, energy, and patience to draw up a satisfactory plan, but there is no substitute for knowing if the business ideas are workable. Furthermore, a thorough business plan outlining solid ideas will help the business owner get a bank loan or attract investors. *(See Chapter 2 for more information on writing a business plan.)*

Adequate Financial Reserve or Backing—Adequate working capital is necessary for success in any new business. The rewards of any business, both emotional and financial, are often directly proportional to the amount of carefully considered risk that is taken.

Education in the Area of Interest—Business owners should take advantage of every opportunity to learn more about the horse industry and their area of specialization. Some good educational opportunities include auctions, competitions, subscribing to magazines or newsletters, taking classes, and attending seminars.

Assessment of the Industry Climate—Business owners should be aware not only of what is happening in their specialty area, but in the industry as a whole.

Building a Reputation—Every business has an image. The way owners, managers, and employees conduct themselves leaves an impression, and determines whether customers return.

Help From Professionals—Owners should not only seek professional advice before starting a business, but whenever they anticipate problems. At the first sign of a problem, it is important to their business' success that they engage the services of an expert.

Developing Marketing Abilities—It is not necessary to be a marketing genius to attract customers. However, business owners should be aware of effective methods of promoting their businesses. *(See Chapter 4 for more information on marketing.)*

Up-To-Date Plan—Once the business plan has been written and implemented, be sure to stay on top of changing conditions and to adjust the business plan accordingly.

In addition to these guidelines, the business owner should address the following issues:

1. Know exactly where all money is going.

2. Always have a current profit and loss statement.

3. Create a six-month profit and loss projection.

4. Be able to justify major expenditures.

5. Protect all business investments.

6. Apply as many sound business principles as possible.

7. Pay as much attention as possible to inventory control and conservation, business expenses, management, books and records, and providing an impeccable service or a superior horse (or equine product).

SUMMARY

A new owner should not be discouraged if he or she has followed all of these guidelines for success and the business still does not show a profit for the first few years. Much of the horse industry operates on long-term profits, which means a few years down the road, a business owner's perseverance is very likely to pay off.

Making a business venture economically feasible is a matter of common sense, sound business principles, and thorough planning. The next chapter will discuss the various components of a solid business, and will teach the new business owner (or potential business owner) how to write a workable business plan.

2

PLANNING FOR SUCCESS

Fig. 2–1.

Every business should have a written business plan. The process of researching and designing a detailed plan allows the owner to see in advance if a business venture is feasible. Preparing the business plan will also help to establish goals and evaluate the likelihood of making a profit. Those who start in business without proper planning will find themselves making decisions based on something less than the whole picture. A business plan is a must.

In order to know if the horse operation is likely to make a profit, it is imperative to know what has happened in the past, its present situation, and future plans. In addition to being a good tool for goal setting and planning, a well-written, well-prepared business plan can also be used to attract investors. When a bank or other financial institution is contemplating loaning money to the horse business, a formal business plan can present the entire business picture for their consideration.

Writing a formal business plan requires a lot of time and effort. It is important that the business plan set forth the entire business concept and it must show, in detail, how business objectives (and profit) will be accomplished. This does not mean that the business plan needs to be complex. In fact, a simple, straightforward plan is usually best. This business plan can also be a key factor in proving profit motive to the Internal Revenue Service, a topic that is discussed in the next chapter.

INTERVIEWS

For the person who is starting a horse business for the first time, it is advisable to begin by conducting some interviews. Before writing a business plan, question as many people as possible who are well established in the horse business in the same area of the industry. Many people like to share their experiences and are willing to cooperate.

The following list contains examples of some of the questions you might want to ask during the interview:

- How long has the business existed?

- Who runs the business?

- What is the form of doing business? Is it a family endeavor?

- What is the major product or service?

- How many horses are involved?

- Who are the customers? What percentage are regular customers?

- How many employees are there? Full- or part-time?

- What are the future goals of this business?

- What kind of advertising is used?

- What is the biggest headache of this business?

- What is the greatest reward?

PLAN FORMAT

Before writing the business plan, organize all the information. It is important to present the information in a professional format, as it will help the owner portray a professional image. The plan should have a cover sheet stating the name of the business and the date, followed by a table of contents page. The body should include all the specifics for operation.

Introduction

This section is the first part of the plan and is a simple statement of the type of equine operation. Be as specific as possible.

Objective

Write a paragraph or two describing, in general terms, the overall objectives of the business. Briefly state the goals of the business and how these goals will be accomplished. This section should be an overview of the horse business and should be well thought out and complete.

Operation

This is the backbone of the business plan and should include the following sections:

Summary of Horse Industry: Details on the specific aspect of the horse industry in which the owner is involved will be included in this section. The informations needs to be presented so that anyone reading the plan can understand the owner's involvement in that segment of the horse industry. Facts about business conditions should be included to show income potential. This could encompass purses or prizes, and sales results. It would be advantageous to include trade magazine articles, trends in the market place, studies conducted by breed organizations, and anything else that would affect the forecasted profitability of the operation.

History of Operations: Describe the initial development of the horse business detailing how the owner became involved with horses. Include photographs, along with recent appraisals of all the horses, equipment, facilities, and land. It is important to cite the information that convinced the owner a profit could be made in this particular aspect of the horse industry.

Start-up Plans: Included in this section are the initial arrangements for the business such as locating property, horses, equipment, and supplies. A realistic estimate of the amount of money needed to begin operations is also needed here. (How will the horse venture be financed? Will it be from savings? Loans?) Also included is the form of business entity: will the business operate as a sole proprietorship, partnership, or corporation? Finally, state when the business officially begins operations.

Facilities: State where the horse operation is to be located and any special features such as access to a major racetrack. Establish whether the facilities will be leased, purchased, or held in some other form. There should be a thorough description of the facility that lists all improvements and equipment. This description should include details of each part of each facility, especially any labor saving or cost saving devices. It is best to assume that those reading the plan are not familiar with a hot walker and other such equipment.

Breeding or training facilities should be described in some detail, noting any special labor saving or safety devices.

When pasture and feed crops are part of horse facility, this will need to be detailed. The amount of money saved by having the pasture and crops needs to be noted as well.

Photographs of the facilities adds to the usefulness of the description. And having an expert's opinion as to the profit potential of the operation and the adequacy of the facilities is also advantageous. Valuation of the property by an expert appraiser is a crucial planning tool.

Inventory of Horses: To present a current picture of the operation it is necessary to include a complete listing of all horses. Included in this listing would be horse's name, date of birth, registration number, the horse's use and current fair market value. The number of horses to be used in the operation should be stated here also. For an ongoing business, it is helpful in presenting a current picture of the operation. Where the horses are held for sale, the selling price would be shown. For insured horses, the amount of insurance will be noted. If any of the horses have been appraised, this appraisal value should be noted as well.

Market, Advertising, and Promotion: Define the market for the business. (What types of customers will be served? What is the market for the product or service? What is the image to be projected? How is this business better than the competition?) State the avenues for promotion for this business and the targeted audience for advertising. Determine an advertising budget and include the cost here.

Businesses that already have an advertising and promotional program in place can provide an analysis of their existing strategy. This could include a record of sales over a certain period and a summary of the costs of marketing during that same period. Samples of advertising and promotional activities could be included to give the reader an idea of what has been carried out in this area.

It is important to explain what methods are used to generate income in a horse operation. This is something that potential investors, bankers and the IRS are equally concerned with.

Time frame: Write a formal statement of business goals year by year for the first five years of the operation. This should be quite specific and should include financial goals.

Management

The management section of the business plan covers the persons who will be running the business. It should contain a detailed résumé of the owner, partners, or other managers. Expertise related to horse operations is important and should be noted in detail here, as well as expertise in other fields. Past accomplishments and plans to increase expertise in the future should be set forth. Professionals whose services are to be used may also be included here.

Financial

The financial part of the business plan contains two sections. The first section details the initial investment needed to cover start-up costs. It includes the cost of purchasing or leasing the facilities. The horses needed to start the operation and their costs are also stated. A list of vehicles, equipment, tools, tack, animal care supplies, and the cost of each item should be listed. Other items that might be included here are the cost of improvements or renovation to facilities, the cost of establishing pastures, and the cost for irrigation or water supply. Be sure to include all start-up items and their costs.

The second section consists of income and expense projections. This section should be in the form of an income statement, listing all sources of expected income and all anticipated expenses, and showing the net income or loss. These income and expense projections cover a five-year period, starting with the year the horse business goes into operation. Making projections takes quite a bit of work. It is necessary to estimate not only the amount of items needed, but also their costs. Careful attention must be paid to estimates, keeping them as realistic as possible. An existing business could include some years of history, along with the five-year projection.

USING THE PLAN TO ATTRACT INVESTORS

All the effort expended in putting together a thorough and professional business plan will pay off on its own. It is also vital if it is necessary to find an investor. Finding adequate capital is sometimes a very important step in making the plan become a reality. Statistics have shown that 90% of new businesses that fail do so because of undercapitalization—not necessarily for start-up, but to keep the business operating until it begins to turn a profit. Unless the owner(s) have enough capital to cover costs for the first few years of the business, securing some kind of investment or loan may be necessary.

When trying to get a bank to invest in a horse business, the owner should remember to focus on short-term, realistic goals. Lofty, long-range plans are a turnoff to the potential investor as they may seem too speculative. Also, estimate costs as accurately as possible. When in doubt, make sure the estimate presented to the potential investor is on the high side so there is room for error. It is much easier to later inform investors that they owe less, rather than more than they originally expected.

Securing capital for any new business is sometimes problematic. Investors (and owners) want to see profit and success, and losses, however reasonable, are hard to explain. Moreover, investors may be so uneducated about the horse industry that they may be difficult to convince. A solution to this problem would be to educate them. Bring in books, magazine articles, or other professional evidence that supports the business plan.

The following factors will likely be emphasized by investors:

- the owner's personal experience in the field

- the owner's personal net worth

- the size of the business

- the average profitability of similar businesses

- the amount of assets the owner brings into the business

- the amount of liabilities (debts) the owner has

- the assets and qualifications of any business partners

- the owner's profit projections

A new business owner has the option of making a loan secure, which means the bank or other investor can take a certain amount of the owner's property as collateral if he or she fails to make the necessary payments.

Clearly, developing a good business plan is one of the most important aspects of a successful horse business. The following pages show a sample of a professional business plan. This plan is not meant to be copied exactly, but can be used as a guide to draft a thorough plan for almost any kind of horse operation.

Thoroughbred Breeding Farm

Business Plan

Thoroughbred Breeding Farm

Table of Contents

Introduction

This facility is to be a Thoroughbred breeding farm standing three stallions at stud and holding up to 30 broodmares. The farm will also have the capacity to accommodate 20 outside mares.

Objective

The objective of this business is to breed and raise quality Thoroughbred racehorses, primarily by our own stallions and out of our own mares. Of the above-mentioned horses, a 3-year-old stallion with an excellent pedigree and race record has been purchased. Also, a quality 3-year-old stallion with an excellent pedigree and race record has been leased for the duration of the upcoming breeding season. We have purchased 10 broodmares (3 of which are proven) at the recommendations of several top breeders and racehorse trainers. We plan to purchase 10 more broodmares before November 1. We will also breed as many outside mares as possible. We have already had inquiries about breeding 3 outside mares to the leased stallion.

A 4-year-old stallion will be purchased in the second year. We also expect 15 foals to be dropped the second year. Within three years, there will be at least 20 top quality foals. The best fillies will be kept for breeding, and a colt may also be kept. The remainder of the foal crop will be sold annually at weanling and yearling sales. Barren and less desirable mares will also be sold, with the proceeds used to purchase replacements. By the fifth year, we will have two valuable studs, one of which is homebred, 30 broodmares, and a foal crop of 20. Our stallions can service our mares as well as (conservatively) 50 outside mares. This aspect of our business will be limited by space, not stallion service.

Operation

A. Thoroughbred Breeding In The Horse Industry

No matter their actual birthdate, all Thoroughbred horses are considered to be a year older on January 1 following their birth. For this reason, Thoroughbred mares are usually bred to deliver their foals during the early months of the year. That way they will be more mature and will have an advantage at racetracks. Until age three, most races are categorized according to age. Due to the fact that these horses reach their racing peak when they are approximately four years old it is considered best to have foals born during the months of February and March. Since the gestation period for horses is 340 days, the most active months for breeding Thoroughbred stallions to broodmares are during February, March, and April. Accordingly, the first months are the busiest time of the year at a breeding farm. All major activities of breeding are accomplished during this time period. Broodmares about to foal are cared for, foals are being born, and breeding for next year's foal crop is underway.

When mares are retired from racing, most of them are kept for breeding. However, only the very best stallions are kept, and quite often these young stallions are syndicated. The best racehorses are usually the most successful stallions in the breeding barn. They most often stand at stud at breeding farms that specialize in the care and handling of stallions. The worth of a stallion and the stud fee he commands are definitely tied to his performance at the racetrack as well as his conformation and pedigree. This is particularly true of young stallions who do not have any of their get at the racetrack. The older proven stallions are in strong demand, however, and most breeding farms find it necessary to limit the stallion's breeding season to 55 broodmares.

Broodmares are bred every year during their breeding life. Some of these mares have been retired from racing at an early age because of some unsoundness and will be bred as young as two years of age.Others will be retired from racing at age four or five. Cost of a broodmare varies greatly depending upon pedigree, conformation, racing performance, and whether or not she has produced any race winners.

The foals produced by these broodmares are considered for the yearlings sales the spring following their birth, with about 20% being chosen for sale at that time. This is an important source of revenue for the owners. These foals are usually born in the early spring, with about 75% of the mares producing a live healthy foal. The mare is rebred for the following year when the current foal is a month or two old, and the foals are weaned from their mother in the fall when they are four to six months old.

Although they may not reach their true racing potential until age four or older, race training for Thoroughbred horses begins at age two or perhaps three years.

B. History of Operations

One of the principals in the general partnership, Ms. M., has been involved with Thoroughbred racehorses all of her life. She is the daughter of a well-known racehorse trainer and spent many years at the backside of the track as a youth. Although she likes racing, breeding horses has always been her first love. Over the years she has owned and bred some quality horses that have done well at the track. Mr. Q. also has extensive experience in the horse business, mostly from a lifetime of living on a horse ranch in the Southwest. Each of the principals has been successful in a horse business in the past, and were looking to go into a business partnership when they met two years ago. They found their goals for raising Thoroughbred racehorses to be compatible and decided to pool their resources and experiences in a general partnership. After extensive research of race winners, pedigrees, and an evaluation of the market, they have completed a business plan. Their own experiences and an analysis of the current market have convinced them that there is a great deal of money to be made in the breeding of Thoroughbred racehorses with proven track records.

C. Start-Up Plans

1. The business will be operated as a general partnership.

2. Start-up expenses will be financed partially by savings and partially through a bank loan.

3. The business will officially be in operation November 1st of this year.

D. Facilities

1. The farm is located outside Louisville, Kentucky, within 10 miles of Churchill Downs.

2. A 4-stall stallion barn, a 30-stall broodmare barn with 10 foaling stalls and an examination room, and a breeding shed are already on the premises. A teasing wall will be added before January 1. A laboratory will be constructed near the breeding shed by November of that year. An additional 20-stall barn for the outside mares will be built the third year.

3. The land and facilities are being leased.

4. The 40-acre property has two stallion paddocks, 10 smaller turnout paddocks for pregnant mares and mares with new foals, and three larger pastures for weanlings, yearlings, and 2-year-old mares. It also has a ranch house with an office and two apartments for employees.

F. Marketing, Advertising, and Promotion

1. Our target market is primarily racehorse owners and trainers nationwide who will purchase our sale stock. We will also target local owners of broodmares who desire quality stud services.

2. The farm will advertise its foal crop to coincide with seasonal public sales. We will also advertise stud services and accommodations for outside mares, beginning in the weeks prior to breeding season and continuing throughout the season or until our stallions are booked.

E. Inventory of Horses

Name	D.O.B.	Reg. No.	Use	Value	Ins. Amount
Horse #1	1993	54321	Stud	$125,000	$125,000
Horse #2	1994	54322	Stud	Leased	—0—
Horse #3	1992	54323	Broodmare	50,000	50,000
Horse #4	1992	54324	Broodmare	45,000	45,000
Horse #5	1993	54325	Broodmare	30,000	30,000
Horse #6	1990	54326	Broodmare	75,000	75,000
Horse #7	1991	54327	Broodmare	65,000	65,000
Horse #8	1993	54328	Broodmare	35,000	35,000
Horse #9	1989	54329	Broodmare	88,000	88,000
Horse #10	1990	54330	Broodmare	25,000	25,000
Horse #11	1992	54331	Broodmare	32,000	32,000
Horse #12	1993	54332	Broodmare	29,000	29,000

3. The foal crop and stud services will be advertised separately in *The Blood-Horse* magazine, a premier Thoroughbred racing magazine in the United States. The farm may also advertise in other Thoroughbred publications, papers, and racing programs.

G. Time Frame

1. The farm's first year objective is for the leased stallion to settle 20 farm-owned mares. We will also service as many outside mares as possible. The three-year-old colt injured a hind leg (which ended his racing career) and will not be able to cover mares until next year when he has recuperated. Our stallion manager will use the remainder of this breeding season to train the young stallion in breeding behavior and procedure.

   All horses, whether farm-owned or outside, will have annual reproductive examinations by a competent veterinarian and have certificates that they are reproductively and structurally sound and disease-free.

2. The second year objective is to have a healthy crop of 15 foals in January and February. In February and March, we will breed their dams again to our two 4-year-old stallions. The farm will also attract at least 10 outside mares. Also in February and March, we will halter break the foals and teach them to lead. In late June or July we will wean the foals from their dams and prepare most of them for sale. We will keep the best fillies and perhaps one quality colt to be used in our breeding program when they mature. The remainder of the foal crop (10 – 12 foals) will bring good prices at next year's yearling sales and will promote our business.

   During this year we will build a laboratory in which to perform semen evaluations, blood tests, and fecal examinations. This will cut veterinary costs by at least 20% for the life of the business. We will also purchase additional breeding equipment.

3. The third year objective is to purchase 5 broodmares, attract 15 outside mares, and build a teasing pen. All purchased mares must pass a physical and reproductive examination. We will have our second healthy crop of 15 foals and the same procedure will be used as the second year's crop.

4. The fourth year objective is to have 25 broodmares and two stallions at stud (20 outside breedings, plus covering our mares), with a crop of at least 20 foals.

5. The fifth year objective is to have 30 broodmares, to sell a 7-year-old stallion and keep the other two (7 and 3 years old). The farm will continue to sell the young studs and barren or otherwise unsuitable broodmares, and use the proceeds to purchase more quality mares. We will also purchase breeding rights from other farms and syndicate shareholders to introduce new blood. We will have at least 20 outside mares sent to the facility for breeding. The farm's foal crop will be approximately 20, but will increase in the sixth year.

Management

An experienced stallion handler has been procured to manage the stallion barn. He has seven years' experience in this capacity working at a Thoroughbred breeding farm in New York. A separate barn manager has been engaged to manage the pregnant and foaling mares, and to halter break and wean the foals. She worked as an assistant manager for 10 years at a Thoroughbred breeding farm in Arizona. She also has earned a degree in Broodmare Management from the University of Arizona in Tucson. In addition, three part-time employees have already been hired to provide care to the horses (feeding, cleaning, and exercising as necessary). These responsible young people (over age 17) are the niece and nephews of Mrs. M. and have grown up caring for, training, and showing their personal horses. Two are currently taking classes in Equine Reproductive Physiology and Microbiology. With continuing education and experience, they will eventually be expected to perform palpations and lab work (within three years).

Financial

A. Initial Investment Needed for Start-Up Costs

Lease of facilities	$_____
Lease of one stallion	_____
Purchase of one stallion	_____
Purchase of 20 broodmares	_____
Vehicles, equipment, and tools	_____
Improvements/renovations to facilities	_____
Development cost of building	_____
Establishment/revitalization of pastures	_____
Irrigation/Water	_____
Tack and animal care supplies	_____
Total Investment Needed	$_____

B. Income and Expense Projections for Five Years

	Year 1	Year 2	Year 3	Year 4	Year 5
Income:					
Stud fees					
Mare care fees					
Sales of foals					
Sales of mares					
Lease of mares					
Sales of studs					
Lease of studs					
Other: _____					
Total Income:	$_____	$_____	$_____	$_____	$_____

	Year 1	Year 2	Year 3	Year 4	Year 5
Expenses:					
Feed					
Farrier					
Veterinarian					
Deworming					
Insurance					
Taxes					
Interest					
Bedding					
Transport					
Property maint.					
Utilities					
Vehicle					
Labor					
Waste removal					
Travel					
Advertising					
Promotion					
Telephone					
Prof. services					
Bank charges					
Total Expense:	$_____	$_____	$_____	$_____	$_____
Net Income:	$_____	$_____	$_____	$_____	$_____

SUMMARY

The business plan is a key element in starting a horse operation. Not only does it help the prospective horse business owner to anticipate income and expenses, it provides an objective and realistic guideline for carrying out the plans. Also, it demonstrates to the IRS that the owner is operating the business with a profit motive, and thus the business should be considered a legitimate business (rather than a hobby) for tax purposes.

3

HOBBY OR BUSINESS?

Many horsepeople would be surprised to learn that they do not need years of experience, a large facility, or a lot of horses for their operation to be considered a business. The primary specification of the Internal Revenue Service is that the activity be engaged in with the objective of making a profit. When a profit motive exists, the IRS will consider the equine venture to be a genuine business, and allows deductions of expenses *which are greater than the business' income. If it considers the venture to be a hobby, expenses are deductible only to the extent of the hobby's income.*

Fig. 3–1.

WHAT THE IRS LOOKS FOR
Profit Motive

What determines whether there is a profit motive? The IRS has set up guidelines to make this determination. To be considered as having a profit motive and thus engaged in a business rather than a hobby, the potential business owner should comply with the following nine factors listed in the Internal Revenue Regulations. These factors are relatively easy—just be consistent.

1—Manner in Which the Taxpayer Carries on the Activity

The most important factor in proving a profit motive should always be present to qualify the venture as a business. The horse operation should be carried on like any other business, using sound business practices and keeping accurate and complete books and records.

There should be a detailed business plan that has been researched and well thought out to show how the business owner intends to make a profit. This plan should include operations and management as well as financial projections for a five-year period. Absence of a business plan and inability to demonstrate to the IRS how the equine venture will be made profitable are two significant strikes against the business owner.

Attempts to improve the business by altering methods of operation or abandoning unprofitable methods indicate that the owner has more than a hobby in mind. Thus, it is important to document these changes and improvements. The keeping of accurate and complete accounting records, as well as a daily record of business operations, will help substantiate a profit motive.

2—Expertise of the Taxpayer or Advisors

Understanding the business cannot be overemphasized as a criterion for determining profit motive. It is important to become educated about the industry before beginning business operations. That education should also be continuous—it should continue to keep the owner current with the industry's trends.

There are many ways to do research and gain expertise in the horse industry. Attending seminars, taking classes, frequenting sales and auctions, visiting other operations, reading professional equine books, and consulting experts are a few ways to gain knowledge. Even if an expert is outside the horse industry (such as an accountant), use of that expertise to help the business profit is looked upon favorably by the IRS. Any time an expert is called upon, it should be documented.

3—Time and Effort Expended by the Taxpayer

The amount of time devoted to the horse operation is another factor used in determining profit motive. This is particularly true when the activity does not have recreational aspects. Partial or total withdrawal from other jobs in order to devote time to the horse operation normally indicates that it is engaged in for profit.

However, if the owner does not personally devote substantial time to the activity, but employs competent and qualified persons to carry on the activity, the lack of time spent by the owner does not necessarily indicate a lack of profit motive. A good example would be a racehorse owner, who must employ professional trainers and jockeys to engage in a horseracing business.

4—Expectation That the Activity's Assets Will Appreciate

Included in the profit generated by the horse operation is the appreciation (increase in value) of the assets used in the activity. In a complete appraisal of the operation, the IRS may consider appreciation in the value of land, horses, equipment, and facilities. Therefore, appreciation of assets can be a powerful factor in proving profit motive.

For example, even if a horse business is operating at a loss, the value of the horses that have proven to be successful at breeding, racing, or showing can appreciate to a point that, if sold, they would produce a gain that would more than offset the losses.

However, if land is purchased primarily with the prospect of its appreciation, and the appreciation gains are due to factors not related to the horse operation, the IRS may treat the land as a separate asset. In that case, it would not be considered part of the profit derived from the horse business.

5—Success of the Taxpayer in Other Activities

In determining profit motive, the IRS may consider the fact that a business owner has engaged in similar activities in the past, and has a record of turning unprofitable operations into profitable ones, even though the present operation is not profitable. This factor is not one that the IRS has emphasized recently.

6—History of Income or Losses of the Activity

Showing a series of years of profit is a strong indication to the IRS that the activity is engaged in for profit. On the other hand, a business showing a series of years of losses, particularly during the start-up years, is not unusual and does not necessarily indicate a lack of profit motive. A gradual decline in losses and a series of profit years after the initial start-up period are good indications of a business operated with the intention of making a profit.

Long-term losses may be acceptable to the IRS if it can be proven that the losses occurred as a result of unexpected and uncontrollable conditions, such as accident, disease, theft, severe weather, other involuntary conversions (e.g. property requisitioned or condemned for public use), or depressed market conditions. It is good business practice to keep complete and accurate records of these circumstances, as they may be critical in demonstrating to the IRS why the business continued to show losses.

7—Amount of Occasional Profits, If Any

Occasional, small profits from an operation in which there have been substantial investments and which has a history of large losses are generally not favorable in determining a profit motive. On the other hand, the IRS does look favorably on an operation that generates an occasional large profit, particularly where the investments or losses are comparatively small. The possibility of eventually earning a substantial profit in a highly speculative venture can indicate profit motive.

8—Taxpayer's Financial Status

The fact that an owner does not have substantial income from sources other than the horse operation is generally favorable in establishing profit motive. On the other hand, losses from a horse operation that provide a large tax savings on other income are somewhat detrimental to proving that the activity is engaged in for profit.

9—Elements of Personal Pleasure or Recreation

The fact that owners derive personal pleasure from their horse activity does not necessarily indicate that they are not engaged in a business. It is reasonable to like horses and therefore to choose a related line of work. Most people who engage in a business endeavor do so because it gives them personal pleasure.

An activity will still be considered a business if there are motives in addition to making a profit. A hobby would be charged, however, where no obvious profit motive exists and it appears that "personal pleasure" is the sole objective. In other words, it is very acceptable to enjoy horses and have a horse business as long as it can be demonstrated that profit is the **primary** motive.

TWO-OUT-OF-SEVEN YEARS

Any horse business that shows two years of profit in a specified seven-year period is *presumed* to be engaged in for profit. Under these circumstances, the burden of proving that the business is *not* engaged in for profit (using the nine factors listed above) is placed with the IRS. However, if the operation does not have two years of profit in seven, it is not necessarily presumed that there is *not* a profit motive, but in this case, the owner will have the burden of proving the profit motive exists (also using the nine factors listed above).

Somewhat reassuring is the fact that the presumption for horse activities has remained two out of seven years while the presumption for all other business activities has been reduced to three out of five years. In essence, the IRS has given horse business owners a break in allowing them more time to show a profit.

How It Works

Under the two-out-of-seven year presumption, after the business achieves its second profit year, the owner will not have to defend the profit motive for that year and the remaining years of the seven-year period (whether those years are profitable or not). For example, if an operation shows a profit in 1995 (its first year) and again in 1998, the presumption of profit motive covers only the period from 1998 through 2001. The owner would have to be prepared to defend any losses deducted before 1998, as the profit motive during that time could be subject to challenge by the IRS.

It should be noted that:

- A presumption does not guarantee that the IRS will regard an activity as a business.

- Failure to achieve two years of profit during a seven-year period does not mean that the IRS will automatically determine the operation not to be a business.

- For the presumption to apply, the same kind of business activity must be conducted during the profit years and the loss years.

Special Presumption

New horse operations may choose a "special" presumption, which covers the first seven years of the operation's existence. With this presumption, the IRS essentially defers an audit of the operation for the first seven years. If there are at least two profit years by the end of the seven-year period, the operation will be presumed to be a business for *all* of the years in the seven-year period. However, without two profit years, the owner must be prepared to defend the operation as a business for the entire seven years.

This special type of presumption can be used by an operation only once and must be applied for within three years of the due date of the first tax return. One drawback to this presumption is that it puts a "red flag" on the owner's tax return, which invites an automatic audit at the end of the seven-year period. Failure to prove two profit years at this audit may invite the IRS to take the position that the activity is a hobby.

The regular two-out-of-seven presumption operates whether an owner elects to use the special presumption or not. If an activity expects to show two profit years immediately, there is little need to use the special presumption. The last five years will automatically be covered, and the owner will not have the burden of proving a profit motive exists.

If the business does not expect to make a profit until the sixth and seventh year, electing the special presumption would seem more desirable. However, as this election carries more risk and responsibility, owners should not elect the special presumption without first consulting a tax professional.

PLANNING FOR A PROFIT YEAR

Common reasons for an IRS hobby-loss challenge is a number of consecutive years of cash basis losses (see *Chapter 12 for more information about cash basis*). An operation that can show periodic profits may be able to avoid such a challenge. Ten or more years of losses could make an operation a candidate for audit. Showing an honest profit year whenever possible will not only help to avoid an audit, but will also strengthen the position of the operation as far as profit motive is concerned.

Operations that are using the cash basis method of accounting have the advantage of flexibility in planning their income and expenditures for any one year. There are various ways to plan for a profit year. Any method used must be well thought out in advance.

Reducing expenses in the profit year can be accomplished by postponing legitimate business expenses to the next year or by prepaying them in the year prior to the targeted profit year. For example, a breeding operation can pay breeding fees in full at the time of booking, which usually occurs in the year preceding the breeding. Other expenses such as large quantities of hay can be paid for in advance before it is taken out of the field, thus reducing the expense in the year it is actually used.

Probably the best way to demonstrate a profit year is through the sale of horses at a gain. Sometimes it makes good sense to sell one of the more costly horses at a profit to keep the business in the black. Then at a later date one or more good prospects could be purchased as replacement horses. Also horses held for sale could be grouped and sold all in one year. However it is accomplished, increasing sales during the profit year should be planned well in advance.

Another way to produce a profit year includes the sale and lease back of horses. This method would be of value to a breeder who wants to sell a stallion but wants to use the horse for an additional year or two. The stallion could be sold, thus creating income for the operation. The stallion is then leased back for a year or two.

The additional income should more than offset the expense of the lease payment, causing more income for the profit year.

A WORD OF CAUTION

The IRS has developed three tests to be met to be able to deduct expenses in the current year that will not be used until the next year. They are as follows:

- The expenditure must be a payment for the purchase of a supply rather than a deposit. It will not be considered a deposit when it can be shown that the expenditure is not refundable and is made pursuant to an enforceable sales contract.

- The prepayment must be made for a business purpose and not merely for tax avoidance. The prepayment should result in some business benefit. Examples of business benefits may include: gaining a better price, or being assured of an adequate feed supply.

- The deduction of such costs in the taxable year of prepayment must not result in a material distortion of income.

EXAMPLES OF TAX COURT CASES

During the 20 years between 1978 and 1998, there were more than 100 court decisions as a result of hobby-loss challenges to persons involved in horse operations. There were 26 horse-related court decisions published during the five years between 1993 and 1998. Of these decisions, only seven cases were racing breeds, and the owners lost three of these. On the other hand, non-racing breeds are much more at risk, and this is most likely because racehorse owners have an excellent source of possible earnings in racing purses and in the enhanced value of racehorses.

The following are eight examples of horse operations that were audited by the IRS and were found not to have been engaged in for profit. The taxpayers appealed their cases to the Tax Court with the following results.

Hoyle v. Commissioner, T.C. Memo 1994-594

In 1997, Mr. Hoyle, a Philadelphia lawyer, purchased a 392-acre farm in Queene Anne's County, Maryland, called Waverly. He hired a professional farmer to work the land, hired an accountant to set up farming books, made improvements to the land, and engaged in numerous farm-related activities. These activities included cultivating soybeans, crabbing, horse boarding, offering horseback riding lessons and hunting expeditions, breeding and selling game birds and horses, and racing Thoroughbreds. Mr. Hoyle spent most, if not all, of his weekends at the farm and communicated with the professional farmer on-site about three or four times a week, for a total of 500 – 700 hours spent on farming and farm management activities per year.

Mr. Hoyle sustained losses in every year during the period of 1977 – 1992. These losses totaled $2.4 million for that 16 year period. The IRS disallowed the losses in 1978 – 1985.

The IRS took the position that "the farming and holding of the land are separate activities unless taxpayers purchased and held the land with the intent to profit from its appreciation, engages in farming on the land, and farming reduced the cost of carrying the land." The Tax Court disagreed, saying that the IRS test applies only where the land is purchased or held primarily with the intent to profit from increases in its value. Based on Mr. Hoyle's testimony that he thought the land would appreciate in value when he bought it for farming, but that he purchased the land for farming, the Court found that the taxpayer's primary intent was to operate a farm. Thus, the Court concluded that the activities at Waverly, including the holding of the property to benefit from its appreciation are all part of a single activity for purposes of Section 183 (hobby-loss provision).

As of August 1985, the farm had appreciated in value by $787,113 since its purchase. Interest and taxes on the land for the same period totaled $807,580. The farm losses for the period 1977 – 1985 totaled $1,121 million, including the carrying cost of the farm.

Having concluded that land appreciation could be considered as a favorable factor the Court turned to other factors that supported Mr. Hoyle's profit motive:

1. He made efforts to increase the value of the farm through various improvements and several soil conservation projects.

2. A large portion of the losses came from interest costs associated with the land and if land carrying costs were eliminated, he earned an operating profit in 1977, 1978, and 1982.

3. His anticipation of profits was supported by the fact that he realized a gross profit when the land-carrying cost became minimal (the Court stating that an occasional small profit for an activity generating large losses was nonetheless important).

4. He changed the way he operated the farm and regularly experimented with new sources of revenue.

5. He had good books and records.

6. He regularly sought advice on how to improve his farm prospects and consulted other experts.

7. The lack of detailed projections of feasibility studies did not evidence a lack of profit motive.

8. The losses constituted a larger percentage of Mr. Hoyle's income than one would expect a taxpayer to be willing to sustain merely for the pleasure of having a farm as a hobby.

9. The waterfront farm was not a vacation home and did not offer more than incidental personal recreation.

The Court concluded by stating that this was one of those cases where they were satisfied that, despite the substantial losses, the taxpayer had a bonafide profit motive.

Joe and Robert Machado, T.C. Memo 1995-526

Issue #1: LaBarbara. In 1983, Joe and Robert Machado and four other individuals formed the "LB" partnership to purchase a broodmare. It was a general partnership with each brother owning a 12.5% interest. The partnership purchased LaBarbara, a brood-mare that was stabled in Kentucky. The managing partner, Mr. Hellman, maintained the books and records and paid all expenses.

LaBarbara was bred to a number of stallions, but the record did not indicate how many foals she produced. The partnership showed losses in each of the years 1983 – 1988. The Machados' share of these losses was $43,000 each, which was deducted on their respective tax returns.

The IRS denied the Machados deductions of the partnership losses because they determined that neither of the two brothers "materially participated" in the partnership; therefore, the partnership losses were not deductible by reason of the passive loss rules. The IRS also imposed penalties for negligence, substantial understatement of tax, and a 25% additional penalty for late filing of their tax returns.

The court had to decide whether the Machados materially participated in the horse activity. Quoting from the regulations, the court noted that the Machados would be treated as "materially participating" in the activity "if based on all the facts and circumstances, the taxpayer participates in the activity on a regular, continuous and substantial basis during the taxable year" and "the taxpayer participated in the activity for more than 100 hours during the taxable year."

The Machados argued that they did materially participate because they researched possible stallions for breeding with LaBarbara, met with other partners to discuss which breeding options to pursue, and voted on which stallions to breed to LaBarbara.

The court pointed out that the only evidence of the Machados' participation in the LB partnership was the testimony of one of the brothers that he spent hundreds of hours researching potential stallions and the 1988 calendar log that reflected entries for 15 phone calls. This led the court to conclude that the evidence did not establish that the Machados spent over 100 hours participating in the partnership. Thus the losses were not deductible because of the passive loss limitations.

Issue #2: Breeding/Racing Business. In 1984, the Machado brothers began, as informal partners, to purchase, breed, and race Thoroughbreds. Joe became interested in horses from his betting on horse races and Robert had taken a horseback riding class in college. Their primary business was the Machado Trucking Company located in California.

During 1980 through 1984, the brothers bought five broodmares, sixteen racehorses, and one share in each of two stallions. They boarded their horses in California. Before purchasing a horse, the brothers would research the bloodlines and racing records. They won $133,542 in purses during the 1980 through 1984 period. They realized no income from their breeding program during that period.

After 1984, as racehorses they had purchased in earlier years became too old to race, the Machados used the older racehorses as stallions for their broodmares. Their broodmares produced 11 foals that were trained and raced.

During the period 1985 – 1988, the Machados won $7,316 in racing purses. They realized no income from the breeding program.

In 1989, the Machados decided to terminate their horse activity. Three horses were sold at auction in California prices that ranged from $200 to $400 and the remaining horses were sold or given away in 1990.

Year	Gross Receipts	Expenses	Losses
1980	$0	$37,474	$37,474
1981	$17,566	$63,034	$45,468
1982	$43,050	$202,386	$159,336
1983	$48,820	$263,952	$215, 132
1984	$24,106	$180,234	$156, 128
1985	$2,250	$175,314	$173,064
1986	$0	$133,140	$133, 140
1987	$934	$106,998	$106,064
1988	$4,132	$110,141	$106,009
TOTAL	$140,858	$1,272,673	$1,131,815

Fig. 3–2. The Machados' income, expenses, and losses during 1980 – 1988.

Racing and breeding records were kept on a calendar. Expenses were kept on a handwritten ledger and on a computer database that was also used by the trucking company. Expenses were not allocated between racing and breeding. Income, expenses, and losses for the years 1980 through 1988 were as shown in Figure 3–2.

The $1,132 million of losses were deducted by the Machados on their tax returns. The IRS disallowed the losses on the basis that the horse activity was not a business.

In dealing with the question of whether the Machados horse breeding and racing activity was engaged in as a business, the court concluded that the Machados did not establish, by a preponderance of the evidence, that they engaged in their horse activity "with an actual and honest or good faith profit objective."

This decision was based on a finding that:

1. The Machados devoted a minimum of time to the activity.

2. They did very little advertising to sell horses produced by their mares.

3. They did not establish that any of their broodmares or race-horses appreciated in value or were likely to appreciate in value to the extent that they could earn an overall profit and recoup losses incurred over a 10-year period.

4. They did not present any credible evidence that changes they made to the operation of the activity would likely make the activity profitable.

5. They did not present sufficient evidence to show that the losses were due to customary business risks or unforeseen circumstances.

Shane v. Commissioner, T.C. Memo 1995-504

Mr. Shane worked as a full time computer programer for Baltimore county, making $35,000 – $37,500 per year. He also had

Year	Loss
1986	$35,631
1987	$26,990
1988	$39,834
1989	$32,996
1990	$39,324
1991	$36,039

Fig. 3–3. Shane's losses for the years 1986–1991.

several thousand dollars of other income. During his college days, he had taken off from school to gain the experience necessary to obtain a horse trainer's license, which he utilized in Maryland, Delaware, Pennsylvania, West Virginia, and New Jersey.

In 1982, he acquired his first Thoroughbred in a claiming race, following a two year period over which he studied racehorses. His horse proved profitable, winning $65,000 during the first 18 months. By 1987, Shane owned eight horses.

In 1988, following several years of poor results with the racing side of his enterprise, Shane began to concentrate his attention on horse breeding, keeping horseracing as a peripheral part of the overall activity. He began breeding his mares to top-rated Maryland stallions. However, prior to the time of trial, taxpayer had not sold any foals.

While Shane managed the financial aspects of his horse activity through his personal checking account, he used a computer program to keep an accurate and detailed record regarding the training, care, and pedigree of his horses.

Shane's expectations to become a successful breeder did not prove out. During the years 1986 – 1991, he incurred and deducted the losses shown in Figure 3–3.

The IRS challenged the losses for 1990 and 1991. When the case went to the Tax Court, the court ruled that Shane had engaged in the activity with an actual and honest objective of making a profit.

As proof that Shane operated in a businesslike manner, the court pointed to his computer program, his dual purpose bank account to keep bank fees low, his change of direction to breeding away from racing, and his meticulous records regarding the training and care of the horses. While the IRS argued there was no business plan, the court responded by stating that nothing in the Code, regulations, or case law requires a business plan with the degree of formality alluded to by the IRS.

The Court concluded that Shane's expectations that he would

experience appreciation value of his horse was a primary factor underlying his motivation for maintaining his horses. The fact that no foals had been sold prior to the trial did not diminish Shane's expectation, according to the Court, especially since his horse breeding operation, which began in 1988, was well within the 5 to 10 year start-up phase recognized in previous court decisions. The court went on to say that the business of breeding and racing horses in undoubtedly highly speculative and risky. Thus, the court found that Shane's failure to make a profit was not a determinative factor.

Shane's modest income led the court to conclude that it was unlikely that he would embark on a hobby costing thousands of dollars and entailing much personal labor without a profit objective. While the court recognized that there is no question that taxpayer enjoyed working with his horses, it nonetheless concluded that it cannot be said that he had any more or less enjoyment from his horse activity than customarily should be expected from an entrepreneurial undertaking.

Charles O. and Barbara K. Givens, TC Memo 529

Charles Givens purchased a 40-acre farm in Mount Vernon, Indiana for the purpose of breeding Tennessee Walking Horses. He had "dreams of raising the next World Grand Champion."

Givens had a background involving horses. For eight years he assisted his father, who owned and operated a horse stable. Givens had owned two horses and a pony and attended numerous horse sales. He had also discussed the feasibility of raising breeding horses with his father and others in the business.

When Givens purchased the Mount Vernon farm, he spent an average of 25 hours a week doing chores and maintenance, and became personally involved in every aspect of the operation. He maintained detailed records of all farm transactions and used his personal account to pay all expenses. He did not open a separate checking account under the farm's name.

Year	Income	Expenses	Depreciation	Total Loss
1	$420.00	$3,611.87	$467.70	($3,659.57)
2	$375.00	$6,023.11	$1,075.07	($6,723.18)
3	$1,680.00	$139.06	$786.50	($4,707.95)
4	$120.00	$5,495.31	$1,977.52	($5,699.68)
5	$120.00	$4,536.21	$1,445.23	($5,861.44)
6	$1,920.00	$3,330.96	$2,118.00	($3,528.96)

Fig. 3–4. Part of the Givens' tax records for the six years of operations. (This is not the complete return—the figures may not add up.)

Before he purchased his first breeding horse, Givens sought the advice of a horse trainer and breeder. He continued to seek advice from knowledgeable people during the course of his operation.

During the first three years, Givens acquired a stallion and four mares. The stallion proved to be unacceptable for breeding and Givens subsequently paid breeding fees for his mares. Over six years, four foals were born. One of the mares produced three of the foals. Despite repeated attempts at breeding, two of the mares were unable to conceive. The broodmare that Givens thought most valuable died due to a virus in September of the sixth year. Upon reviewing the six years of losses, Givens decided to discontinue the horse operation. The records show losses as shown in Figure 3–4.

At issue was whether the taxpayer's horse operation was engaged in for profit. The Tax Court found that Givens had conducted his horse breeding activity in a businesslike manner. Although he did not maintain a separate checking account for his business activity, he did keep separate, detailed records.

His willingness to change the farm's operations in an attempt to achieve profit shows he acted in a businesslike manner. He purchased a stallion believing it would reduce expenses. He bred his mares with the stallion and advertised the stallion's availability to other horse owners for a stud fee. Unfortunately, the stallion was not of the right temperament for breeding and was traded for a mare.

Givens had substantial experience with horses, having grown up on a farm with horses and having owned several himself. He did not have experience breeding show horses, therefore he sought the advice of experts and followed that advice. This factor was considered in his favor.

The Tax Court ruled that Givens was entitled to fully deduct expenses and depreciation which resulted from the horse breeding activity.

Charles R. and Helen J. Stubblefield, TC Memo 480

Charles Stubblefield rode and showed Quarter Horses for five years before starting his own business. During this time, he was recognized by the American Quarter Horse Association as a qualified judge. After he stopped showing, he continued to ride for pleasure and traveled to various states to judge Quarter Horse shows. The Stubblefields' son, Scott, was also an accomplished horseman. By the time he was 15, Scott was already training and winning professionally.

Scott was 22 when the Stubblefields purchased 17 acres near Tyler, Texas. The "Stubblefield Farm," which was purchased in an attempt to establish a nationally recognized Quarter Horse operation, originally had very few buildings and little fencing. A small apartment was constructed on the premises. Four years later, a 2,400-square foot home was built. A show barn was constructed the following year. Scott and his wife lived on the farm rent free.

Scott was designated as the trainer, and he and his wife acted as the farm managers. Scott never received a salary, nor

Year	Income	Expenses	Net Loss
1	$1,759.86	$10,349.48	($8,589.62)
2	$00.00	$30,444.95	($30,444.95)
3	$1,262.90	$20,479.69	($19,216.79)
4	$6,605.82	$60,052.83	($53,447.01)
5	$00.00	$35,815.00	($35,815.00)
6	$5,783.06	$26,489.25	($20,706.19)

Fig. 3–5. Part of the Stubblefields' tax records for the first six years.

was he reported as an employee. (However, he did receive a large portion of the income.) Charles Stubblefield was involved in the operations of the farm only in the capacity of reviewing the expenses and filling in at the farm when Scott was away. Stubblefield did not consult with other experts, despite the continued losses he was sustaining. Nor did he consult with Scott, or ask him to make any changes in the operation.

Year	Adjusted Gross Income
1	$72,655.46
2	$41,174.98
3	$65,648.86
4	$280,198.58
5	$180,773.00
6	$319,075.19

Fig. 3–6. The Stubblefields' adjusted gross income for the first six years.

The income reported on Schedule F by Stubblefield was from judging fees and the sale of horses. He paid all the operation's expenses, but did not receive any of the income from breeding and training fees or prize money, which Scott generated. The advertising and promotion of the farm did not associate Charles Stubblefield with the facility. Records of operations were not maintained. Schedule F of the Stubblefield tax return shows the losses as shown in Figure 3–5.

During a six-year period, the Stubblefields' adjusted gross income on their tax returns was as shown in Figure 3–6.

Eight years after the business began, the Quarter Horse activity was abandoned, and the farm was offered for sale. The purchase price of the farm had been $60,000, with additional funds spent for improvements, bringing the total investment to somewhere between $220,000 and $240,000. Due to the farm's location, its value had appreciated and an offer of $500,000 was received.

The Stubblefields possessed the ability to train and show horses successfully and they acquired the knowledge to run a successful operation. Had they used this expertise, a profit motive may have been found. However, despite growing losses, no effort was made to change or improve the operation.

Charles Stubblefield was not significantly involved in the farm's operation. However, he continued to ride the horses for pleasure, thus supporting the recreational aspect of his involvement in the activity.

The court determined that the appreciated value of the land was due to the location, and not because of the horse activity. The fact that, when purchased, the land was not set up for a horse activity, and residential dwellings were constructed before any horse facilities, led the court to conclude that the land had been purchased for its eventual appreciation.

The Stubblefields were not able to produce books and records of their Quarter Horse operation. Although Stubblefield maintained that he and his son were involved in an informal partnership, the fact that Scott received most of the income and his father paid all the expenses *was determined to be a diversion of income.* The fact that Stubblefield retained Scott, although he continued to operate at large losses, was determined to be evidence that a profit motive did not exist.

The Tax Court ruled that the Stubblefields did not have an actual and honest objective of realizing a profit from their Quarter Horse operation.

Richard L. and Carole A. Eisenman, TC Memo 467

In March of their first business year, Richard and Carole Eisenman purchased three purebred Arabian mares for $7,500.

Year	Expenses	Depreciation
1	$5,910.53	$2,678.71
2	$6,499.63	$2,225.45
3	$10,046.23	$1,397.51
4	$10,225.00	$892.00
5	$5,560.00	$158.00
6	$5,404.00	$143.00
7	$4,188.00	$89.00
8	$4,737.00	$37.00
9	$4,477.00	$49.00
10	$4,822.00	$00.00

Fig. 3–7. Part of the Eisenmans' tax records for the first 10 years.

They made this purchase after studying trade magazines and consulting with persons knowledgeable about the breed. They had visited many ranches and shows and had examined between 50 and 80 horses before making this purchase. The Eisenmans had owned horses before buying the Arabian mares and would continue to own a number of pleasure horses which their daughters rode. Neither of the Eisenmans rode horses.

The Eisenmans bred two mares (the third was not of breeding age) in March of the second year. They were bred to a stallion which the Eisenmans carefully researched and selected. He had won five national championships. One of the mares produced a foal the following spring, which the Eisenmans named Hi Bolt. The other mare did not successfully breed. Four years after they were purchased, all three mares were sold for $9,000. Hi Bolt was trained and was shown successfully.

Early in the tenth year, the Eisenmans had Hi Bolt evaluated by an Arabian breeding and training expert. The expert appraised Hi Bolt's value to be between $20,000 and $25,000. He also recommended that she be retrained, bred, and shown to increase her value. He felt that Hi Bolt was crudely trained at that time.

The following April, another trainer was engaged to train Hi Bolt for show. One year later, an offer to purchase Hi Bolt for $55,000 was received and rejected by the Eisenmans.

The Eisenmans maintained a ledger that detailed all the expenses for the Arabian horses. These records were kept separate from those of the family's riding horses.

The Eisenmans reported the deductions in connection with their Arabian horse breeding activity as shown in Figure 3–7.

The Eisenmans did not devote much of their personal time to the horse breeding activity, but employed others who were more knowledgeable to manage the Arabians.

The Tax Court found that the Eisenmans had engaged in the

activity with a profit motive. They had conducted the activity in a businesslike manner, kept accurate records, developed some expertise, and relied on competent people to train and care for the horses. They consulted experienced advisors before making critical decisions and invested considerable sums in Hi Bolt's training, even though neither of them rode. Also, the real possibility that the horse breeding operation *could realize an overall profit upon Hi Bolt's sale* led the court to rule that the Eisenmans were entitled to the deductions for their Arabian horse breeding activity.

Virginia L. Wardrum, TC Memo 121

For seven years, Virginia Wardrum and her daughter, Merry Lynch, were involved in raising, training, and showing horses. During this period, Merry won over 300 ribbons and 30 first place trophies in competition.

Wardrum worked hard at the horse activity, spending 15 – 20 hours a week keeping records, maintaining the facilities, purchasing feed and supplies, transporting horses locally and out of state for competitions, and tending to the horses' daily needs. She sought the advice of experts in setting up her horse operation.

Merry was responsible for training the horses. This took as much as 40 hours a week. She was paid a small salary for her services. She had extensive knowledge and experience, having been taught by many top trainers. She apparently had aspirations of becoming an Olympic rider.

Wardrum had owned seven horses, but never more than four at a time. They were all bought and sold for small amounts of money. When Merry went away to college, she took two horses with her.

The court ruled that Wardrum was not engaged in this horse activity with a profit motive. She sustained losses each year and was not able to establish just how she hoped to earn a profit. It did not appear that her daughter would earn sizable amounts of prize money from competition, nor that the horses would appreciate in value. Wardrum did not take in boarders or train for others. All of the expense and work were geared toward improving Merry's skills and helping her to become an Olympic-class equestrian.

Dennis R. and Bereneice Seebold, TC Memo 183

After purchasing four horses in one year for pleasure, Dennis and Bereneice Seebold decided to start an Appaloosa horse business the following year under the trade name "Triple S." They knew it would take several years to make their business profitable, but thought that it would provide income for later years. In preparation for going into business, Bereneice Seebold read many books, attended a horse clinic, and consulted with experts on the Appaloosa breed. They also consulted with their CPA about the business.

Even though both Seebolds worked full-time jobs for many years, they each still managed to devote at least 40 hours a week to the Appaloosa operation. They did nearly all of the labor themselves rather than hiring to have it done.

The Seebolds regularly advertised their Appaloosa farm, offering horses for sale, and boarding, training, and stud service. Spider Speed was purchased as a breeding stallion and became the symbol for Triple S. His cost was $1,512, and his value appreciated to approximately $25,000. The farm produced 20 foals.

While the Seebolds did not always maintain a separate checking account for their Appaloosa farm, they did keep separate ledgers of Triple S activities.

The Seebolds also engaged in raising turkeys and geese. However, they discontinued this aspect of their operation because it was not profitable.

Although the Seebolds sustained losses for six years with their operation, they projected a profit of $8,000 – $10,000 in year seven.

The Tax Court found that the Seebolds operated their farm in a businesslike fashion in their keeping of books and records. Discontinuing the non-profitable turkey and geese portion of their operation also showed that they were operating in a businesslike manner. No personal pleasure or recreation motive was found, as the Seebolds expended a great deal of hard work and effort in their operation and did not ride the horses.

The court found that the Seebolds' income from other sources was not significant when compared with the Triple S losses, and their plans for income in later years was in the couple's favor. The court also found that the Seebolds sought the advice of professionals to help develop their abilities as Appaloosa horse farmers. The expected appreciation of their horses, increased breedings to Spider Speed, and increased sales of foals were considered in the Seebolds' favor in having a profit motive.

WHAT TO DO IN CASE OF AN IRS AUDIT

The IRS selects returns each year for random audit. Among those selected are those with large losses from hobby type enterprises. A number of horse businesses are selected for audit because of their doubtful nature as a business or because of their large losses. Those who have been operating in a businesslike manner, have kept good records, and are demonstrating a well-defined profit motive should have nothing to worry about.

A horse operation must be ready to deliver unbiased information to establish the profit motive when confronted with an Internal Revenue Service challenge. This information should include a formal business plan along with financial statements and detailed accounting records. The owner should also provide a record of time and effort put into the business. This could be a simple spiral notebook with dates and happenings noted. Communications from experts and/or advisors that show the owner has sought outside advice regarding major business decisions should also be included.

The first thing that happens when a taxpayer is selected for audit is an audit letter is received. This letter has a deadline of 10 days to respond to the "person to contact." When contacted, this person will schedule the audit and answer any questions. *Do not disregard this letter!* If the contact letter is disregarded the auditor has no choice but to do the audit based on the information on the return. In that case, an audit report will be issued and most likely there will be a significant addition to the taxes owed for that year. It is still possible at this stage to contact the auditor and make an appointment. When there is no response from the taxpayer, the account will be sent to the collection section. This section of the IRS has the power to file liens, against taxpayer property, attach business and personal assets, and levy bank accounts.

The person doing the audit may or may not have an understanding of the horse industry. Be prepared to completely explain the horse operation, but do not assume that the auditor is ignorant of such matters.

There can be various results to an audit. It may be that no changes are made to the tax return or it may be that a refund is due because all allowed deductions were not taken. Usually additional tax is assessed because returns that are chosen to be audited have a high possibility of additional tax being owed.

It is important to carefully select the person who is to prepare the tax returns, because your tax preparer or accountant can appear in your place during the audit. This person must have a power of attorney to be legally entitled to discuss personal matters. He/she must be completely apprised of all circumstances pertaining to the horse operation and the return in question. A conscientious CPA will have clear principles of what should and should not be on a tax return.

Although audits can be delayed for a time, it is best to just bite the bullet and schedule as soon as possible. The IRS likes the time to be within 30 days of the first contact. This will be no problem for those who have maintained good records; for those who have not, no amount of time will make any difference.

The audit notice will designate items to be examined and will request needed records. Audits are for a particular year but can be expanded to include other years if deemed necessary.

Do not make the audit a difficult situation. Do not bring more records than are necessary for the audit. Provide only what is requested on the audit notification. In most cases audits are preformed in the auditor's office, but if the records are too large to transport the auditor will come to the business location. When there is an unusual situation, it is best to talk to the person doing the audit in determining the location.

The deciding factors used by the IRS in determining whether the horse operation is a hobby or truly a business include: operating in a businesslike manner; having a business plan, a separate checking account, and well-kept records; and of course, demonstrating a profit motive.

If the horse operation incurs large losses, it is almost certain to attract the attention of the IRS, and it is likely to receive a letter requesting an audit. Although an audit is not a pleasant experience, it does not have to be a disaster as long as the business has been operating with a true profit motive and records are in order.

AVOIDING CHALLENGE BY THE IRS

If the horse operation is selected for an audit by the IRS and found not to be operating for profit, there may be substantial consequences. Let's suppose that in the year 2001 the IRS is auditing tax returns of a horse operation for the three years 1998 through 2000. This process could last through the year 2003, if there is an appeal and a trial. Then suppose the three years being audited are determined by the IRS to be a "hobby" rather than a true business. The next three years (while the audit, appeal, and trial are taking place) will almost always be considered a hobby as well. In that case the horse operation could be liable for six years of back taxes, including interest and penalties. Needless to say, this could destroy the horse business.

Sometimes the determining factors in succeeding in a challenge by the IRS are basic things like advance planning and written records of all aspects of the horse business.

There is a variety of business ventures in the horse industry, and yet the basic principles are the same when confronting a hobby-loss audit by the IRS. These basic principles follow.

Separate bank accounts and accurate records for the business.

It is important to always use a separate checking account for the horse business. It is also wise to hire a professional to help set-up the financial and business records, and to review them from time to time. When the IRS auditor is given good records that clearly show income and expenses, the appointment may end quickly.

A formal and well-written business plan.

There is no rule requiring a written business plan, but if a properly written instrument can be presented the horse business will have more credibility. Numerous recent cases emphasize the presence or lack of such a plan. Written budgets and income forecasts are vital items to include in that plan. It is important that this plan existed prior to when the IRS Audit was initiated.

If taxpayers can show that when the business was not proving to be profitable, they made major modifications to a business plan in an effort to create profits, years of losses may be forgiven. Taking time and effort to rectify problems with the horse operation is simply contradictory to a hobby motive. Because of this it is always best to attempt to improve a losing business by changing it in some manner.

Disproving the recreational or personal pleasure motive.

The IRS hobby-loss challenge is based on the assumption that horse operations are oftentimes carried on for the pleasure of the owners rather than for profit. Because of this, the personal pleasure or recreational motives involving horses can be touchy. It would be wise to take measures lessening the appearance of such motives. Using the business horses for family pleasure will most likely affect the case. There have been owners, however, who have succeeded in court cases, even though the family was actively pursuing showing of horses. But there have been other similar cases unfavorably decided. Horses used for personal pleasure or recreation are always at risk in an audit situation.

Adequately time and money spent on the business.

The taxpayer's position will be better if a written record of time invested in the horse business is maintained. In addition to ordinary chores like cleaning stalls, feeding and grooming horses, these records should contain other activities like conferring with trainers or veterinarians, attending horse affairs or seminars, keeping business and horse records, meeting with possible customers, and reviewing the business plan. Almost all cases mention amount of time and effort expended in the horse business, and the law likes actual physical work and genuine effort made in pursuing a profit.

The courts are also more favorable toward owners who devote a substantial amount of available income to their operations. Decisions have gone against owners who devoted less than 10% of available income to the operation, but those who invest 20% or more in the horse operation will usually be held as truly in business for profit. The thinking is that no responsible person would spend so much time and energy on a hobby.

Consulting with experts on a regular basis, and continuing education as part of the business.

It is wise to talk to experts before beginning any horse activity. Once the business is up and running it will be necessary to employ a good accountant and other appropriate professional such as a veterinarian and trainer. These professionals should then be consulted routinely about business decisions and other matters. It would be wise to keep a written record of these consultations. And affidavits can always be obtained later from them if needed for audit purposes.

It is important to continue to learn about the horse industry in general and especially the area of the owner's business. This can be accomplished by membership in horse organizations, attending seminars and clinics, and reading trade magazines as well as taking formal classes in colleges and universities.

Keeping records of unexpected reversals

Every horse business has unplanned hardships that could be from the outside or industry-wide. Or it may be something happening to this horse operation only. When the misfortune affects the entire industry, it will be well recorded by various sources. If the hardship is specific to their business, the owners need to keep a detailed record. This written record helps in an audit situation because it substantiates what happened to cause the reversal in the business. The owner should document all deaths from whatever cause, all illnesses and injuries, and any abortions and lack of conception by mares. Examples would be: a prized mare aborts twins because one has died in utero and caused an abortion at six months; the entire herd comes down with a virus that results in death to several horses; or a valuable stallion is struck by lightening. All of these reversals need to be clearly outlined in the business records.

Creating a profit year when feasible.

When the horse operation has several years of losses, a year showing a profit will help in proving a profit motive.

As discussed earlier, creating a profit year can be accomplished in several different ways and needs to be planned for in advance. In addition to reducing expenses by prepaying them, increasing sales of horses, and the sale of lease back of horses, another way to create a profit year is by lessening the depreciation expense. This is done by not purchasing horses or other depreciable property during the planned profit year.

Every taxpayer is liable to audit by the IRS and even the most well-run horse operation may be chosen at random. This is where record-keeping and planning prove valuable in establishing a profit motive.

SUMMARY

Knowing what the IRS looks for in a business can help owners address those factors in their business plans, and avail themselves of the significant tax advantage associated with engaging in a business rather than a hobby. Hopefully, the Tax Court case examples have shown some mistakes to avoid, such as failure to employ more qualified help or recruit expert advice when needed, building an extravagant house before building any horse facilities on land that was purchased for a horse business, and demonstrating more personal interest than profit motive while operating at a loss.

Most hobby-loss cases brought against businesses are dismissed on appeals. However, keeping accurate and complete records and following the guidelines outlined in this chapter will make proving a profit motive to the IRS easy and straightforward.

4

MARKETING TECHNIQUES

Fig. 4–1.

To become competitive in the horse business, the owner must have a product or service that is in demand, know where the potential customer base is, and be able to sell the product or service to the potential customers. If a business can start out with a well-established customer base, less energy and finances will be spent on advertising and promotion. Some businesses face losses in the start-up phase due to the lack of clientele. But by evaluating the needs and desires of potential customers, promoting the product, and using professionalism to develop a good client base, it is easy to make a new horse business successful.

91

MARKETING STRATEGY

Simply stated, marketing is the anticipation and satisfaction of the needs and wants of a potential customer group. In other words, marketing is filling a need or a desire. To be successful in the horse business (as in any other business), it is important to provide a service or product that is desired, and also somewhat necessary.

Surveys show that there are a great number of horse enthusiasts in the United States. The majority of horse owners have one or two horses they keep in their backyard or at a public facility. Some people who like horses want to learn more about them. They read books, visit web sites, attend seminars, clinics, shows, races, open houses, auctions, sales, and just about anything else having to do with horses.

In addition to the steady need for well-bred horses, there is also a demand for instructional schools, training and boarding facilities, and related services like tack shops and feed stores. Within each market group, all businesses provide a service and depend on some type of sales.

Identify the Market and Serve It

The first question to ask is, "Does anyone want this service or product?" No matter what the location or what kind of business is to be started, analyze the need for what will be offered. How many customers will need this service, and to what extent? What types of customers can be expected?

The quality of competition should also be considered. If the business stays a step ahead of what people need or want, it can rise above the competition. The success of the business in drawing customers depends on what is done to recognize a need, provide a service or product to fill that need, and then promote that service or product.

Choose a Location

In selecting a location, keep in mind the clients or customers the business will be serving. For example, a racehorse trainer would receive much more exposure, and consequently more business, training at a public racetrack than at a private facility. Moreover, racehorse trainers and owners will find that start-up costs are less expensive at smaller tracks (but the purses are also smaller), and it is easier to get stalls at the track in the summer.

Other considerations in choosing a location may be:

- easy to find

- economic climate of the area

- room for expansion

- convenience of supplies and services (feed store, farrier, vet)

Appropriate zoning for the area where the business is to be established should also be taken into consideration. To find out the zoning for a particular piece of property, call the county courthouse or a local real-estate agent. Before committing to purchase the property, check with the city or county health department to see if there are any special health requirements that must be met by a horse facility. Also, have an attorney or title company conduct a title search to make sure there are no other restrictions that were placed on the property by a previous owner.

Create an Image

Every business has an image. The manner in which customers and prospective customers are treated when they visit, the cleanliness of the facilities, the attractiveness of the location, and the quality of the service or product delivered, all help form the image of the business. All employees should be mannerly, calm, friendly, and attractively dressed. Experienced horse handling enhances the business' reputation for competence. It is possible to create an image for a new facility or change the image of an existing one by improving one or more of the above factors. Moreover, a business owner can promote the business on the property. An attractive entrance, displays of awards or certificates, clean, well-manicured barns and paddocks, and a professional atmosphere all enhance the business' reputation.

PUBLIC RELATIONS

Good public relations consist of promotion and attraction. Promotion means informing the public about the operation's existence, specific features, location, and area of expertise. In planning a marketing program, it is important to keep in mind that there is much more involved than just attracting new business. The way the business owner presents himself or herself carries through the entire operation. Because people will do business with those they have confidence in, it is essential to build good rapport with potential customers.

Also it is important to have a plan that allows for the success and enjoyment of the customer. This success may be in the form of owning a winning racehorse, learning how to ride, breeding exceptional foals, or having a well-trained horse with which to compete.

The customer should be welcome anytime, and should never be ignored. The businesses that focus on the customer and what that customer is looking for will be the most successful. At least as much time and effort should be spent following up with existing customers and keeping them satisfied as is spent developing new business. The development of satisfied customers is the backbone of any successful marketing program.

Word-of-mouth from satisfied customers is still the best means of attracting new customers. And word-of-mouth from dissatisfied customers is the worst publicity. Many times the offended customer will not even complain, but will just go away and not return, not asking for any retribution. In this case, they will most likely tell all their friends their tale of woe.

MARKETING PROGRAM

The most valuable marketing tool one can have is a good reputation; not just as being honest and straightforward, but also regarded as knowledgeable and capable in their area of the horse industry. The necessity of maintaining an identity in the horse world business exists as long as the business is in existence. One way an identity is established is by planning and developing a marketing program.

First, the business must be identified by a sign in plain view. For the business to be remembered, business cards should be given to all potential customers and acquaintances who might recommend the horse operation.

Business cards should be suited to the business they represent and must include not only the business name, but address, telephone number, fax number, and e-mail address. Because people do keep and use them, business cards must present the operation in such a way that people will remember. In addition to giving business cards to potential customers, they can be included in correspondence. The idea is to keep the business name in front of the buying public.

How does one produce a business card? Finding the right design for the card is the first step. The business logo (discussed later) and slogan are a good start. Take these ideas to a printer with all the pertinent information. If the business does not already have a logo the printer can help create this also. Most printers have desktop publishing and can design everything on the computer while the owner watches. Remember that it is best to keep the business card simple and uncluttered.

Have a business logo designed that is attractive and simple. Along with business cards, have letterheads and envelopes printed with a matching design. Use them for all business correspondence.

The price of business cards, letterheads, and envelopes can be sky-high or quite inexpensive. Printers can furnish an assortment of paper samples. The best choice of paper is bright white (or color) of 100 to 150 pound stock. Since good design, quality printing, and quality paper are not necessarily expensive, it is possible to have something nice without spending a lot of money.

Invite potential or past customers to visit the business facility where they can see the entire operation. Be sure to pass out business cards and any other available information on the operation. A few days after the visit, send a note of thanks and offer to be of help when needed.

It is important that the owner of a horse operation is an active participant in local activities and area associations related to the business. This is a good way to show leadership ability and to become involved with potential customers. Volunteer, make yourself useful, and get the job done.

Off course nothing can replace personal contact and word of mouth, but eventually advertising and promotion will become necessary as the business grows. This is the time to have good promotion and advertising programs in place to continue the growth.

The problem many horse businesses face is insufficient advertising and marketing effort. Without advertising, customers are not informed about the business.

The question is not whether to advertise and promote. There is no choice. Without advertising and promotion the business will never get off and running. Advertising is essential to keep the business going and growing.

PROMOTION

Every minute, perhaps without realizing it, somebody is selling something by promotion. Newspapers and magazines are filled with press releases or stories about events planned to promote a person, product, or service. Radio and television offer live voices and images in their promotion. Even a person talking to a friend may be promoting a product or service just by saying its name.

To successfully promote a horse business, a business owner must do two things. First, create a favorable interest in the operation, and second, stimulate action on the part of the desired population. In planning promotion, know what the final objective is.

Avenues for Promotion

Many people confuse promotion with advertising. Although advertising a horse facility or service in a newspaper or breed publication is helpful, it is not necessarily the most effective method of promotion in the horse industry. Horseraces, shows, and other competitions provide another important arena for promotion of horses, services, or facilities. Business owners should have their horses participate in as many of these events as possible—provided their horses can be expected to win. Attractive and clean transporting vehicles with the name, logo, location, and telephone number of the business can transport the horses to each event—they serve to promote as well.

Breed associations also provide avenues for promotion. They often sponsor shows, races, contests, and educational programs. Business owners should participate in as many of these events as possible. Subscribing to breed magazines or newspapers ensures that the owner knows about the events well enough in advance for good planning. Attending a sale or auction—even without any intention to buy—is an opportunity to see and be seen, to talk with other people in the industry, and to learn about current market conditions.

Business owners can also sponsor their own events: open barns, grand openings, horse shows, sales, and clinics are other avenues for promotion. For example, holding a fun show or clinic in support of a particular group serves to introduce people to the facility and hopefully enhances the desired image. By holding a raffle or drawing, it is possible to obtain the names and addresses of the people attending. These names can then be used for future mailings and contacts.

Sometimes business owners are hesitant to sponsor an event at their place. They know it will help business, but do not know how to promote and attract a large enough crowd to make it a success.

Promoting an event need not be all that difficult. It starts with a good plan at least six months in advance. First, establish a budget, because the amount available to be spent determines the kind of plan to be put together.

Next, determine the interest area. This can be done by looking at a map and finding an area in close proximity to the location of the event. All horse enthusiasts within the area are prospects to attend.

Then research media coverage in the area. Included are horse publications, radio and television stations, and local newspapers. Now decide how to reach the proper people with promotional messages. It may be in the form of a press release, or perhaps a feature story about the owner and the operation. Interviews on radio or television are often used to spark interest in the event. Handbills posted in critical locations, listings in coming events calendars and broadcasts, and paid advertisements can all be beneficial. And don't forget promotion by word of mouth.

The best way to start is with a press release. A couple of months before the event, a short, matter-of-fact statement with contact information should be mailed to all media outlets, and to other horse enthusiasts who will be happy to promote the event. Next, print hand bills and distribute them in all directions in the designated area at least a month ahead of the event. Another news release should be mailed about a month after the first one. This news release should expand on the first one. Include an announcement of something important, like a special guest. A third release with something new added could be mailed a couple of weeks before the event.

Dates of the event should be listed with all coming events in local newspapers and newsletters. It is a good idea to have radio stations announce the event because they make these announcements many times, and this is a very effective method of advertising.

A couple of weeks before the big day, contact radio and television stations to set up interviews. Be sure to invite the media representatives to cover the event, issuing free tickets. Attracting reporters to an event and getting them to write a story on it can be a valuable source of free advertising.

Do not forget about word of mouth advertising. Make sure everyone involved with the operation is fully informed about what is going on, and ask them to spread the word. Telephone county and local leaders who deal with horse people and invite them to attend urging them to tell others about the event.

If the operation's budget allows for advertising, place ads in local newspapers a week or two prior to the event, and run broadcast spots two or three days before. The advertising should inform people the event is something interesting and exciting that should not be missed.

ADVERTISING

Every advertisement should work hard to attract the readers and proclaim benefits. There are basically two kinds of advertising used in the horse industry. The first kind of advertising is used when there is something to sell, such as breedings, training, lessons, horses, etc. This type of advertising explains that there is something available now, and urges the reader to act immediately.

Then there is the advertising that is designed to create interest in a business and build awareness, even though the operation may not have anything to sell at the time. This form of advertising endeavors to increase familiarity and to instill in the readers' minds the benefits of doing business with the advertiser. Even though the advertiser has nothing to sell immediately, the advertising lays the ground work for future sales. This type of advertising should be powerful, compelling, and engaging enough to attract attention and hold it until the point is made. It should explain why someone would want to business with the advertiser and should highlight the benefits the operation has to offer.

The question is not which type of advertising to use; an operation can benefit from using both types. The real question is how to make every advertisement attention-getting, exciting, with benefits for the reader, and designed to create interest in and awareness of the horse operation.

Advertising Budget

To get the best results from the allotted advertising dollars, it is important to have an advertising plan. As a general rule, expect to spend 10% of the expected return on advertising. If a horse is to be sold for $2,000, plan to spend about $200 on advertising. If the stud fee is $1,000, figure how many breedings are reasonably desirable and calculate the total income from that number of breedings, using around 10% of that amount as the advertising budget. The same can be said for training and boarding services: calculate the desired income and use 10% of that amount as the advertising budget.

Importance of Good Record Keeping

The advertising budget will go much further if the business owner maintains records from year to year on where the advertising dollars went and which avenues were most effective in attracting the right customers. Using these records, the business owner can decide which avenues of marketing to avoid in the future, which to allot more of the budget to, and which should remain the same next year. The records could also show the business owner what kind of customer is being attracted. With this information, the owner can increase the advertising targeted at those customers. Or, the owner may wish to emphasize different aspects of the business so as to attract a different, and hopefully more profitable, set of customers. Good records of the year's advertising and promotional expenses will also help at tax time.

Choosing a Publication

What is the best publication for advertising? This decision depends on what is being advertised. A publication with a large circulation is not as important as reaching the people who are interested and ready to purchase the kind of horse or service being offered. In other words, concentrate on the targeted market.

When offering a horse for sale, running ads in several publications for a short time, especially during public sales, will probably bring better results than running an ad for a long time in just one publication. (Running the same advertisement for a long time may cause buyers to wonder what is wrong with the horse.) Breeding farms have a defined season when advertising is most effective: stud services should be advertised just before (and continue throughout) breeding season; a crop of foals should start being advertised just after they are dropped. When advertising services such as training or boarding, it is best to use a series of advertisements or year-round advertising.

Creating an Advertisement

What type of advertisement to run depends on the publication and the advertising budget. For example, an advertisement offering a horse for sale or breeding should include every positive thing possible about that horse:

- successful prior breedings
- an excellent pedigree
- outstanding relatives
- successful offspring
- awards earned
- records held
- winnings
- race times

A map to the business is helpful. The location, telephone number, web site address, and person to contact should, of course, also be included in every advertisement.

The first thing an ad should do is get noticed. The reasons ads get noticed are headline, illustration, pleasing design, and the benefits being offered.

For an ad to attract and hold the reader's attention only one main benefit should be offered at a time. Trying to convey more than one idea to the buyer is distracting. It is better to use different ads for different concepts. The headline should feature the benefit, and it should also be illustrated. The text or copy must clearly set forth the benefit and tell where and how it can be purchased.

Dynamic Illustration

Photos and illustrations greatly enhance the impact of an ad. An ad without an illustration will probably go unnoticed. Every reader is attracted to a dramatic action photograph. It should show enough action to capture the reader's attention and at the same time promote service or product for sale. The picture needs to be more than just a quick photo, and this is where a professional photographer may be needed. If the selling price of the horse or service warrants it, using a professional photo for the ad may be justifiable, but a quality amateur snapshot can also bring good results.

Be creative when advertising breeding stock, it is not necessary to show the sire and dam. A cute picture of the foal will more than suffice. Pictures of people can also be incorporated into the ad, as buyers are interested in the owners as well. Some have used illustrations such as drawings, cartoons, and other artwork to advantage, but nothing works as well as a quality photograph.

Short, Catchy Headline

Good headlines are so important that professional advertisers often write the headline before the ad copy. It must tell why anyone should be interested and also explain the illustration. Powerful headlines work with pictures to grab the attention of the reader and make them want to continue reading. One might get an action photo of the horse and combine the picture with a headline that both tells the name and explains the main benefit of the business. This concept can seldom be accomplished in a couple of words, however, headlines are best kept short and catchy.

Interesting Ad Copy

Good advertising copy along with headline and illustration can capture the reader's attention. It is the job of advertising copy to propel them toward making a purchase. The ad copy must answer questions, arouse reader's interest, inspire confidence, and motivate to buy: the ad's primary purpose.

There should be a clear intent for the copy, and it must be convincing. It must be presented in such a way that the reader is sure it is real. It is also important to present the main idea more than once, as repetition works to get the message across. Giving assurances and proof build confidence. Also it is wise to guarantee the product when possible.

An effective ad must conclude by asking for business or using phrases like "Call Now" or impose a specific time limit, detailing the price and inviting a response. Make it easy to contact the proper person for details and to make a purchase. Provide names of real people and several ways to contact them: phone, fax, e-mail, etc.

Business Logo

Creating an attractive logo is one of the initial components of a marketing and advertising program, because the reader immediately identifies the logo with a particular horse business. The logo should be clear and unmistakable and should carry the name of the business. It should not be complex or ornate. For that reason "clip art" does not make for professional logos. For the best logo with original artwork, the services of a commercial design artist may need to be engaged. But this is not the only way to have a logo designed, as others with art talent offer this service as well.

When a logo is used for advertising purposes, it is usually presented with information pertaining to the horse business. This would include name, address, telephone and fax numbers, and e-mail address of the owner as well as directions to the business.

Ensuring Good Response

Getting personal information from the reader so they can be included on the potential customer list of the business should be relatively easy.

Everyone likes to get something for nothing. Most people will respond to something new and free, especially if it is something interesting that will assist them in their business enterprise of personal recreation. Getting people to respond to a printed advertisement can be just as simple as having them fill out a coupon for the free offer. The information on the coupon can then be used as a sales lead.

The free offer could be a "how to" booklet, information on breeding problems, or details of a specific new feature at the advertiser's horse facility. In addition to free information, a small gift can be mailed to those who respond. Be careful not to offer such a grand gift that people will respond just to receive it when they have no actual interest in what is being marketed. It should be nice enough to cause interested parties to respond quickly.

Every person who responds should be sent the information and gift as soon as the request is received. Include a personal note of thanks offering to be of help if they have questions. When a response appears especially promising, a telephone call should be made to follow up.

The names and addresses of the persons who have responded will then be added to the file of potential customers. Whenever a mailing goes out from the horse operation, they can be included with the regular customers. Sales leads provide a viable means for a business to acquire new customers and must be acted upon quickly.

In addition to identifying prospective customers, response advertising can be used to gauge the effectiveness of different avenues. For example, the same advertisement can run in several magazines at the same time. When this is done, it is necessary to print an identifying symbol in the coupon. This way it will be possible to know which publication the response is from.

By using this method, it won't be difficult to find out which advertisements are generating the most replies. To determine the most cost effective ad, figure the cost of each response. This is accomplished by dividing the cost of the ad by the number of replies it generated. This will enable the owner to focus spending for ads where they do the most good, and eliminate it where it is not productive.

Avoiding the Exaggeration Pitfall

In an effort to impress possible customers and generate more sales, some people embellish the truth and promise more than can be delivered. However, this practice is not wise because it can backfire on the business owner.

Then there are some who overstate the truth without even thinking. Their concern is to make sure their advertisements stand out above the rest. So they use slogans like "a cut above" or "the best in the nation" confident this is the proper message to send. These advertisers will need to be ready to meet the expectations they have generated in the prospective buyers.

Not that it's likely perspective buyers will confront the advertiser. It is more likely the disappointed buyer will complain to others when they discover they have been misled, and will not be inclined to have future business dealings with the advertiser.

Customers will not be disappointed if the advertisements are honest and clearly state the true features of horse or other products. Of course, superior qualities and advantages need to be stressed, but it is best to forget trying to impress and to concentrate on telling the truth. Interest in the product can be created with advertising copy that is well written without misleading the buyer. Ads that oversell the product may gain the sale but will lead to less business in the long run.

"Non-Traditional" Advertising

Some of the "non-traditional" ways of advertising are very practical for people in the horse industry. These methods would not necessarily replace the more traditional but would supplement them.

One of the newest methods of advertising and promotion is the Internet. Having a web site can be quite advantageous for a horse business when it is done correctly. As in regular advertising the first impression must be good enough to generate genuine interest. The greatest sales advantage to a web site is that the advertiser can have a detailed dialog with a potential customer. This is something that cannot be done with the more traditional methods of advertising.

Moreover, it is often possible for a business to purchase advertising space on another horse-related web site. This ad can be just as effective and more economical that traditional print advertising. In fact, many horse sites offer free classified ad space.

It is not enough to just upload the site and wait for potential customers to find it. The Internet address or URL must be actively promoted to elicit the right sort of response. Start by including the address in all online and printed horse listings and search engines. Then link it to as many other horse business web sites as feasible, and list the e-mail address in all traditional advertising.

Any marketing method offered should be checked out before a decision is made spend those advertising dollars. Make sure potential customers are the ones being reached. The vehicle chosen must cover the area near the business and attract the right kind of people. As there is no point in advertising where potential customers do not exist, it is best to find out what type of readers are attracted to the advertising medium in question. Figuring the cost pre thousand potential customers reached will allow the business to gauge its effectiveness.

Once the advertising medium has been selected, it is a good idea to check their effectiveness. Create an e-mail address specifically for that medium, so when a potential customer e-mails for more information, you know which ad they are responding to. Keep careful records of these methods to avoid confusion.

Keep in mind that it does not matter much where the prospective customer gets the message. It doesn't matter if the business uses traditional advertising or the very latest in non-traditional marketing, as long as they get the message and get it with some kind of regularity. Exploring various methods of advertising and promotion will allow the business to research the effectiveness of each marketing vehicle.

SUMMARY

Successful marketing includes all of these strategies as well as developing a rapport with customers. One contact with a potential customer or client is usually not sufficient to build such a rapport. Follow-up contacts are usually necessary to attract business. Generally, people who return for more of the product or service offered are satisfied customers, and their opinions within the horse industry are the best form of advertising and promotion.

5

BUYING
&
SELLING HORSES

Regardless of which area of the industry they are involved in, most horse business owners buy and sell horses. This process can be simple or complex, depending on the cost of the animal and the terms of the agreement between the buyer and seller. This chapter outlines the legal aspects of buying and selling, and explains various types of sales and sale contracts. It details what provisions should be included to best serve both the buyer and the seller.

Fig. 5–1.

BUYING HORSES

Purchasing horses is a process that needs the same careful consideration as any other major business decision. Because most buyers are generally very enamored with horses, expert guidance is often needed for the selection process to be thorough. It is not always easy to buy the right horse, and it may be difficult to resell a horse that is purchased hastily and turns out to be unsuitable. Because of the investment involved, it is important that the selected horse or horses meet the needs and desires of the buyer.

When purchasing a horse for an owner or client, keep in mind the activity for which it is being purchased and the price range that has been set. The buyer/agent should be well informed about the quality and type of horse that will best suit the client's needs. Purchasing a horse without carefully considering the intended use could later cause unnecessary problems.

Uninformed buyers can easily misunderstand laws pertaining to the sale of horses, especially in the area of seller responsibility, and obligations of an agent and the veterinarian performing an examination of the horse. Because they are uneducated about these things, they may not be aware of their own responsibilities and assume guarantees and warranties are automatically offered. They may not do all their homework and end up with problems when the horse turns out to be somewhat less that expected. So they will most likely blame the seller, veterinarian, or agent and may even initiate a lawsuit.

Using an Agent

Quite often the first contact a newcomer to the horse industry has is with a sales agent. Consequently these agents are crucial in the horse industry. The sale will certainly be lost if the agent makes a mistake.

These agents are in a difficult position. They want to see the horse sell for a large amount because they work for a commission;

at the same time, they are working for the buyer to obtain the lowest price possible. The first problem the agent has with this is that buyers rarely have confidence in him/her even though they are entirely honest and forthright. And the agent is penalized dollar-wise when he/she does get the better bargain for the purchaser.

When engaging an agent for the purpose of purchasing a horse, look for one with a good reputation. There are many ways an agent could take advantage of the buyer and private treaty sales have even more potential for problems. Agents are not regulated or licensed in any way, so the buyer needs to choose with great care. There are plenty of temptations for agents to be less than honest, so it is important that they have basic integrity. The fact that they have income from other sources will also protect them from being lured into less than honest business deals.

The agent chosen should also be knowledgeable about the fair market value of horses and of course, must know where the good horses are to be found.

It is important for the agent to have an eye for good horseflesh and plenty of contacts within their sphere of the horse business. And it is a real plus if the agent has actual hands-on experience within that sector of the horse business. It can happen the agent will lose time and money in futile pursuit of that perfect horse. Even when the agent has warned the buyers of the pitfalls of certain horses, they may become enamored with the horse and disregard all the agent's warnings and end up with the wrong horse. They then criticize the agent because of a bad deal.

In an industry where deals are made with a handshake and many agreements are unofficial, it is relatively easy for an agent to yield to the temptation and overcharge the buyer. And many times the seller's agent is also taking a large commission on the same sale. This obviously leads to a much overinflated price for the buyer.

Blank agent's authorization forms are quite often found in sales catalogs. Never sign one of these forms, not even when the agent is well known. More than a few people have ended up buying horses for much more than they were worth because they signed a blank form. When the purchaser is unable to be at the sale, it is no longer necessary that an agent's authorization form be signed in advance. This was once the case but because of modern technology, sales companies who have all the appropriate paperwork in advance will now allow a buyer to bid on a horse over the telephone. This way the buyer has control over the bidding and can avoid problems later on.

Determining who is honest is not always an easy task. Perhaps the best way to find an agent with integrity is to check with others in the horse industry, and benefit from their experiences. It probably will not take very long to find an agent with a reputation for honest dealings.

There are certain matters that need to be taken into consideration when engaging an agent:

- The kind of horse and price range the purchaser is looking for should be well understood by the agent.

- The agent is to furnish the buyer with an impartial and educated opinion on the worth of the buyer's choice of horses before the sale. The agent should be aware of the prevailing atmosphere of the sale and should be able to relate this to the buyer.

- Confidentiality is of utmost importance to the buyer. The agent should not disclose any of the pertinent facts about the buyer's intentions.

- It is important that the horse being purchased has met veterinary examination requirements prior to the sale.

- Know the agent's fee up front. The going rate for an agent's services is about 5% of the net purchase price. It must be clear that the agent is working for the buyer and not some seller. To be safe, keep the money in an escrow account until the sale is final.

- It is the agent's job to secure the best price for the buyer. Before any money changes hands, verify the sale with the seller. This will avoid any side deals or double dealings.

- Before transporting the horse, the agent must secure mortality insurance.

- When all the legal paperwork is completed the monies can be released from the escrow account.

- The buyer may bid via phone, providing all the paperwork is in order.

Veterinary Prepurchase Exam

Regardless of the type of horse or where it is being purchased, it is wise to have a veterinarian examine the animal prior to sale. Although trainers can evaluate performance and breeders the reproductive value of a horse, when it comes to the most decisive factor in purchasing a horse-the animal's overall health and physical condition-an expert veterinarian should be employed.

Not every purchase examination is the same. The intended use of the horse will determine what tests the veterinarian performs. A 2-year-old gelding that is being evaluated as a racehorse will need a far different examination from a 7-year-old mare that is being considered for breeding purposes. Both would receive a comprehensive physical exam, but the gelding's would stress lameness tests and the mare's would include a complete reproductive assessment.

The buyer should select a qualified veterinarian who is thoroughly familiar with the discipline for which the horse is being purchased. The cost for anything more than a basic prepurchase examination can range from several hundred to several thousand dollars. The seller should agree to having the horse's present veterinarian consulted. Accompanying the veterinarian to the exam will assure that another horse had not been substituted for the exam procedure. A written description of the results of the exam should be presented by the veterinarian, so that everyone involved can be aware of the findings.

Deciding what should be included in the prepurchase examination requires clear communication between the prospective buyer and the veterinarian. The buyer should:

- Choose a veterinarian who is familiar with the breed, sport, or use for which the horse is being purchased.

- Explain to the veterinarian the expectations and primary uses of the horse, including short-and long-term goals (for example, racing, then breeding).

- Ask the veterinarian to outline the procedures that he/she thinks should be included in the examination and why.

- Establish the costs for these procedures.

- Be present during the prepurchase exam. The seller or agent should also be present.

- Discuss the findings with the veterinarian in private.

- Ask questions and request further information about the vet's findings, if necessary.

The purchase exam is meant to furnish facts about the horse's present medical condition. It is not the duty of the veterinarian to give or withhold authorization on the sale of the horse. Keeping in mind the use for which the horse is intended, the veterinarian will give counsel to the prospective buyer about how conformation may affect its performance.

The purchase exam cannot reveal all the facts about a particular horse because it is like a photograph and can only provide information that is true about the horse on that day. There are many factors that have contributed to the horse's condition that may not be evident on the day of the purchase exam. Even so, the information from this exam can be very important. The purchase exam can keep the buyer from acquiring an unsatisfactory horse and thus save money and avoid disappointment.

There is no set way to conduct a purchase exam. Each individual buyer must decide with the veterinarian as to what is needed. The following is a list of suggestions:

- The horse's medical history, including worming, vaccinations, and feeding will be reviewed.

- The horse's mouth and teeth will be inspected.

- The ears, eyes and nostrils will be examined.

- The body and limbs will be palpated.

- The lungs and heart will be listened to.

- Respiration, pulse and temperature will be checked.

- An evaluation will be made of the horse's confirmation.

- Blood samples will be drawn for Coggins/other tests.

- Feet will be observed and checked with hoof testers.

- Flexon tests will be carried out on the joints.

- The horse's behavior will be scrutinized.

- Without warm-up, the horse will be observed traveling in a straight line and in small circles, and under saddle at a walk, trot, and canter.

More tests will be recommended by the veterinarian if there is cause to believe that the horse will not be suitable for the intended use. Tests could include urine and blood analysis, x-rays of the legs, nerve blocks, and endoscopic and ultrasonic examinations. These tests are used to confirm the seriousness of a problem or establish a diagnosis. These are all discretionary and may be the recommendation of the veterinarian or the choice of the prospective purchaser.

All horses used for breeding need tests to ascertain their reproductive condition. Prospective broodmares will be palpated rectally to inspect the reproductive system to determine any structural problems. A uterine biopsy and culture can establish the health of the uterus. All stallions should be teased and collected to ascertain fertility and libido. Then the sperm will be checked for count, motility, and viability.

In making a realistic decision about the purchase of a horse, it is important that the buyer completely understand the results of the veterinarian's examination. When discussing the results with the veterinarian, note the following items:

- The buyer has a right to get a second opinion, but owes both veterinarians a fee.

- There is no such thing as a perfect horse.

- A horse's performance may not be seriously affected by some medical conditions or conformation faults.

- Where the horse requires special care, the buyer must decide if this fits their requirements and budget.

By providing objective, health-related information, the equine practitioner can be a valuable partner in the process of making a purchase decision. Money spent on a purchase exam is a good investment even if the buyer decides not to purchase the horse. It can prevent a lot of headaches and trouble and spending of even more dollars later on.

Beware of Fraud!

Individuals who sell horses are usually honest and upstanding. However there are those who have given the term "horse trader" a bad name. Most people in the industry will come in contact with this type at some time. They use all manner of deceptions and can be quite crafty in their illegal pursuits. In fact, they are so clever that even seasoned buyers can fall for their schemes. But because of their naivete, new buyers are often the prime targets for crooked dealers.

For the scam to be successful the crooked seller needs to get the victim's confidence. The term "con man" comes from this ability to gain the trust of buyers through the use of false promises and claims. When the buyer does not verify these and takes the con man at his word, the scam is successful. It may be some time before the buyer realizes the truth—that the horse purchased is not what it was made out to be.

There is nothing new under the sun and horse sale fraud is nothing more than modernized versions of old scams. If a horse deal seems to good to be true, it usually is. No one likes to be "had," therefore all buyers need to be aware of the possibility of being deceived.

False Documentation

In this scam, registration papers from horses sold to killer buyers come into play. Scam artists can buy these papers for a few dollars, match them up with similar horses and then sell them to unsuspecting buyers.

It is the little difference like a marking that is the wrong shape or a white hoof that is not there, that will be caught during a thorough examination of the papers. Sometimes merely contacting the issuing registry that will reveal fraud. There have even been attempts by these scam artists to convince registry officials to misrepresent records for their benefit.

Medicated Horses

Using medications to conceal bad behavior or physical problems like lameness is undoubtedly the most common scheme of the con artist. Another method is to withhold feed from a high strung horse to make it appear more calm, or to overwork the same horse so that is appears safe for even a child or beginner to ride.

Bait and Switch

The old bait and switch scam has been around for years and this is the way it works: a very attractive item is advertised, but it does not actually exist. Instead a product of lesser quality is offered in hopes of capitalizing the deceived buyer's desire to purchase. Perhaps the ad is for the kind of horse most would only dream about and the price advertised is well within most horse lovers' means. Of course when the prospective buyers arrive they are told that the horse has just been sold, and they are pressured to look at other horses that just happen to be for sale.

Swapped Horses

A horse is purchased and delivery is part of the deal. But when the horse is delivered it is not the same one that was purchased. In fact, it is much lesser quality. When he or she tries to acquire the original purchase, the buyer will find that the seller has disappeared.

Agent Fraud

Overcharging of both buyers and sellers is the most common fraud committed by agents. This is easily done where the clients have been working without any documentation. The agent can charge excessive commissions or they can report an inflated amount for the horse's sale price and keep the difference along with the commission. These markups have been known to increase the price of horses dramatically.

False Impressions

Some fraud is simply a matter of the seller trying to create a false impression by presenting the horse in a dishonest manner. Included in these methods of deception are standing a horse on a grade to give the appearance of being well balanced, hiding hoof and ankle flaws in tall grass when showing, tacking up a bridle-shy horse ahead of time, or warming up a chronically sore horse before the prospective buyer arrives.

Don't Ask, Don't Tell

If the buyer does not ask, the sellers are not usually bound by law to tell all about the horses they have for sale. This means that the buyers must be very precise in the questions they ask the seller, or they may end up with something that they did not bargain for.

Make the Deal

Armed with this knowledge of all the possible sources of fraud and deception, the prospective horse buyer is ready to start looking for that special horse. Following the guidelines presented here will enable the buyer to be well prepared.

Know the Needs

Before actually looking for the horse to buy there are certain things to be considered. First of all, what is the planned use for the horse? Not just in the present, but also in the future? What is the most desirable characteristic looked for in the horse? Is there one breed that best meets all those characteristics? What amount can be spent on the purchase? Make a list of the answers to these questions.

Realistic Expectations

It is of utmost importance to consider realistically the abilities of the buyer, both as a rider and as a handler/trainer. Just as in humans, there is no perfect horse. Every horse has flaws, some quite small and insignificant and some rather large that have to be overcome or managed. All purchases carry some risk and each requires some compromise.

Use a Safety Net

The decision to purchase a horse cannot be made by the veterinarian nor the agent. While they should give the buyer an honest appraisal of the horse at the time of the sale, they cannot be held responsible for the decision to buy or for what happens after the sale is made.

If the buyer is not qualified to judge horses or negotiate sales, someone should be called upon to assist. This can be as uncomplicated as asking a knowledgeable friend to be with them as they complete the buying procedure. This person can help in the evaluation of the horse and it's suitability, evaluate the seller, and be present during sales negotiations.

When the prospective buyer is inexperienced, the solution should be through a well-informed agent. Once the agent has been found, get several references, find out the agent's fees and commission, and get a written agreement. It may be necessary, especially in high dollar purchases, to hire an attorney who is familiar with the equine law to draw up the agreements, thus protecting the buyer's investment.

Thorough Preparation

When it is time to inspect the horse, the buyer should bring along the written list of questions about the horse. The list can then be referred to and questions checked off as each is answered. The seller must be specific as to the use of the horse. If the horse is trained, the seller should state the discipline for which it is trained. And, as discussed later in this chapter, the intended use of the horse must be clearly stated so that the UCC's warranty provisions will cover the sale.

Check Out Training and Temperament

The inspection of a horse may take more than one session. This is to enable the buyer to establish if the horse has the ability, training, and temperament that meet the buyer's criteria. This should not be decided in a hurry, nor should the buyer end up being a pest. Be alert for signs of drugging, slow movements and responses, a distended penis, and sluggishness.

Drug Testing

The only way to be certain the horse is performing normally while being investigated is to have it tested for painkilling and mood-altering drugs. The buyer will not want to have every horse tested, but when an appropriate prospect has been found, a drug test can be carried out as part of the veterinarian's prepurchase examination.

Check out the Guarantee

Not every seller will offer a money-back guarantee. This does not mean that there is something to hide, as the seller may honestly not be in the position to do so for various reasons. Also, sellers must protect themselves from harm that may occur when the horse has left their control. Still, it is wise to inquire about the return policy, in case an exception can be made for a particular horse. Before bidding on a horse at an auction, the buyer should be well aware of all terms and warranties offered with the sale.

Deliberate and Confirm

Do not feel pressured to make a purchase. Allow time to check up on all the seller's claims. This may involve returning two or three times to take another look, unannounced, if possible. Calls can be made to others who can confirm that the horse is as the seller has presented it. This could be previous owners/riders, veterinarians, trainers, breed associations, or registries.

Put It in Writing

A written agreement should include not only the horse identification information and payment terms, but also all the negotiated items, and applicable statements made by both the seller and the buyer. (See the section on paperwork later in this chapter.)

SELLING HORSES

Skilled salespeople present a good impression of their business as they are selling a horse. That is, if the buyer has confidence in the integrity of the seller and the reputation of the business, the horse will be more easily sold. *(See Chapter 4 for more information on marketing.)*

To ensure that the seller receives top dollar, horses should be fit, well fed, and properly groomed. The owner should have all the necessary legal documents, health certificates, and registration papers in order.

Every horse business must decide at some point which horses to sell and which to keep. This is true no matter the size of the horse operation, dollars invested, amount of business know-how, or number of horses involved. The owner also must decide whether to sell privately or at public auction. If the horse is to be sold at auction, the owner must further decide which sale to use, and which consigning agent to hire.

These decisions depend on why and what is to be sold. Perhaps the owner is selling some of the best horses because the market is rising, or maybe it is time to cull the herd. Sometimes horses are sold to raise capital to purchase major equipment, or to pay off the debt on equipment bought last year. Another reason may be to prove a profit motive to the Internal Revenue Service. The reasons for selling horses involved are as varied as the horse businesses themselves. Selling the right horse at the right time is vital to both short-term and long-term business success.

Deciding Which Horses to Sell

The most important aspects of selecting horses for sale are the overall goals and financial obligations of the business. With these considerations firmly in mind, the owner can appraise the conformation and temperament of the horses being considered for sale. So before deciding on any form of sale, the business plan needs to be consulted. This is another important reason to have formal written business plan (*see Chapter 2*). The plan will contain projected income and expense for the current year. Included in the income items will be projected sales of horses. Meeting the projected amount of sales is vital to the profit for the year.

Using the business plan, the next action is to look at the amount needed to break even. Adding 25% to that figure will permit some margin in case the horses fail to bring the expected price or become sick or injured. With this new amount needed from sales, then the owner can determine how many horses need to be sold in the current year.

The next step is to assess each individual horse's conformation and marketability. It is important to keep in mind the following points:

- How would this horse be classified from a conformation viewpoint? Is this a lesser horse, a middle horse, or one of the best?

- Has this horse peaked in its desirability and athletic ability or will it continue to improve and sell for more money later on?

- Is this the time to cull some of the lesser horses, or wait to see if they improve?

- Is this the best time to sell this horse, or will this particular bloodline be more popular at a later date?

- Is it better to sell a broodmare now or wait and sell her with the foal at her side next year?

In contemplating this last question, it is necessary to keep in mind the age of the mare and the desirability of the foal. These factors could determine their future market value. When the mare is in foal to a well-known stallion, it may be wise to keep her until after she foals because the value of the foal may be considerable. But, if she has been bred to an unknown stallion, it may be better to sell her before the foal arrives.

Deciding Where to Sell the Horses

Because selecting the appropriate sales method can determine the amount of money received for the horses, great care must be taken in the selection. Comparing the sales results of various sales in prior years can help in choosing the right one.

Since money chases the top of the sale, horses should be chosen from the best in conformation and pedigree for a public sale. (Public sales are discussed more thoroughly later in this chapter).

First narrow the choice of sales down to two and then consider the following questions:

Large or small sale: The horse may stand out better at a small sale, where it would be lost in the crowd at a large one.

How popular is the sale? The seller needs to consider who will be attending this sale. There is no point in using a sale that historically tops at $20,000 if the horse to be sold has a much higher value.

Does this sale offer some sort of specialty? There are sales that are geared to promote a certain breed or class of horse.

Where are the potential purchasers? Since each buyer will attend only a few sales, the seller must concentrate on those and sell horses at a sale where these potential purchasers will be hoping to buy.

What is the best time of year? For example most yearling sales are anywhere from June to October. The foaling date may determine when to place it in a sale. A yearling born in May will need more time to develop and would be placed in a later sale as opposed to a yearling born in February.

Deciding on the Consigning Agent

At this point, there is only one more decision to make: Which agent will represent the seller at public auction? This is a very important question and the answer may determine whether a profit is made on the sale of the horse. As with accountants and tax experts, it is extremely important to choose an agent with utmost care. *(See Using Agents in this chapter.)*

Sellers: Motivated for Better or Worse?

Every equine discipline is subject to disappointing horse sales at every level. There are four basic problem areas that cause unsatisfactory sales:

The horse is a lemon–In other words, the horse has serious behavioral or physical problems that are discovered after the sale has been made.

Lack of communication—Those parties involved in the sale have misinterpreted the warranties, agreements, or responsibilities to others participating in the tale.

Buyers fool themselves—The buyers have purchased a horse that

125

is not suited for their abilities, purposes, or pocketbook. Because of this, they cannot give it the proper care and/or use.

Scams—Sellers intentionally set out to deceive the buyer.

Some sellers become less than honest when the pressure is strong enough. The reason for this is the amount of time and effort it takes for the sale, and the frustration when the horse remains unsold for a long time. The cost of upkeep, advertising, showing the horse to many prospective buyers, and arranging for prepurchase exams takes a lot of time and money that could be spent elsewhere. Then there are people who just want a free ride, back out of deals at the last minute, or do not show for appointments. Sometimes the strain causes the seller to make a sale that is less than honest.

Overly cautious veterinary reports tend to overstate every minor health or soundness problems. This practice has led some sellers to think of these examiners as "doctors of doom" and fear they will emphasize each blemish as if it were a lethal defect. Reasons for extreme caution of the veterinarian is the fear of lawsuits, which the horse seller has no problem understanding. Nevertheless, the sellers can feel quite impotent when faced with generally adverse reactions generated by the prepurchase examination.

There is almost no way to hold a seller accountable when dishonest tactics have been used in a horse sale. In all types of business dealings, those run in an honest and reputable manner will be the ones to attract repeat business. And this is true in the equine industry as well. However, a large number of horse sales are a onetime occurrence. For example, auctions where sales are made between people who never meet, onetime events by individual sellers, bargains made by traveling traders, and sales involving a seller who is in the horse business for just a short time.

The Uniform Commercial Code provides the only regulation of horse sales, other than perhaps the state licensing of veterinarians involved in the sale.

126

THE UNIFORM COMMERCIAL CODE

What does the Uniform Commercial Code (UCC) have to do with buying and selling horses? The UCC is a set of laws adopted by all states (except Louisiana) that governs the purchase and sale of goods and covers the responsibilities and rights of the seller and buyer. Horses offered for sale are considered goods, and the same state statutes apply as for the sale of any other goods, including warranties and guarantees. (Business owners who are buying or selling horses in Louisiana should seek legal advice to determine their rights and responsibilities.)

Part of the provisions of the Uniform Commercial Code protect the horse owner's "security interest" in the horse. Simply stated, that means that a person has a valid interest in, or right to, a horse that he/she owns or partially owns.

For example, horses under consignment may be open to attachment by creditors of the consignee. That means that where the creditor has mistakenly assumed that the horse is owned by the consignee, and has extended credit based on that assumption, the creditor may take the horse as security. For their own protection, horse owners should file a UCC-1 Form in the state and/or county where the horse will be located. (UCC-1 Forms are for sale at most office supply stores.) Filing this form in accordance with the Uniform Commercial Code division of sales protects the owner from the consignee's creditors by perfecting the owner's security interest in the horse. *(Appendix A contains an example of a UCC-1 Form.)*

When to Perfect a Security Interest

When a horse or other property is sold and full payment is not received immediately, the seller should "perfect" a security interest in the animal to protect against default of payments. For example, at the time of an installment sale, the seller and buyer should complete a UCC-1 Form. This form states the name and address of the seller and buyer and describes the goods used as security (the horse or other asset). When this form is filed with the state or county where the sale has taken place, the seller holds a perfected security interest in that horse. In the event the horse is moved, the UCC-1 Form needs to be filed with the new state or county.

Just how this perfected security interest protects the seller is evident in the following story:

> A horse was sold at an auction by Mr. Crandall to Mr. Fields. An installment purchase and security agreement, as well as a UCC-1 Form were signed by both parties.
>
> Two days later Mr. Fields sold that same horse to Mr. & Mrs. Moore. During the time that the auction paperwork was being processed, and before Mr. Crandall filed the executed UCC-1 Form, Mr. Fields filed a UCC-1 Form signed by Mr. & Mrs. Moore. Consequently, Mr. Fields perfected his security interest in the horse, and his interest superseded Mr. Crandall's.
>
> None of this came to light until almost two years later, when Mr. & Mrs. Moore had completed paying for the horse and wanted the registration papers. Because Mr. Fields had filed bankruptcy in the meantime and had not made the required payments to Mr. Crandall, the registration papers were not released to him. So Mr. Crandall had the papers, Mr. & Mrs. Moore had the horse, and Mr. Fields held a perfected security interest in the horse.
>
> Because Mr. Fields held the security interest in the horse, Mr. Crandall was not in a position to repossess the horse for non-payment. Mr. Fields could not provide the registration papers because he had not paid off his debt to Mr. Crandall. Mr. & Mrs. Moore had a horse that they neither had clear title to nor the registration papers for. And Mr. Crandall most likely will never receive the unpaid balance for the horse.

If a UCC-1 Form had been filed immediately, the above incident would not have happened. Mr. Fields actually was doing the correct thing when he promptly filed this form. Had Mr. Crandall filed his UCC-1 Form before Mr. Fields, he would have been the first in line for the horse, and could have repossessed it for non-payment of the debt. In that case, Mr. & Mrs. Moore would have lost out, even though they were unaware that Mr. Fields did not have clear title to the horse.

Before buying a horse, the buyer should check with the office of the County Clerk or the Secretary of State (in the state where the horse resides, and/or the state of the seller) to make sure there are no other security interests in that horse. Otherwise, the buyer may pay for the horse, yet have no grounds for ownership when the person holding the security interest repossesses it. If the seller holds a security interest in the animal, and the buyer has de-faulted, the seller has the right to repossess the horse as long as the action is not considered breaching the peace. In other words, if repossession of the horse would involve breaking and entering, the seller would have to obtain a court order to repossess the ani-mal. A less dramatic alternative for the seller may be to perfect a security interest in a more secure asset of the buyer, such as an automobile, rather than using the horse for security.

Once the buyer has paid for the horse, the seller provides the buyer with proof that the security interest has been canceled. This is accomplished by filing a UCC-2 Form and sending the buyer a copy of that form, indicating that the security interest has been released. (UCC-2 Forms are also for sale in most office supply stores.)

WARRANTIES FOR THE BUYER & SELLER

When a horse is offered for sale, the seller warrants (guaran-tees) that the horse is free of any security interest or lien of any third party, that the horse's title is good, and that the seller has the right to transfer the title. This is considered an "implied warranty," because the average buyer would assume these conditions are true. If these conditions are not true, or if the seller has any doubt about the horse's title being clear, then it must be indicated in writing to the buyer that none of the above warranties are being made.

The Uniform Commercial Code imposes the responsibility for making the title good on the seller. If the seller has failed to inform the buyer of a defect in the title, and/or the seller is unable to correct the defect in the title, the buyer may have a damage claim against the seller.

Implied warranties also encompass the animal's fitness for a certain purpose. For instance, if the seller knows the buyer is looking for an event horse, and the buyer makes a purchase based on the seller's recommendation, the seller is warranting that the horse is fit to walk, trot, canter, and jump.

When a seller makes actual verbal or written statements or promises about a horse to a buyer, these "express warranties" become a part of the purchase agreement, and the seller has in effect guaranteed that the horse conforms to these promises or statements. It is not necessary that the seller use any special word such as "guarantee" to create an express warranty. Nor is it necessary for that to have been the intention. This type of warranty is not derived from the seller's opinion of the horse's value, but rather the seller's statements about the horse's ability or training.

An example of an express warranty would be a seller stating that the horse was "show ring ready." For the seller's protection, it should be clearly stated in writing just what is being sold. If the seller does not want to guarantee the horse for any specific activity or use, then a statement to that effect should be a part of the bill of sale or purchase agreement. Popular terminology for this purpose is that the horse is being sold "as is" or "without any guarantee" or "without any warranty." In other words, what you see is what you get. However, even the acknowledgment that the horse is being sold "as is" does not offer the seller absolute protection from fraudulent misrepresentation charges.

The amount of money being spent and the intended use of the

horse determine the warranties or guarantees a seller may be willing to make. Horses purchased for a few hundred dollars do not usually carry any kind of guarantee, but are bought "as is." The more money the buyer is willing to spend, the more guarantees the seller may be willing to make. Because guarantees impose a risk on sellers, they may expect a higher price for horses that they are willing to guarantee.

When a horse is being purchased for breeding, the buyer may want a guarantee on the horse's fitness and ability to produce offspring. Here again, the amount of money paid for the horse may determine the seller's willingness to make a guarantee. Of course, the best and safest way to ensure that the horse being bought is of the ability and condition desired is for the buyer to arrange for a veterinary examination (discussed earlier in this chapter).

All warranties or guarantees should be clearly spelled out in the purchase agreement between the buyer and seller. This could be a simple bill of sale for the horse "as is," or could be a more complex purchase agreement that would necessitate the help of an attorney. If the horse being purchased is a high-priced one, it would be best to seek legal advice.

PUBLIC SALES

Thousands of horses are bought and sold each year through public sales. Probably the most significant advantage of public sales is the convenience; having a variety of horses in the same place makes it easier for the buyer to find the "right" one. However, other buyers are competing for the same horses, and they may have more money to spend. Also, the anonymity of the public sale makes it risky. No guarantees are given to buyers, and complete veterinary examinations are usually not allowed before a sale. Nevertheless, public sales are a vital part of the horse industry.

When consigning horses to a public sale, the seller may have to pay a consignment fee and sometimes a fee for conditioning (a sales agent prepares the horse to look its best for sale). Usually, the sales agent will also receive a 5% – 10% commission on the final bid. The time required for Thoroughbred sales preparation varies from 30 to 90 days. Because of the consignment and conditioning expenses, the horses should be of a quality to bring a good price. It does not make sense to consign a horse to a sale where the sales price would be eaten up by the conditioning and consignment fees. However, not all sales require the conditioning time and expense; less prestigious sales may only charge the consignment fee.

Each sale has its own terms and conditions, which should be clearly understood by the buyer and seller. These terms and conditions cover such things as risks and warranties, bidding, buyer's payments, defaults of purchase, delivery to buyer, taxes, withdrawal rights, insurance, stabling, and credit terms available. Because most public sales require payment in full within 30 minutes of the sale, and the seller should have no security interest in the horse after it is sold, it is unnecessary for the seller to file a UCC-1 Form.

The seller should evaluate the location and timing of the sale, how the sale is promoted, and how the animals are promoted, as these factors will affect the price range of the horses being sold. The following sections discuss the most common types of public sales.

Select Sales

The select sale is the most prestigious type of public sale because only the finest horses (in terms of breeding and conformation) are nominated. A panel of experts in the breed examine all nominated animals and select "the best of the best" for the sale. (This type of sale takes its name from the fact that this process of elimination narrows the selection considerably.) Needless to say, the horses in select sales bring high prices, as these sales attract buyers from around the world. An example of a select sale is the

---

Examples of Implied & Express Warranties

Implied Warranties:

- The horse is free of any security or lien.
- The horse's title is good, and the seller has the right to transfer it.
- The horse is fit for a particular purpose.

Express Warranties:

- The horse is "race trained."
- The horse is able to produce offspring.
- The horse is "show ring ready."

Fig. 5–2. While implied warranties are protected unless there is written evidence to the contrary, express warranties should be clearly stated in writing to protect the buyer and the seller.

Keeneland July Select Yearling Sale held in Kentucky. This sale features many of the top Thoroughbred yearlings in the world, and it is not unusual to see a sales price exceed $1 million.

Open Sales

Registered horses that do not qualify for select sales are usually sold in open sales. There are more open sales than select sales simply because there are more horses with average pedigrees and conformation on the market. Also, the only requirement for open sales is that the horse be a registered Thoroughbred, Standardbred, Quarter Horse, etc., and that the owner pay a cataloging fee. Horses sold at these sales are generally more affordable than those sold in select sales.

Sales of Two-Year-Old Racehorses in Training

The advantage of buying a horse at this type of sale is that two-year-olds are generally only 60 – 90 days from their first race. Although two-year-olds are more expensive than yearlings (as their prices reflect training fees and increased maintenance expenses), the buyer can get a better idea of what the horse is capable of at this stage. Knowing this, some people do nothing but buy yearlings to resell as two-year-olds, hoping to make a profit. This practice is called "pinhooking."

Sales of Older Horses in Training

With this type of sale, there is an advantage in that the horse has at least made it as far as the racetrack, or has a horse show record. However, the buyer must consider why a horse would be sold at this stage in the game. Sometimes a horse is sold because a partnership has dissolved or an estate is being liquidated. However, sometimes a horse being sold is not doing well enough to earn its keep. Or, the horse has sustained an injury, and its pedigree is not good enough to justify retaining the animal for breeding. Occasionally, a buyer can pick up a horse at this type of sale and campaign successfully at a different racetrack, a lower level of competition, or in a different sport entirely.

Breeding Stock or "Mixed" Sales

As the name suggests, all types of horses can be found at these sales—weanlings, yearlings, broodmares, stallions, etc. Anyone involved in breeding might be found at this type of sale. (Home-bred horses sometimes bring the greatest satisfaction, because breeding them involves heightened anticipation due to the amount of time spent waiting before there is any return on the investment.)

Before the Sale

Several weeks before attending any public sale, call ahead to the sales company and obtain a catalog. Fill out the credit application (located in the front of the catalog), take it to the bank for verification and notarization, and return it to the sales company. Be sure to check with the sales company to ensure that your credit has been approved.

A buyer should always read the conditions of sale, which are listed in the sales catalog. They contain important information such as how much time the buyer has to give notice of rejection after having a purchased horse examined by a veterinarian, and what kinds of guarantees are made on the horses sold. Sale warranties are typically very limited in length and coverage; at best guaranteeing soundness of eyes, bones, reproductive capacity, and wind.

Before the sale, the buyer should review the catalog and somewhat narrow the choices to those horses with desirable breeding that fall within an acceptable price range. Although it is impossible to know how the bidding will go, a person can often judge the price range of a young horse by looking at the stud fee. For example, a good "rule of thumb" is that weanlings often go for two times the stud fee, whereas yearlings tend to go for four times the stud fee. Buyers would also be wise to note what, if any, paid up engagements the horse has, or if any futurity races have been booked and partially paid for.

Ideally, the buyer should arrive a day or more early at the sale to examine interesting prospects. The buyer should ask each horse's handler to walk and trot the horse out so it can be inspected for conformation (particularly the legs) and way of going. It is a good idea to mark comments in the sales catalog for each animal inspected. For example, if the buyer disapproves of a horse after this preliminary inspection, a definite "no" should be marked next to that horse in the catalog. Making notes in the sales catalog ensures that the buyer will not confuse several horses and bid on the wrong one.

During the Sale

Unless you are really an elite professional, never buy a horse without examining it first. When tempted to bid on a horse that looks attractive in the sales ring and is going for what seems a ridiculously low price, remember that very often (but not always) there is a reason why no one else is bidding on it.

Buyers should also have decided ahead of time what their price limit is on each horse that has been inspected and approved. If they have extra time, they might examine some horses that appear above their price range. Each sale has its own "personality," with some having high prices and some being lower than usual. Even within a particular sale, if a good horse comes in at a time when there is little buyer competition, the buyer may be able to get the better animal and still stay under his or her price limit.

When it comes time to bid, the buyer should pick one bid spotter and stick with that person. This way, the bid spotter gets accustomed to the buyer and can detect subtle bidding signs. (If consignors see an eager bidder, they may attempt to run up the bid.) It also avoids a situation where two bid spotters are taking bids from the same buyer. (Occasionally, buyers have discovered they have been bidding against themselves!)

It is good for a new buyer to attend a few sales before actually becoming involved in bidding. It takes time to get used to the procedures and habits of a particular sales company. For instance, if a buyer puts in the highest final bid, but the amount is less than the secret reserve price (the price at which the consignor has agreed to sell the horse), the auctioneer may "up" the horse's price to the next increment.

After the Sale

Once a horse has been purchased, many sales companies require that a buyer settle up (pay for the horse) within 30 minutes.

The buyer will not get the horse's title at this time, but the sales company will give the buyer a stable release form, which allows the new owner to transport the horse from the sale grounds. If the buyer's check does not clear, the sales company, which has perfected a security interest, will repossess the horse.

Next, get a veterinarian to examine the horse. If the horse is not as it was represented in the catalog, it may be returnable (usually up to 48 hours after purchase). It is a good idea to line up a veterinarian ahead of time when planning to purchase a horse at a sale. Often, the veterinarians on the sale grounds are busy and may not be able to examine the horse in time.

Buyers should come to the sale prepared to take a horse home. That means having a trailer or van lined up, or having feed, water, and buckets available, and a groom to take care of the horse. If the sale is far from the horse's final destination, the buyer may need to make arrangements to board it somewhere along the way.

PRIVATE SALES

A private sale allows the buyer and seller to come to a private agreement on the sale/purchase. Horses advertised in breed magazines, newspapers, at the local feed store, and at competitions are often sold through private treaties. Sometimes, a buyer will make an offer for a horse that has not been advertised, and if the price is right, the owner might agree to a sale. A distinct advantage of private sales is that the horse may be subject to a complete veterinary exam before the sale. Also, prospective buyers have time to mull over the good and bad points of the horse and negotiate with the owner for a price with which they are comfortable.

Selling Horses Through a Farm or Agent

Many owners do not want to consign their horses to a public sale, yet are not prepared to market their animals themselves.

They may find a trustworthy agent who specializes in buying and selling horses for individuals. Alternatively, training or boarding facilities that have a lot of activity or visitors may take horses on consignment.

When a horse is consigned in this manner, the owner places the horse with the trainer or farm with the understanding that the horse will be sold for a set price. The agreement is therefore not only for the sale of the horse, but for boarding the horse as well. Since the horse is offered for sale, it needs to be kept in saleable condition. Sometimes a requirement for this type of agreement is that the horse remain with the consignee (the farm or trainer to which the horse is consigned) to be conditioned for sale. As with public sales, this cost may be unjustifiable unless the horse is valuable.

Keep in mind that because the consignee is able to charge board for the horse, there may not be the incentive to make a great effort to sell it. For this reason, it is wise to negotiate an amount of board that closely matches the consignee's cost of keeping the horse. All matters about the horse's feeding, care, and exercise should be spelled out in a consignment agreement, as well as the selling price and any other terms. The amount and timing of payment to the consignee should also be clearly set forth and understood by both parties.

Because of the risks involved in consigning a horse privately, this type of consignment agreement should be entered into with care. The owner should be well informed about the management and the facility to which the horse will be consigned.

Leasing to Buy

Leasing horses with the option to buy can be very successful. Horses may be offered for lease for a specified amount of time, with the intent that if the lessee (rider) and horse are compatible, a sale will be made. It is advantageous for first-time buyers to consider short-term leasing as a means of "test driving" a prospective purchase. If the horse selected proves unsuitable, the lessee may return it and look for another one. This is not the only way to lease horses, but it usually results in a successful private sale.

While a leasing-to-buy program can be beneficial to both parties, it takes a lot of organization and planning on the business end, and would most likely be offered in conjunction with lessons or other training programs. *(The sample lease agreement in Appendix A contains an option to buy.)*

SPECIAL TYPES OF SALES
Selling a Stallion and Retaining Breeding Rights

If a stallion is being sold and the seller wishes to retain the right to breed certain mares to the stallion after selling him, a written agreement with the new owner(s) should be arranged. But it is poor protection for the seller if the buyer sells the stallion to a third party or if ownership of the horse changes hands for some other reason.

With proper wording in the contract, it is possible for the original owner to create a security interest in the breeding rights of the stallion. The contract should clearly state the number of breedings retained per year and whether the seller has the right to sell these rights to another. These points also need to be stated on the UCC-1 Form, which the seller should file for the retained breeding rights.

The contract should state the remedies available to the seller if the breedings are not provided as agreed. These remedies might include a monetary penalty and provisions for repossession of the stallion if the conditions are not met. Filing a UCC-2 Form clears the title from the retained rights when the contract has been fulfilled.

Selling Unborn Foals

The sale of an unborn foal does fall within the Uniform Commercial Code definition of "goods" for sale. That means, when sold by persons who are in the business of selling horses, the unborn foal is considered to be guaranteed by the seller as meeting the criteria of horses in the marketplace. Unless so stipulated in a contract between the buyer and seller, the foal is warranted by the seller to be marketable. A foal born deformed or with permanent defects would not meet this criteria, and in such a case the buyer may not be held to the agreement to purchase the foal.

If the seller is an expert in a certain area of the horse industry, and the buyer is relying on that expertise in purchasing an unborn foal for a specific purpose, the seller has given an implied warranty that the unborn foal will be suitable for that use.

If the seller is making no warranties on the unborn foal, then this should be stated in the purchase agreement. As with the sale of any horse, it is necessary to state that the foal is being sold "as is" or without warranties. This written statement would protect the seller from any implied warranties.

The agreement between the seller and buyer should state what happens if the mare aborts the foal, the foal dies at birth, or the foal is born deformed. Is the buyer entitled to another foal out of that same mare or a different mare? Will any deposit that has been made be refunded? Answers to such questions need to be set forth in writing.

The written agreement should also detail who is responsible for the care of the mare and foal while the foal is still nursing, where the mare and foal are to be kept, and what happens if the mare dies. Furthermore, it should outline the payment terms for the unborn foal. *(Appendix A contains an example of a purchase agreement for an unborn foal.)*

The Installment Method

Buying and selling horses over time has become quite common. This is particularly true of high-priced animals, but even a moderately priced animal may be sold using the installment method. An installment sale is simply a way of acquiring property immediately, but having the payments spread over a period of time. Usually equal payments are made yearly, quarterly, monthly, or any other period agreeable to both buyer and seller.

Because the buyer normally takes physical possession of the horse, the seller must have some way of retaining rights to the horse until it is paid for in full. Without the right to repossess the horse in cases where the payments are not made as agreed, the seller would be without means to collect the unpaid balance.

A common misconception about securing an interest in a registered horse is the importance of retaining registration papers. Although this method is quite effective in collecting the money due in most cases, it does not really provide the seller with the necessary security interest. *Registration papers do not represent full legal ownership of the horse, but only prove the horse's breed registration and parentage.* Retaining registration papers is of little legal value to the seller should the buyer sell the horse to another party or lose the horse to creditors.

Location, Use, and Care of the Horse

In addition to outlining the terms of payment and perfecting a security interest, there are other issues that may be involved in the purchase of horses under the installment method. These are the location, use, and care of the horse.

If the horse is moved, the seller needs to know. Obviously, the seller wants to protect the security interest in the horse by filing UCC-1 Forms in the location where the horse is residing.

Both the use and care of the horse are issues about which there may be difficulty in reaching an agreement, especially if the seller has definite requirements for these matters while still holding a security interest in the horse. For instance, the buyer may not like to be restricted in the use of the horse, or the particular care of the animal (as defined by the seller) may prove to be impossible.

Any specific requirements should be spelled out carefully in the installment purchase agreement to avoid misunderstandings. Likewise, penalties for any departure from the agreed upon use and care should also be a part of the agreement. (There are cases where horses have been repossessed for the buyer's failure to provide the agreed upon care.)

In preparing an agreement, it should be spelled out as to which state laws are to apply. Usually, the laws of the state where the seller resides are applicable. Another matter that should be covered in the installment purchase agreement is what happens when there is a breach of contract, and who is responsible for attorneys' fees in case of legal action.

Understanding the problems that may arise, and being aware of the need for proper writing of installment agreements, can save the buyer and seller much distress. *(See Appendix A for an example of an installment purchase and security agreement.)*

Claiming a Racehorse

Claiming is a way for a racehorse owner to obtain already-racing horses that can provide an immediate return on the investment. Most large racetracks hold about nine races per day, many of which are claiming races. All horses entered in a claiming race are eligible to be claimed at a certain price. A claiming race may be, for example, for $5,000. The racehorse's owner must accept the risk of losing the horse at that price. The person claiming the horse is also taking a risk: the horse may be running with an injury that will not allow it to race many more times, and the claimant is not allowed to have a vet examine the horse beforehand.

When first entering a racehorse business, one typical plan is for the owner to acquire about 60% of the stock through claiming. The remaining 40% of the horses might be purchased as yearlings and homebred. Well-claimed horses provide the owner with immediate income; the yearlings' training can be carefully controlled; the homebred animals can be nurtured from conception to racetrack.

Before claiming a racehorse, it is best that the new owner finds a qualified racehorse trainer to help select it. Hire a trainer the way any employee is hired—check references, ask for outside opinions, study his/her racing record, and pay an unexpected visit to the place of business. A neat shedrow, a communicative and cooperative attitude, intelligence, and sound horsemanship are all good qualities in a racehorse trainer.

Handler's lifetime statistics can be reviewed with one of BRIS's (Bloodstock Research Information Services) reports, making it possible to determine the trainer's qualifications.

The owner should consult the statistics (for races and workouts, if available) in the Daily Racing Form for likely claiming prospects. Also among the factors to consider are:

- pedigree

- management (previous owner and trainer)

- racing level

- earnings

- turnover (how many times the horse has been claimed)

- age

- racing patterns

- how well the horse may run at the next level up

When claiming racehorses, owners should look for a variety of talents and racing characteristics, so as to have a good chance of winning as many races as possible.

After reading all the outside information, it is time to watch the horse in its morning workout. It would be a good idea to bring along a small video camera for later review. Watching and clocking the horses allows the owner to see how the horse was working, what the surface was like that day, how much hold the rider was using, what the horse's fractions were, what equipment was used, the horse's condition at the end of the workout, and whether the trainer seemed satisfied.

To claim a racehorse, many tracks require that the claimant already own a racehorse that has run in that race meet. The trainer can usually help the new owner to qualify. The claimant must submit the claim at the Racing Secretary's Office, usually 15 minutes before post time of the race in which the horse is scheduled to run. The claimant must be prepared to take the horse immediately after the race, whether the horse wins or loses, runs sound or returns lame. If the claimed horse wins, places, or shows, the original owner, not the claimant, receives the purse money.

Here are some of the good characteristics to look for, and the bad ones to avoid.

- Speed and staying power. Speed is a natural ability while staying power is acquired through training.

- Uniformity. A horse that runs in the money 60% of the time is a very consistent runner.

- Ready to peak. Horses go through cycles of peak performance, falling off and peaking again. It is best to acquire a horse on the way toward winning form.

- Workouts. Although these do not always show the horse's true ability, they do give an idea of what the trainer is working on.

- Petigree? Good breeding is not everything. Many well-bred horses are running as cheap claimers.

- Training? Many trainers have good caliber horses racing at average priced racetracks, preparing them for difficult competition and higher stakes.

There are various reasons for a racehorse running in claiming races. There may be a problem with injuries that causes its performance to suffer considerably. Or perhaps it is a matter of not having the natural capacity to race at a higher level. Most racehorses are claimers because there is no other place for them to race and they need to earn a living.

Claiming can be a good place to start profitable ownership in the business of horseracing.

Claiming Restrictions

A person may not enter a horse in a claiming race if that horse has an outstanding claim, lien, or other security interest against it. The only exception is if the person entering the horse in the race submits written consent to the entry by the person(s) holding the claim, lien, or other security interest.

Most racetracks limit the claimant's options concerning the horse for at least 30 days. For example, the new owner must race the horse at a level no less than 25% more than the price at which it was claimed. Therefore, if the horse was claimed at $5,000, it must be raced at $6,250 or higher for 30 days. Depending on the horse, it may have less chance of winning at that level, but will probably not be claimed away from the new owner. Other limitations imposed by the Racing Secretary are: 1) the horse may not be sold, and 2) the horse may not race at another track for 30 days, sometimes longer.

Usually, the only condition under which a claimed horse may

be rejected by the claimant is if the horse is selected for drug testing after the race and tests positive for a prohibited drug. The claimant usually has 72 hours from notification of a positive test result to refuse to accept the horse.

Whether or not the horse undergoes a drug test following the race, the new owner should have it examined by a veterinarian, including blood tests, fecal exam, of the horse's airways, gait analysis, and x-rays. If it is discovered that the horse has a chronic unsoundness or some other ailment that will render it unable to win races, the new owner may enter it in a lower claiming race (after 30 days) in hopes of getting rid of it. Unfortunately, many other trainers will be wise to this scenario and will counsel their owners not to claim the horse.

WHAT ABOUT THE PAPERWORK?
Bill of Sale

Whenever horses are bought or sold, there should be a bill of sale. This may be just a simple handwritten note, but is necessary for both seller and buyer. Anyone buying a horse should insist that a bill of sale be executed so that ownership of the horse may be properly transferred. Even if the horse is being given away, it is necessary to have a written document to that effect. Also, all registration papers should be transferred at this time to prevent confusion later.

A bill of sale need not be complex. It should contain the names and addresses of both the seller and the buyer, the amount of money being exchanged, and the horse's description. The bill of sale should also state that the seller is the owner and has the right to sell the horse. *(Appendix A contains an example of a bill of sale.)*

Purchase Agreement

When a more expensive horse is being sold, a more detailed purchase agreement may be needed. This is particularly true if the seller is making additional warranties or guarantees as to the horse's abilities or suitability for a particular purpose. *(Appendix A contains an example of a purchase agreement where a deposit has been made.)*

Consignment Agreement

A consignment agreement minimizes the risk of dispute between the seller, buyer, and consignee. This contract defines the agreement for the sale of the horse and outlines terms for the horse's board, care, and exercise.

A buyer may request to see documents proving that the consignee has the right to sell the horse—that the horse has not, in fact, been stolen, or is being sold without authorization. However, it may not be in the seller's best interest for the buyer to see the actual consignment agreement. Therefore, it would be wise for the seller and the consignee to have a separate document, called a Limited Power of Attorney, drawn up. This document, when signed and notarized, grants the consignee permission to act on the seller's behalf in selling the horse. If the buyer requests documentation, the Limited Power of Attorney can be shown to him or her without compromising the agreement between the seller and consignee. *(Appendix A contains an example of a consignment agreement and a limited power of attorney form.)*

Authorized Agent Form

Sometimes, owners will have their trainers go to sales and purchase horses for them. In these situations, the owner fills out and has notarized an authorized agent form (located in the front of most sales catalogs). This form authorizes the trainer or other agent to act on the owner's behalf, using the owner's credit during the time period specified on the form. Therefore, it is recommended that this form only be used when a solid relationship has been established between the buyer and the agent. These authorized letters must be on file with the sales office before the start of the sale. *(Appendix A contains an example of an authorized agent form.)* As mentioned earlier, caution is advised when signing a blank authorized agent's form.

Installment Purchase and Security Agreement

This type of agreement is commonly used when a horse is sold using the installment method. Details of the agreement are clearly stated and the seller is granted a security interest. The buyer agrees to complete the necessary UCC-1 Form to perfect this security interest. Care should be taken in this type of agreement to ensure the understandings of both seller and buyer are adequately stated. Where the horses involved are very costly, it may be wise to seek the advice of an attorney. *(Appendix A contains an example of an installment purchase and security agreement and a UCC-1 Form.)*

Promissory Note

In addition to the installment purchase and security agreement, a promissory note is necessary. This note specifies the terms and amount of payments to be made. It also states prepayment rights, rof the holder of the note, and remedies in case of default by either party. *(Appendix A contains an example of a promissory note.)*

SUMMARY

Buying and selling horses is a common activity for many people in the horse industry. Knowing what to buy, when to buy it, and how to negotiate payment is necessary to succeed in this area. The contracts printed in Appendix A show the kind of information many horse professionals include in their agreements. Business owners who want to design similar contracts for their own operations would be wise to withhold their signatures until all documents have been reviewed by their attorneys.

6

SERVICES
&
CONTRACTS

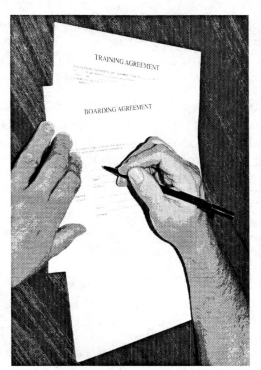

Fig. 6–1.

Whenever a horse is boarded, bred, or sent to a professional trainer, a written contract between the owner of the horse and the person providing the service is recommended. This contract should be signed and kept by both parties.

All contracts should contain details for proper care of the horse and conditions for the service provided. That way, conflicts can be avoided, while both parties are protected in case a term of the contract is unfulfilled. This chapter discusses the most common types of contracts in the horse industry—boarding, leasing, breeding, and training agreements—and gives the reader a basic understanding of what provisions these agreements should contain.

DEVELOPING A CONTRACT

Although it is possible to have a verbal contract with another person, it is highly recommended that any agreement be set forth in writing. Often, people have different perceptions of what was included in a verbal contract, and these different perceptions could result in conflict.

A good way to develop a written agreement is to have both parties draw up the contract they want, with the final draft being a compromise between the two. If only one person writes it, the contract will tend to favor that person's interests. Having both parties actively involved in drafting the contract also avoids a situation where someone signs it without reading the "fine print" and is legally bound to a clause he or she did not want. Once the contract is signed, and some form of payment has passed between the parties, the agreement is considered legally binding.

When putting agreements in writing, keep in mind that the most common weakness of contracts is ambiguity. People who have had little experience with legal matters or contracts often do not anticipate or provide guidelines for special problems that may be encountered later. The wording of a contract need not be complex, but the more specific the wording, the better. It is best to have an attorney help to draft important business contracts.

When asked to sign a contract, some people become defensive, as if their word is not good enough, and contracts are just used to take people to court. Then, there are those people who will sign a contract without reading. They may begin to read but because of the difficult language, they just give up and sign. Contracts have a reputation for archaic language that is hard to understand.

The terms of every agreement between people involving performance of service, or transfer of money or goods, should be put in writing for very good reasons. First of all, having all particulars in writing will prevent the parties from having differing views of what the agreement was really about. Even very intelligent people can view the same incident and come up with different descriptions of what happened. A similar phenomenon can happen when people are selling, training, boarding, or leasing horses unless all the details are written into the contract.

Let's assume that Barbara Bielby is selling several of her broodmares. Jim Fisher has been looking for just what she has for sale. After they discuss the horses at length, Jim decides upon one mare. The price is right, and Barbara has agreed to have the horse delivered to Jim's farm after he brings a check for the full amount to her the next day. The deal is made and they shake hands. Unfortunately, the mare was badly injured while being delivered to Jim's farm. Now there is a dispute over responsibility because they each had a different view of when the ownership of the mare was transferred. Barbara assumed that the mare was Jim's property when he made the payment. Jim thought the mare was his when it was delivered safely to his farm. There would be no dispute if they had a written contract that spelled out when the transfer of ownership was to take place.

Confusion can also arise over what is included in training. When it comes to training the contract must specify who is to do the training: the trainer only or may an assistant train part of the time. It is best to define any terms that could be interpreted in more than one way. Every item must be stated in the agreement and in detail, covering all circumstances and exactly what is being provided. When an agreement can be cancelled, it is best to list all circumstances that would lead to that and include what amounts of deposits and prepayments will be refunded.

It is not necessary to have an attorney draw up the contract. And even when an attorney is used it is best for that parties involved sketch out just what is being agreed upon. Then the attorney can review the agreement to ascertain that it meets with the state law and is fully enforceable. Contracts that are used routinely in the business such as board and lease agreements and liability releases also should be reviewed by an attorney. The more money involved, the more important it is to have an attorney. To avoid the likelihood that the contract will every have to be part of a court case, make sure everyone completely comprehends and acquiesces to all the terms before they are put into writing.

Before signing any contract each party involved should be certain they have read it thoroughly. Every question should be answered, nothing should be assumed, and everything should be clarified. It is better to discover any problem areas ahead of time, before any money has been paid. When there are disagreements that cannot be resolved, it is best to not sign a contract.

Amounts exceeding a certain value are not enforceable unless in written form. Not all states have the same requirement, so it is best to check with the individual state laws to ascertain the amount. Also it is necessary to have waiver of any warranties put in writing for the waiver to be enforceable. And all amendments to the original agreement are not enforceable unless put in writing. People remember things differently so when it is agreed that the original contract should be modified in any manner, the amendment must also be in writing and attached to the original. When there is a disagreement that becomes a legal dispute, the original contract with written amendments will prevail over any verbal agreements.

To avoid an expensive legal battle, consider the following:

- First, get everything in writing.

- Make sure the contract is understandable.

- Be sure the contract meets state requirements.

- The contract should be properly completed.

- Keep the contract in a safe place.

- Do not assume a contract does not have any value.

- Consider contract terms and its effect.

Contract Language to Consider

Indemnification Language
One party agrees to reimburse the other for a damage or loss.

Equine Activity Liability Act
A set of laws that some states have enacted to bear on liabilities in the equine industry. These may need to be researched.

Using Model Contracts Carefully
It must be realized that examples of contracts found in this and other books and in office supply stores are only a good place to start in developing a contract and are not meant to be the finished product. The major concern is that these examples will not include language pertinent to the applicable state laws. Because they are meant to cover a multitude of circumstances, they cannot possibly take into consideration all situations.

Disputes
Detail how disputes will be resolved.

No Oral Agreements
A good contract contains language to prevent one of the parties

from claiming that the contract was changed by a verbal agreement before or after it was signed. For example:

- A statement that the contract is the complete presentation of the agreement between the parties;

- A statement that the contract replaces any earlier agreements between the parties; and

- A statement that the contract can only be changed by a written agreement signed by both parties.

Confirm Authority

Check authorization by a corporate party. When one of the parties to a contract is a corporation, it is necessary to confirm that the individual representing the corporation is authorized to execute a contract on its behalf. The way this is accomplished is to use language in the contract that states the individual signing for the corporation has absolute authority to secure the corporation and has been properly authorized to enter into this particular transaction.

Releases

Not every court will enforce a signed release of liability. It may help to consider the following:

- Call the waiver or release what it is. Having the title clearly spelled out at the top of the form will lessen the chance that the signers will claim that they do not know what they were signing.

- Clearly state who is being released from liability. Where others in addition to the horse professional are involved, include all parties who are being released.

- In accordance with Equine liability laws now in effect in many states, a **WARNING** notice must be posted on signs and stated on releases involving horse activities.

State Law

When it comes to the laws of individual states, legal advice can be useful in preparing horse related agreements. Laws differ from state to state in some respects. For example, the stableman's lien law may differ under each state's law. These are laws that control when the horse boarding facility can sell horses to recover some of the board bill that has gone unpaid.

Attorney Fees

The contract should stipulate who will pay the legal fees and court costs in case of a dispute.

Insurance

Insurance requirements need to be included in the contract. For example:

- **Leases.** A lease can specify, for example, who will maintain liability, mortality, and major medical and surgical insurance on the leased horse while the lease in effect.

- **Boarding Contracts.** Stables can require customers to provide the name of their horses' mortality insurance carriers and emergency phone numbers. This might become important if the stable needs to notify the company (in the owner's absence or on the owner's behalf) that an insured horse has become injured or ill.

It is more costly to have an oral agreement dispute go to court than it is to engage a knowledgeable attorney to at least review a written contract. And sometimes insisting on a written agreement can reveal the other party's intent. Paying close attention to details can make a good deal of difference and should not be neglected.

BOARDING HORSES

A good boarding facility is one that can be trusted. Some qualities of a good boarding facility include a proper and consistent feeding and turnout schedule, good-sized and clean stalls, a safe turnout area, and employees who are knowledgeable, reliable, and have good attitudes.

In Great Britain, the British Horse Society is a powerful governing body in the horse world. It is responsible for licensing boarding and riding stables so that the public can be assured of high standards among licensed facilities and instructors, and can avoid those facilities that are not licensed. In contrast, the American Horse Shows Association (AHSA) offers a riding establishment certificate for stables, farms, partnerships, or syndicates with at least one owner who is a member of the AHSA.

The AHSA's goals in offering the certification are:

- to upgrade the care of horses, equipment, and facilities

- to increase public awareness of quality horse stables

- to create nationally uniform requirements for horse stables

However, at this time, certification is not based on the quality of the facility. Other associations have also developed guidelines for stabling operations, but they can only make suggestions. They do not have the influence or effectiveness of their counterpart overseas. Some states may require riding stables or other equine facilities to be licensed, and the regulations vary considerably.

It is not easy to run a boarding stable. The hours are sometimes long and the work is hard. It takes a lot of time and effort to manage someone else's horses in a capable and efficient manner. And it requires skill and diplomacy to handle the horse owners. The objective is to have happy and healthy horses and pleased owners, while maintaining a profitable business.

Safety Considerations

Of prime importance is the condition of the facility. This includes barn, fences, riding areas, shelters, and parking space. All must be safe and accessible. Every part of the facility must be inspected. The owner's horses may have never caused any problems, but outside boarders are sure to have some bad habits and will test and try their new surroundings. When inspecting the facility, think of all the ways a horse could damage something or be harmed in some way. It is also necessary to provide space for the horse owner's tack. If there is not a lot of space, limits may need to be set on how much can be brought in.

Practical Matters

Other items to be considered are parking for horse trailers, a telephone for the boarders to use, restroom facilities, and refrigeration for medications, food , and drink. If these are not already in existence, decide whether they can be provided.

Do not rely on a handshake as a binding contract. Decide what services are to be offered to the boarders and the rate charged for each service. Some may request full-care, others self-care, and still others something in between, or even field board. Make sure boarders understand up front what is meant by each of these terms. If daily grooming, bathing, and clipping are to be offered the charges for these need to be noted separately and added to the regular monthly board. In addition, there may be some people who want things like special rations, supplements, hoof preparations, blanketing, fly spray, bell boots, or splint boots when turned out. The boarders may not be able to be around when the farrier or veterinarian comes to work on their horses. The owner of the boarding stable must make a decision as to which treatments and services are part of the regular board and which require a special fee. All fees and services need to be listed in typed form and given to all prospective boarders.

Make sure all transactions are recorded. The reason for the business is to make a profit; the owner cannot afford to work for nothing. When the operation is large enough to require even part-time help, the cost of the help needs to be factored into the boarding fees. The boarding agreement will state when all fees and charges must be paid. It will also state who is responsible for each area of the horse care. A waiver of liability will be included in the agreement. The stable owner should keep a record off all deworming, shoeing, medications, etc. for each horse boarder.

Barn Rules

Rules for riding and handling horses may be added to the boarding agreement and posted in a conspicuous place in the facility. Work will be easier and everything will run more smoothly when the boarders do their part and clean up after themselves and their horses. This includes rules like closing gates, riding only where designated, putting away barn and riding equipment, and using halters and leads on their horses.

The owner needs to set precise times of operation for the boarding stable. The boarding agreement should clearly state rules about visitors and guests of the boarders who will be riding their horses. It is important that all owners of horses, guests and riders be apprised of the rules of riding and general operation. These parties should also have signed waivers or indemnity releases. And the stable owner must be notified when a guest is riding a boarder's horse.

The owner should not become too familiar with the boarders, but must keep a professional distance. This is not to say that the owner should be unfriendly, but it must be clear to the boarders who the owner is, and they must not be allowed to question the owner's authority. When a boarder is regularly breaking the rules, it will be necessary to ask them to take their horse and leave.

Boarding Agreements

Boarding horses requires written agreements that state the rights and responsibilities of the facility where the horse is boarded as well as the rights and responsibilities of the horse owner. The boarding arrangement may be a very simple turnout situation or may involve full service.

A boarding agreement should cover the following points:

- **Fees for feed and for any optional services.** These fees should be clearly stated, indicating the amount of monthly board and the due date. The stable should collect the board fee in advance to avoid carrying a boarder for 30 days without payment. Optional services might include turnout, blanketing, exercise, grooming, and supplements.

- **Right of lien.** This section covers the stable's right to retain or even sell the horse if the fees are not paid. This issue is covered in more depth at the end of this chapter.

- **Description of the horse(s).** This is a basic part of any agreement, and should include items like name, age, sex, breed, color, markings, height, and registration or tattoo number.

- **Description of the facilities and care to be provided.** This section should include provisions for feeding, shelter, and any other special instructions.

- **Fees.** Farrier and veterinarian fees are the owner's responsibility. They are not included in the monthly boarding charge.

- **Emergency care instructions.** The owner should provide the stable with a copy of the horse's insurance policy as well as the name and phone number of the preferred veterinarian.

- **Risk of loss** due to injury, sickness, death, or theft of the horse. It should be clearly stated that all risk of loss is to be borne by the horse owner.

- **Hold harmless.** The horse owner agrees to hold the stable harmless in case the horse causes damage or injury.

- **Termination.** This section outlines under what circumstances the agreement can be terminated, and what happens in case of a default.

(Appendix A contains an example of a boarding agreement.)

LEASING HORSES

People in the horse industry have been leasing breeding and racehorses for many years, and leasing other performance and pleasure horses is becoming more common. Some riding stables are dropping hourly rentals of riding horses for longer-term leasing. Other stables offer horses for sale or lease, using the lease to open the door to a potential buyer. A lease can be a very profitable arrangement from both the lessor and the lessee's standpoint, and is no different from leasing other types of personal property to be used for business purposes.

The terms of a lease can vary greatly to meet the different needs of both the lessee and lessor.

Leasing Agreements

A lease is a contract whereby one pays for the use of another's property. This contract should be drawn up very carefully for the protection of both the lessor and the lessee. The following terms are included in the lease agreement:

- **Term of the lease.** The date the lease begins and ends needs to be clearly defined. A lease may be for less than one month or for several years.

- **Description of the horse(s).** This is a basic part of any agreement, and should include items like name, age, sex, breed, color, markings, height, and registration or tattoo number.

- **Fees.** Also called "consideration," the fees charged and the due dates of the payments are stated here. Sometimes people are looking for good homes for horses they cannot sell and will lease the horses for free. The lessee is normally responsible for all expenses, however.

- **Horse's Earnings.** When a racehorse is leased, the earnings are usually split between the lessee and lessor. The manner in which these earnings will be divided should be clearly stated in the lease. The split can be anything the parties agree on, but the usual range is 20%–40% to the lessor and 60%–80% to the lessee. Because the horse is racing in the name of the lessee, the winnings are generally paid to the lessee, so it will be necessary to state in the agreement just when the lessee is to pay the lessor's share.

- **Various Expenses.** The lessee generally pays the ordinary expenses such as board, training, farrier, racing fees, routine veterinary charges and any miscellaneous costs.

  Other than routine veterinarian charges are usually apportioned between the lessee and lessor, with the lessee being responsible for a set amount and the lessor paying the remainder.

  Due to the fact that both the lessee and the lessor have financial interests to safeguard an amount for insurance needs to written into the lease agreement. Spell out who is responsible for paying the premiums and who can collect on a claim.

  The party responsible for transportation expenses should be clearly stated in the lease agreement.

- **Option to Buy the Horse.** State in the lease agreement how the lessee goes about exercising an option to purchase the leased horse. (Leasing to buy arrangements are popular, and are also covered in Chapter 5.)

- **Claiming Races.** When the lessor is willing to let the horse race in claiming races, the minimum amount of the race and the distribution of the claiming price must be stated in the leasing agreement.

- **Lessor's Right to Examine the Horse.** It would be wise to include a section in the agreement allowing the lessor the right to examine the horse periodically. The section should also allow for the lease to be terminated if the horse is found to be abused in any manner.

- **Returning the Horse to the Lessor.** Include in the lease who will pay the expense of returning the horse to the lessor. Also state how it will be returned and to what location.

- **Renewal of the Lease.** If the lessee has the right to renew the lease, it should be stated. Also it should be clear if the terms are to remain the same and the time frame for the renewal of the lease to take place.

- **Care of the horse.** It may be necessary to state the care to be given, especially if the horse has any special requirements.

- **Purpose of the lease.** This section clarifies the use of the horse for the term of the lease. It may be desirable to provide a warranty that the horse is suitable for this purpose.

- **Risk of loss.** The agreement should state who is to assume the risk of loss, and who, if anyone, is to insure the horse.

- **Hold harmless.** The lessor is giving up control of the horse and the lessee is required to hold the lessor harmless from any claims of injury or damage caused by the horse.

- **Ownership and liens.** The lessor must own the horse and agree to keep it free from all liens.

- **Default.** If either party breaches the agreement, the other party has the right to terminate the lease. If the lessee is at fault the lessor may retrieve the horse. The lease agreement should provide for reasonable attorneys' fees and court costs to be covered by the defaulting party.

A lease can be as simple or as complex as the parties wish to make it.

It is beneficial to have a clause in the lease that provides the means by which the lessee and lessor can resolve disagreements. It could be a clause that calls for arbitration of the dispute. This would involve having the lessor and lessee each choose an arbitrator and then those two choose another arbitrator. All of the arbitrators should be persons with expertise in the horse industry. Having the third arbitrator make a decision is usually much easier and less costly than taking the dispute to court.

Remember that these are generic guidelines for horse leases, and it is best to consult with an attorney or CPA when preparing a lease of any kind.

Recording the Lease

The lessee should be aware of restrictions for showing or racing a leased horse. For instance, there must be an official lease form attached to the horse's registration certificate on file with the State Racing Commission before a leased horse may be entered in a race. In some states, the lessee must have an owner's license to enter a leased horse in a race.

If a business owner leases a horse with the intent to show that horse, he or she should check with the breed registry and show organization to determine the regulations surrounding leased horses. If showing leased horses is allowed, the lease agreements will probably need to be on file with the organization which is hosting the show. For example, the AHSA accepts a lease as ownership except in Amateur-Owner classes. However, the lease must be registered with them (for a small fee) to be eligible for showing in approved shows.

Some states require that any leased horse be recorded with the state or local government. This precaution is taken to protect the lessor from the possibility of the lessee selling the horse to a third party. *(Appendix A contains an example of a lease agreement.)*

BREEDING HORSES

There are two main types of breeding contracts. The first is where a mare owner contracts with the stallion owner for the services of that stallion in breeding the mare. The second type of breeding agreement is the lease of a breeding stallion to stand at stud at the lessee's horse facility. There are three other types of breeding contract discussed as well—leasing a broodmare, foal sharing, and leasing a broodmare on an every-other-foal basis.

Contract for Stud Services

This contract simply states that the mare owner is entering into an agreement with the stallion owner for the breeding of the mare. Agreements of this nature occur on a regular basis throughout the horse industry. The fact that this type of contract is common does not eliminate the need to be thorough in its preparation. The following are the major items involved in a breeding agreement:

- **Fee.** This is the stud fee and varies as to the breed and value of the stallion.

- **Payment.** The time of payment is an important feature. Some stallion owners demand payment in advance, with a nonrefundable booking fee. Others require half of the fee in advance, with the remainder to be paid after breeding.

- **Veterinarian certificate.** This certificate guarantees that the mare or stallion has no transmittable disease or infection.

- **Care and feeding of mare.** Provision for feed, shelter, turnout, and exercise of the mare and the related fees should be clearly set forth.

- **Veterinarian and farrier.** The responsibility for veterinary and farrier care should be spelled out in the agreement.

- **Care of the horse.** It may be necessary to state what kind of care is to be given, especially if the horse has special needs.

- **Live foal guarantee.** Most breeding agreements include a provision for a situation where the mare does not produce a live foal. Careful attention must be paid to the definition of "live foal." Generally, a reasonable live foal guarantee lasts up to 72 hours after the mare gives birth.

- **Risk of loss and hold harmless.** Who assumes the risk of injury, sickness, or death of the mare or stallion should be spelled out. If the mare is going to be bred on the stallion owner's property, which is typically the case, both owners should be concerned that either the stallion owner or the mare owner has adequate liability insurance to cover injury to third parties or property.

- **Registration.** It should be clearly stated in the agreement that the stallion owner is responsible for executing the necessary registration documents.

- **Termination.** Failure of either party to fulfill the provisions of the agreement may terminate the agreement.

Booking Contract

The stallion owner may also require the mare owner to sign a booking contract. A booking contract adds to the general terms of the breeding agreement by including more specific details. For example, the contract may state the mare owner's rights if the mare fails to produce a live foal, or if she or the stallion dies, or if either one is rendered incapable of breeding. It should also state under what circumstances a mare will be rejected or tested and treated for genital tract infection.

Information Form

An information form for mares that travel to the stallion owner's farm may also be necessary. In this document, the mare owner lists the horse's description and pedigree, medical and breeding histories, and any special feeding instructions. It is also helpful if the mare owner lists any habits the mare has and emergency instructions in case the owner cannot be reached.

(Appendix A contains examples of a breeding agreement, booking contract, and information form.)

Leasing a Breeding Stallion

The lease of a stallion to stand at stud is similar to other horse leasing agreements, although particular attention should be paid to the purpose of the lease. One important issue to clarify is who has the right to register the foals.

It is also wise to insert a provision for a "Lessor's Lien" in the agreement for the protection of the lessor, in the event the lessee does not make payments as agreed. The lessor's lien provides the lessor with a first lien on any foals produced from the lessee's mares, under the terms of the lease. This type of lien would not apply to foals from mares not owned by the lessee, however. *(Appendix A contains an example of a lease for a breeding stallion.)*

Leasing a Broodmare

Like a stallion lease agreement, a broodmare lease agreement has many of the same provisions as a regular lease, but the purpose is for breeding as opposed to performance or riding. Usually the lessor owns both the mare and the stallion to which she is bred, and the lessee will own the foal when it is born.

The lessee takes the mare to his or her farm after breeding, and the mare remains there until the foal is weaned. For the term of the lease, the lessee is responsible for the mare's maintenance and that of the foal. In addition, a fee is paid to the lessor for the mare's services. *(Appendix A contains an example of a lease for a broodmare.)*

Foal Sharing

Foal sharing is an accepted custom in the horse industry. This is where both the mare owner and the stallion owner agree to a breeding without any money changing hands. There is no payment of stud fees nor is the mare leased. When the foal is born, it belongs to the two owners equally. When the foal is sold, the two owners share the profit. Or they may agree to keep the foal and raise it for racing, split the earnings, or use it at stud and split the stud fees. This is the most common type of foal sharing.

The same two owners may enter into a similar but different foal sharing agreement. Instead of owning the foal together, they may choose to repeat the breeding and own foals separately in successive years. Suppose it is decided that the mare owner will get the first year's foal, and the stallion owner the second year's. Deciding who will own which foal can be easy as flipping a coin. The ownership of Bold Ruler, the great 1960s Thoroughbred stallion, was decided just this way.

Or an owner might have two mares to send to the same stallion for breeding. When the foals are born, one would belong to the stallion owner, the other to the owner of the mares. In either of these cases, it would be necessary to decide ahead of time who would own which foal, and this would need to be incorporated into the written agreement, or breeding contract.

Another form of foal sharing is where the foal is sold and both the owner of the mare and the stallion get a predetermined amount. When the money received in more than that amount the owners divide the excess equally.

Advantages of Foal Sharing

Most often it is the mare owner who proposes this type of arrangement. Although stallion owners would usually choose to sell their breedings at the established price, there may be times when they will be open to foal sharing. It may be good business to enter into this type of arrangement when the stallion's book is not full. Foal sharing agreements in a case like this would allow the owner to fill the stallion's breeding season and thereby attract good mares. The owner of the stallion that is in high demand would not be inclined to foal sharing agreements.

A good candidate for foal sharing might be a recently retired racehorse with a respectable race record and an appealing pedigree. His owner could enter into foal sharing agreements to attract the quality of mares needed to establish a good reputation as a breeding stallion.

Foal sharing agreements have advantages for both the mare and stallion owners. This may not seem to be an attractive option for breeders, but it is a way to attract good mares to the stallion and produce good prospects for the sales ring. When the agreement calls for the get to be sold and the money split between the owners, it can benefit both the owner of the mare and the owner of the stallion. And when the progeny are bringing in more than two times the stallion's breeding fee, it can be well worth trying foal sharing as an option. It would be wiser to split the sale price that to accept the stud fee, if, for example, the sale price was $175,000 and the breeding fee $50,000. But there is always the risk that the foal will never reach the sales ring because of death or injury; or when it does go to sale, it may not bring the hoped for price.

Another benefit for the owner of the mare is that the foal sharing agreement allows the mare to be bred to a stallion that may not be possible otherwise because of the high stud fee.

Foal Sharing Agreements

Foal sharing agreements, like any other business contracts, need to be carefully prepared with an eye to avoiding any problems down the road. And like any other business dealing, it is best to know the party before entering into a contractual agreement.

The contract for foal sharing should cover the following:

- Listing of parties involved.

- Description of stallion and his ownership.

- Description of mare and her ownership.

- Designation of parties responsible for expenses of the mare, the stallion, and the foals.

- What happens if the mare is sold?

- Who has control of the foals?

- What insurance is carried on the mare, stallion, and foals?

- The mare's breeding condition.

- What happens if the stallion or mare is not able to fulfill the commitment of the contract?

- And most important, the disposition of the foals. If sold, at what age? What reserve and who gets to set it? If competing, in whose name will it compete? Who chooses the trainer? How will expenses by allocated? What happens at the end of horse's athletic career?

(Appendix A contains an example of a foal sharing agreement.)

Every-Other-Foal

A less common type of breeding agreement is where a mare is leased on an every-other-foal basis. In this situation, the owner of the mare and stallion (lessor) breeds them, then sends the mare to the lessee. When the first foal is born, it belongs to the lessor. The mare is then rebred to the stallion. The lessee continues to care for the mare during the second pregnancy, and the second foal belongs to the lessee. This process could continue for as many years as the lessor and lessee agree upon.

Although such an arrangement sounds like a lot of time and effort expended to obtain one foal every other year, it is a desirable arrangement for the lessee when the value of the foal would otherwise make a purchase impractical. The arrangement is beneficial to the lessor because he or she gets the first (and every other) foal without expending any time, effort, or money on the mare.

There is normally no exchange of money or property in leasing on an every-other-foal basis. The lessee may be required to maintain a minimum amount of mortality insurance on the mare during the term of the agreement, with the lessor listed as the insured. *(Appendix A contains an example of a lease for a broodmare on an every-other-foal basis.)*

Breeding Certificate

A breeding certificate is usually signed by the stallion owner and given to the mare owner. It certifies that the stallion bred the mare on certain dates at certain times. The stallion owner also agrees to execute all necessary documents for registering the foal(s) produced. *(See Chapter 10 for additional information on registration procedures.)* This certificate is the mare owner's proof that the foal was sired by a certain stallion.

When purchasing a mare in foal, the buyer should make sure the stud fee has been paid in full, and the breeding certificate has been completed by the stallion owner. If the stud fee has not been paid, the stallion owner may refuse to complete the necessary paperwork to register the foal. *(Appendix A contains an example of a breeding certificate.)*

TRAINING HORSES

Racehorse trainers are required by the State Racing Commission to pass a written and practical examination for licensing before they are allowed to train racehorses. However, outside of the racehorse industry, horse trainers are usually not required to be licensed. This means that just about anyone can claim to be a horse trainer. Since the horse owner must rely not only on the skill of the trainer, but on his or her honesty and integrity, it is important that the trainer is of good reputation.

An owner who wants to find out about a trainer's reputation need only pay an unexpected visit to the place of business. A competent trainer is intelligent, hard working, resourceful, and employs good grooms, exercise riders, and jockeys. At the same time, once the owner verifies the credibility of the trainer, constantly looking over the trainer's shoulder is discouraged.

Training Agreements

Training agreements between horse owners and trainers have not traditionally been in the form of a written contract. Because trainers are normally engaged to produce a result that is less than tangible and cannot be guaranteed, the owner must generally trust the trainer's methods. However, there are many areas of the owner-trainer relationship that can and should be spelled out in a written document.

For instance, in racing it is normally the trainer's (not the owner's) decision to select the jockey or exercise rider who fits the horse, and to decide where and when the horse races.

Training fees can range from around $20 – $30 per day to over $100 per day, depending on the popularity of the trainer and the type and location of the business. Training fees generally include only training, feeding, and stabling. Extra expenses may include transportation, special training equipment, special vitamins or supplements, racing expenses, and veterinarian and farrier costs.

In addition, many racehorse trainers receive 5% – 10% of the purse when a horse wins a race.

Owners should pay close attention to all extra expenses and make sure as many as possible are noted in the contract. The following points should be part of every training agreement:

- **Description and delivery date** of the horses.

- **Fees and payment.** This section details how much will be paid, what expenses are covered, when payment is to be made, and what happens if payments are late.

- **Trainer's responsibilities and expenses.** It should be spelled out just what activity the training is for and how expenses are to be billed. Also, the type and extent of care that the trainer will give the horse should be covered here.

- **Board and feed.** Special feeding, shelter, and turnout instructions should be included here.

- **Authority to obtain** veterinary and farrier care.

- **Horse out of training.** What happens if a horse is taken out of training temporarily?

- **Racing or Showing.** Under whose name is the horse to be raced or shown?

- **Term and termination.** The length of time training should take and conditions under which training will end should be stated here.

- **Insurance and indemnification.** The kinds and amounts of insurance to be carried need to be described. If the owner agrees to indemnify the trainer, it should be included here.

(Appendix A contains examples of training agreements for show horses and racehorses.)

STABLEMAN'S LIEN

A lien is a right to the property of someone else as security toward the payment of a legitimate indebtedness. Not being paid in a timely manner for the services of boarding, breeding, or training horses can cause genuine cash flow problems for the people providing these services.

Many states have laws to protect the owners of boarding and breeding establishments. Under these laws, the owner of the breeding stallion or boarding stable is given a lien on the horses involved to ensure that payment is made. Liens are available to anyone who boards horses for any length of time, in any size operation. The owner of the stable is allowed to keep the horse as payment of the unpaid debt, or may sell the horse and apply the proceeds to the amount owed.

The stable owner must have actual possession of the horse and must follow the specific procedure set out by the state statute to enforce the lien. Some states' laws allow the lien to be applied to any property of the horse's owner which is in the lien holder's possession. Since some horse registries may not accept a lien sale, but require a court order, it is wise to contact the registry involved to determine its requirements for transfer of registration papers before selling a registered horse. For example, the Arabian Horse Registry requires an attorney's letter stating that the state statutes have been followed in the process of the lien sale before the papers can be transferred to the lien-sale purchaser.

When a Lien Exists. The circumstances under which a lien exists can vary from state to state. Some require the stable owner to perfect the lien before it actually exists. Other states require nothing more than the boarding charges to have taken place. It is important that the stableowner knows what is required by state law before taking any action. Some will require the posting of public notices or filing of an action in court before the boarder's horse can be sold.

Owner Recovers Horse Without Paying Board Bill. Possession of the horse can be a vital factor. Some states require the stableowner to retain possession of the horse to secure a lien. In those states, the lien will be lost if the horse is returned to its owner. Of course, if the horse's owner sneaks onto the stable owner's property and hauls the horse away the lien many not be lost, and there could be trespassing charges for the horse owner.

Refusing to Return the Horse to Its Owner. Usually it is best for the stable owner to retain possession of the boarder's horse. It is important to know the requirements of the state law in this regard. Some clearly allow the stable owner to keep the horse on the business premises; other state laws are somewhat vague. A legal problem could arise for the stable owner who detains horses without the right to do so.

Conducting a State Authorized Sale to Satisfy the Lien. Again, state laws vary; some have time limits for the sale, and some allow the lienholder to conduct the sale. Following the requirements of the law will assure that the sale of the horse is conducted properly. Even if allowed by law to sell the horses privately, the lienholder will usually profit by placing the horse in a state authorized public sale.

Distribution of Sale Proceeds. Before any proceeds of the sale can be distributed, all concerned parties must be taken into consideration. If the state law recognizes statutory liens there may be a payment required to a veterinarian, farrier, or others. When money has been borrowed from a bank to purchase the horse, there will be a security interest held by that bank. Who gets what amount of the proceeds is something that must be resolved by the parties involved.

In all cases, the requirements of the particular state law must be followed to take full advantage of the protection the law offers to stable owners when stuck with boarders who can not or will not pay their board bill.

SUMMARY

Horse business owners need to know their rights and responsibilities, as well as those of their clients. For instance, in the event that a client does not follow the conditions of a written agreement, a stable owner may have a right to the person's horse, or other property, as security toward payment of the client's debt. Fortunately, most misunderstandings and conflicts can be avoided by having written agreements that clarify both parties' obligations.

7

EMPLOYEES & INDEPENDENT CONTRACTORS

Fig. 7–1.

Because horses used in a business—such as performance and breeding horses—tend to be high-maintenance creatures, many owners will have to take on hired help.

But before they do any hiring, business owners should understand their legal obligations to their employees and to the state and federal governments. This chapter will help business owners to distinguish between employees and independent contractors, and will discuss how wages and federal and state taxes should be handled in those and other instances. Also discussed is the process of finding and keeping employees.

CLASSIFICATION
Employees

Anyone who performs services for another person is an employee if the employer controls the method and results of the services performed. Even when the employee is given freedom of action, the employer-employee relationship still exists.

It does not matter what the employer-employee relationship is called. The employee may be called an agent, partner, or even an independent contractor. It does not matter how the payments are determined, how they are made, or what they are called. Nor does it matter if the employment is full- or part-time. Also, there is no employment class difference. An employee could be a manager, superintendent, or supervisor.

Three of the most usual features of an employer-employee relationship are that the employer furnishes the employee with equipment for working (such as tools), a place to work, and the employer has the right to fire the employee.

Independent Contractors

People who pursue an independent trade, business, or profession in which they provide services to the public are probably not employees and are classified as independent contractors. They include:

- contractors/subcontractors
- public stenographers
- certified public accountants
- self-employed trainers

- lawyers
- auctioneers
- veterinarians
- farriers

If the person for whom the services are rendered has the right to control or direct only the result of the work and not the means and methods of accomplishing the result, then the person performing the service is generally an independent contractor.

Misclassifying Employees

Some employers misclassify employees as independent contractors. Clearly it is to the employers' financial advantage to call an employee an independent contractor, thus avoiding the burdens of contributing payroll taxes and reporting wages. Quite often the misclassifying is intentional, sometimes because the business would have a difficult time surviving with the additional burden of these payroll taxes.

The IRS has mounted a campaign to address the issue of misclassification of employees as independent contractors. Those businesses that have misclassified employees will be liable for the payment of back payroll taxes plus penalties and interest. This could prove to be financially devastating to small businesses. And worse, the liability for these back taxes, penalties, and interest could carry over to the responsible parties who could be held personally liable.

For example, racehorse trainers may believe that all exercise riders and hot walkers are independent contractors because of the independent nature of their work and the high turnover. However, depending on the circumstances of their employment, some exercise riders and hot walkers may be considered employees by the IRS, and racehorse trainers are responsible for withholding the appropriate amount for taxes. Jockeys, in contrast, would probably be considered contract labor.

Needless to say, care should be taken in the classification of workers. It may be advisable to have a simple written agreement that both parties sign, indicating either an employer-employee relationship or the hiring of an independent contractor. To help determine whether a worker is an employee or independent contractor, the IRS established 20 factors that indicate whether adequate control exists to constitute an employer-employee relationship. The importance placed on each factor varies with the occupation and the context in which the services are performed. If, after reviewing the 20 factors, an owner is still uncertain about how to classify its workers, the IRS will make that determination. Form SS-8 requests the IRS to determine if a worker is an employee.

Twenty Factors

1. **Instructions.** Is the worker required to comply with instructions about when, where, and how to work? Even if no instruction is given, the control factor is present if the employer has the *right* to give instructions.

2. **Training.** Is the worker trained to perform a job in a particular manner? Independent contractors ordinarily use their own methods and are not trained by those who use their services.

3. **Integration.** Are the worker's services integrated into the business operations? And are those services important to the success or continuation of the business? This factor would show that the worker is subject to direction and control.

4. **Services rendered personally.** Must the services be rendered personally? This factor would indicate that the employer is interested in the methods as well as the results.

5. **Hiring assistants.** Does the business hire, supervise, and pay assistants? Independent contractors hire, supervise, and pay their own assistants. This is because they work under an agreement that requires them to provide materials and labor and to be responsible only for the result.

6. **Continuing relationship.** Is there a continuing relationship between the worker and the company? This factor would indicate that an employer-employee relationship exists. A continuing relationship may still exist even where work is performed at irregular intervals.

7. **Set hours of work.** Does the company set the work schedule? Independent contractors usually set their own hours.

8. **Full-time work.** Is the worker required to devote 40 hours per week to the person for whom he/she performs services? Independent contractors work whenever they choose.

9. **Work done on premises.** Is the work performed on the premises of the company, or at a location designated by the company?

10. **Order or sequence set.** Does the company direct the order or sequence of the work? This factor would show that the worker is subject to direction and control.

11. **Reports.** Must workers submit regular progress reports? Employees must account to employers for their actions.

12. **Payments.** Is the worker paid by the hour, week, or month, as opposed to an independent contractor who is paid by the job or on a straight commission?

13. **Expenses.** Are the worker's business and travel expenses reimbursed? This factor would show that the worker is subject to regulation and control.

14. **Tools and materials.** Does the company provide the tools and materials used by the worker?

15. **Investment.** Employees do not usually make significant investments in the equipment or facilities used in performing services for someone else.

16. **Profit or loss.** An employee cannot make a profit or suffer a loss, but merely collects wages.

17. **Works for more than one person or firm.** Does the worker perform services for multiple, unrelated persons or firms at the same time? An employee usually works exclusively for one company or person.

18. **Offers services to the general public.** Does the worker make his or her services available to the general public? An independent contractor would do this.

19. **Right to fire.** Is the worker subject to dismissal for reasons other than failure to perform? An independent contractor cannot be fired so long as the specifications of the contract are met.

20. **Right to quit.** Can the worker quit the job at any time without incurring liability? An independent contractor usually is legally obligated to make good for failure to complete the job.

HIRING & KEEPING GOOD EMPLOYEES

Every employer is looking for employees who are experienced, motivated and reliable, but this is particularly challenging in the horse industry. While the necessity for labor for farming and other agricultural operations has decreased because of new discoveries and automation, the horse industry has remained labor intensive. In addition to the fact that the requirements for manual labor has continued at a very high level, wages for this type of work remain low and the hours of employment are still quite diverse. For these reasons, horse operations are finding that good employees are difficult to find and keep.

In spite of these problems, there are some horse operations that always seem to get and keep the best employees. And if it is not because the employees are paid higher wages, then there must be other good reasons. If the horse operation can provide work year-round and can pay the prevailing wage, labor management is made much easier by adhering to two basic elements: hire the right people and make them want to stay.

Smart Hiring

It is important to know what each prospective employee wants from a job of this type. It is obviously not the money nor the chance for a lot of days off. What is attracting them to this type of work? This is the most important aspect of hiring, even more important than experience with horses.

Most people who want this type of employment just love horses and want to be involved with them as much as possible. They are enamored with the atmosphere of horses, horse farms, race courses, and horse barns. Some employees may be looking forward to becoming horse owners or trainers and may be eager to learn as much as they can on the job. These employees can be very dependable and useful to the operation while they are continuing to learn.

Creating a Team Atmosphere

A team atmosphere among employees should be a priority of every business owner. This should include all employees, from the least to the most important. The owner should create a team that takes satisfaction in being an employee of this specific operation. This satisfaction can come from the reality that the outfit they work for has a reputation for professionalism. This does not necessarily mean the horses are winning the most or producing the most, but that the horses receive superb care and attention.

185

Most employees perform to the level expected by the employer, and if treated as if they have noting worthwhile to offer they respond in that manner. This definitely will not increase their motivation of effectiveness. In fact, it could make them resentful and rebellious. In contrast, if a team spirit can be created, the employees will make every effort to do whatever is required.

Everyone makes mistakes and it is best to find them out at the beginning. The only means of staying on top of things is to make a continual effort to create a team atmosphere. It is vital to treat employees equally, and not play favorites. If excellence is expected in all aspects of the operation, and employees are rewarded as a group, then group effort will be the result.

The operation will be good one or bad one to work for depending mostly on the person running it. There is an old saying that "one generally gets the employees that one deserves."

Working Student Arrangements

The working student arrangement is common for some business owners. When a student is to train at a particular operation a contract should be signed by both the student and the employer. Terms and conditions must be discussed and agreed upon beforehand. This contract should cover these elements:

- The goal of the arrangement.

- Whether food, lodging and keep of a horse will be part of the agreement.

- The length of the trial period, if any.

- The time-frame of the agreement.

- Amount of money involved.

- Hours to be worked and days off allowed, and if days of competitions are to be counted as days off or working days.

- Method of ending the agreement.

Having a written agreement that is well thought out that both the student and the employer have agreed upon should avoid misunderstandings.

EMPLOYMENT TAXES

Employment taxes include 1) those taxes withheld from an employee's wages, and 2) those taxes paid by the employer on behalf of the employee. The taxes withheld from the employee's wages are federal, state, and local taxes and the employee's portion of the Social Security and Medicare taxes. The employer is required to match the Social Security and Medicare taxes and pay this amount along with the employee's withheld amount. (Independent contractors who are sole proprietors must pay both the employee's and employer's portion of the Social Security and Medicare taxes on their net incomes.)

The other employment taxes are federal and state unemployment taxes. These taxes are based on the amount of wages earned. The employer makes these payments as a contribution to the state and federal unemployment funds.

Is the business of breeding, raising, showing, racing, or selling horses responsible for these employment taxes? The answer is generally "yes," if there are employees as qualified in the 20 factors. However, there are some special rules for agricultural labor that will be discussed throughout this chapter.

All employers must have a Federal Identification Number. This nine digit number is provided by the IRS and can be applied for using Form SS-4. It is now possible to apply by phone and follow up with Form SS-4. When applying by phone, the Federal Identification Number is immediately available. Otherwise it may take 10 days to 5 weeks to receive. The IRS will mail a packet of information and forms necessary for reporting wages and paying taxes. (Some states also require an employer identification number.)

Withholding Taxes
What Are Wages?

Generally, wages include all payments made to an employee for services performed. It does not matter if the payment is called a bonus, commission, or salary; a payment to an employee is considered wages and is therefore subject to withholding taxes. This definition would also include noncash compensation, with certain exceptions.

If meals and lodging are provided to employees as a condition of employment (in other words, for the benefit of the employer) they are not included in the employees' wages. Many horse operations offer employee housing and some even require that the employees live on the premises. Also excluded from the definition of wages are the reimbursed or advanced traveling expenses and meals paid for by the employer. The same is true of working condition fringes, such as special clothing required to be worn. Small benefits such as free drinks and snacks are not counted as wages.

Noncash Remuneration

Noncash remuneration is when an employee is paid with something other than a paycheck or cash. Noncash payments are not always a clear cut matter, and it is important that they are handled in such a way that they meet the IRS guidelines. The IRS is always looking for payments of earnings that are concealed in some way to avoid taxes. Their concern is that income tax and social security taxes will not be paid on true earnings.

For example, it is not uncommon for employees to receive a young horse as a bonus—at Christmas or other occasion. Because the employee is working for the person who is giving the bonus, it is not permissible to call the horse a gift. Even if it was called a Christmas gift, the noncash bonus would be considered the same as cash wages by the IRS. If the employee sells the young horse for, say $2,500, then that amount is treated as if the employee had received cash of that amount. If the employee retains the horse for personal use, then a fair market value needs to be established and that amount treated as cash received. In either case, the dollar amount is treated as wages and must go on the employees' W-2 and have income and social security taxes withheld and other employment taxes paid.

Employers should keep individual payroll records for all employees, in addition to a master record. Both should list wages paid, deductions taken, and quarterly totals. Wages that are paid and reported can then be deducted by the employer as an operating expense.

Income Taxes

Every employee must furnish the employer with the familiar signed Form W-4 Employee's Withholding Allowance Certificate. This form tells the employer how many withholding allowances the employee is claiming and from this, the correct amount of withheld income tax is calculated. Every year, the IRS provides each employer with a Circular E, Employer's Tax Guide, or a Circular A, Agricultural Employer's Tax Guide. These publications contain tables for calculating the amount of wages to withhold.

The federal income taxes withheld from the employee's wages by the employer are paid to the IRS. This payment is made using Form 8109, Federal Tax Deposit Coupon, at an authorized bank. The deposit rules require either monthly or semiweekly deposits depending on previous tax deposits. An employer of agricultural labor is not required to make deposits if the accumulated tax liability during the year is less than $500.

An employer who withholds federal income and FICA taxes (discussed below) files a Form 941, Employer's Quarterly Federal Tax Return. An employer of agricultural labor files a Form 943, Employer's Annual Federal Tax Return for Agricultural Employees. These forms are sent to the Internal Revenue Service Center for the area where the employer's business is located.

Year _____										
Individual Payroll Record										
Name										
Address					**Soc. Sec. #**					
No. of exemptions					**Rate of pay**					
					deductions					
Pay Date	**Check No.**	**Period Ending**	**Salary**	**Gross Wages**	**Federal Tax**	**State Tax**	**Social Security**	**Medicare**	**Net Pay**	
Total 1st quarter										
Year to date										
Total 2nd quarter										
Year to date										
Total 3rd quarter										
Year to date										
Total 4th quarter										
Year to date										

Fig. 7–2. An example of an employer's individual payroll record.

Master Payroll Record

Year _____

Week or Period Ending	Gross Wages All Employees	deductions				Net Wages All Employees
		Federal Tax	State Tax	Social Security	Medicare	
Total 1st quarter						
Year to date						
Total 2nd quarter						
Year to date						
Total 3rd quarter						
Year to date						
Total 4th quarter						
Year to date						

Fig. 7–3. An example of an employer's master payroll record.

The employer gives the employee a Form W-2 Wage and Tax Statement at the end of each year (actually, by January 31 of the following year). The employer also sends a copy of this form to the Social Security Administration. Form W-2 lists the wages earned and the federal, state, and local taxes withheld, as well as the Social Security and Medicare taxes withheld.

FICA Taxes

Social Security and Medicare taxes are imposed by the Federal Insurance Contributions Act, hence the term FICA tax. The law requires employers to withhold FICA taxes from the wages of most employees, and to match this amount from their own funds. The exceptions to this requirement are 1) work performed by children under the age of 18 who have another principle occupation, such as being a student; and 2) agricultural work performed by aliens who are legally in the United States to do farm work. This is of particular interest to horse operations located in areas where large numbers of aliens make up the labor supply. Employers should review each individual's Employment Authorization Card to determine the person's status. *(See the section entitled "Immigration Law" for more information.)*

As with wages for federal withholding tax, noncash payments for agricultural labor are not considered wages. Free room and board furnished to a farm manager or other agricultural laborer is not considered wages for purposes of income or FICA taxes. Also, payments for agricultural labor are considered wages only when they exceed $150 per employee or $2,500 to all employees during the year.

There is a ceiling on the amount of wages that are considered wages for the purpose of Social Security taxes. (There is no longer a ceiling for Medicare taxes.) Once an employee's wages reach this limit, Social Security taxes are no longer withheld. The current ceiling can be found in the Employer's Tax Guide or Agricultural Employer's Tax Guide. FICA taxes are paid together with the federal taxes withheld.

Federal and State Unemployment Taxes

Unemployment insurance is a state and federal tax paid by the employer. This tax is *based on* the employee's wages, not withheld from, nor charged to, the employee. The federal unemployment tax is calculated on the first $7,000 of wages for each employee. Most states also tax this amount for the individual state funds.

For the purpose of unemployment taxes, an employer is 1) any person who paid $1,500 or more in wages in any calendar quarter during the current or preceding year, or 2) any person who employed at least one person during that period.

For agricultural labor there is a special rule. This rule states that a person is an employer only if 1) wages of $20,000 or more have been paid, or 2) 10 or more persons were employed for at least part of a day in 20 different weeks during any calendar quarter in the current or preceding year. (Agricultural labor has the same meaning for this tax as it does for other taxes.)

Federal unemployment taxes are deposited the same way as withheld federal and FICA taxes. Such a deposit is required when the liability is more than $100 at the end of any calendar quarter.

REPORTING PAY FOR INDEPENDENT CONTRACTORS

When using the services of an independent contractor, it is not necessary to withhold and pay employment taxes. Form W-9, Request for Taxpayer Identification Number and Certification, should be requested from each independent contractor and kept on file. This form provides the information needed to report the amounts paid during the year for the independent contractor's services (such as veterinary services). When these amounts total more than $600, they are reported to the IRS on Form 1099 MISC, Miscellaneous Income. The business owner furnishes a copy of this form to each person who received the payments. Some states also require a copy of Form 1099 MISC from employers.

SELF-EMPLOYMENT TAXES

Any individual who operates a business as a sole proprietor or partnership is required to pay self-employment taxes. Self-employment taxes are imposed on the net income of the business. (If the net income for the year is less than $400, no self-employment tax is due.) Self-employment taxes are FICA taxes, just like those withheld from employees. The important difference is that the self-employed person is responsible for both the employee and employer portions of that tax. Self-employment taxes are reported on Schedule SE of Form 1040, Computation of Social Security Self-Employment Tax.

Self-employed persons are responsible for making estimated tax payments quarterly throughout the tax year. Both the FICA tax and the Federal Income Tax should be included in these payments, which are made using Form 1040-ES payment vouchers. The payments should be mailed to the IRS.

IMMIGRATION LAW

The Immigration Reform and Control Act of 1986 was the first major revision of the U.S. Immigration laws in many years. The law is designed to preserve jobs for American citizens and aliens who are authorized to work in the country.

Basically, every employee hired after October 6, 1986, must fill out and give to his or her employer a Form I-9. Filling out this form entails providing the employer with verification of the individual's employment eligibility. The employer must be furnished with and examine documents that establish identity and employment eligibility. Among the documents that qualify are United States Passports, Drivers Licenses, Social Security Cards, and Employment Authorization Cards. The employee fills out the form and signs it, then presents it to the employer with the proper documentation. The employer visually inspects the documentation and then signs the form and keeps it in the employee's permanent file. The U.S. Department of Justice offers a Handbook for Employers—Instructions for Completing Form I-9.

Internal Revenue Service Forms	
FROM EMPLOYER TO EMPLOYEE	• Form W-2, Wage and Tax Statement lists total wages earned, and federal income and FICA taxes withheld. (Also sent to the Social Security Administration.)
FROM BUSINESS TO INDEPENDENT CONTRACTOR	• Form 1099 MISC, Miscellaneous Income reports amount paid to independent contractors, if the amount is over $600. (Also sent to the IRS.)
FROM EMPLOYER/ BUSINESS TO IRS	• Form 941/943, [Agricultural] Employer's Quarterly [Annual] Federal Tax Return reports income to the IRS. • Form 1099 MISC, Miscellaneous Income reports the amount paid to independent contractors, if the amount is over $600. (Also sent to each independent contractor.) • Form 8109, Federal Tax Deposit Coupon is turned in with the withheld taxes to an authorized bank for deposit. • Form SS-4 requests a Federal Identification Number. • Form SS-8 requests the IRS to determine if a worker is an employee or an independent contractor.
FROM EMPLOYER TO SSA	• Form W-2, Wage and Tax Statement lists total wages earned, and federal income and FICA taxes withheld. (Also sent to the employee.)
FROM SELF-EMPLOYED TO IRS	• Form 1040, Schedule SE, Computation of Social Security Self-Employment Tax reports FICA taxes. • Form 1040-ES, Estimated Tax Payment Vouchers report payment of federal income tax.
FROM EMPLOYEE TO EMPLOYER	• Form W-4, Employee's Withholding Allowance Certificate shows how many withholding allowances employee claims. • Form I-9 verifies employment eligibility.
FROM INDEPENDENT CONTRACTOR TO BUSINESS	• Form W-9, Request for Taxpayer Identification Number and Certification provides the business with information needed to report the amount paid to independent contractors to the IRS.

Fig. 7–4. Various forms required by the IRS.

SUMMARY

Not all horse operations are large enough to warrant having employees. For those that find that they cannot operate without hiring some help, care must be taken to follow the guidelines for employees and to make sure that employees are distinguished from independent contractors. Before a business owner hires any employees or pays any wages, he or she should apply for a Federal Identification Number and have all the necessary charts, forms, and information on hand. This can easily be accomplished by seeking the help of a CPA or by contacting the IRS and other federal and state government agencies.

8

AVOIDING LIABILITIES

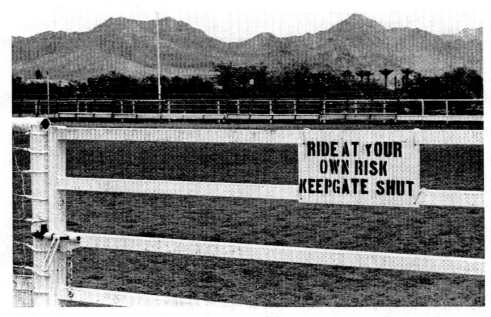

Fig. 8–1.

Most people in the horse industry understand and accept the risks that come with a horse-related activity. The best ways that horse business owners can guard against liability are to be aware of their legal responsibilities, to ensure safe conditions on the property, and to be alert to all activities taking place on the premises. While a good insurance policy can keep the business from suffering considerable losses due to liability, prevention is the key. Exercising a reasonable amount of care in the horse facility's day-to-day operations significantly reduces the owner's risk of liability.

THE OWNER'S LEGAL RESPONSIBILITIES

Having horses (on owned or leased property) can involve special risks and responsibilities. The business owner's primary duty lies in creating and maintaining safe conditions on the property.

When it is known that conditions exist that may prove to be harmful, a warning must be given. This warning should be given in such a manner that a reasonably sensible person can avoid the harm by heeding the warning. When a person who has been warned chooses to ignore it and proceeds anyway, that person has "assumed the risk," and the owner has no responsibility for harm that may occur as a result.

What about horseback riders who use one's property without invitation or permission? Some state laws provide protection to the landowner, arguing the landowner has no responsibility to warn riders of dangerous conditions on the land when the riders are occupying it without invitation or permission. When in doubt about the liabilities of horse ownership in a particular state, consult your lawyer or an insurance agent.

When Is a Horse a Legal Nuisance?

Having horses in a residential or heavily populated area is not legally considered a nuisance. But, if the horse operation interferes significantly with the neighbors' enjoyment of their property, a nuisance complaint may be filed. Horse farms rarely get shut down completely as the result of nuisance complaints. However, if it can be shown in court that a nuisance does exist, the owner may be asked to change the farm's habits or facilities. The following five conditions are the most common factors used to determine whether a legal nuisance exists:

- intolerable noises

- offensive odors

- breeding activity sights and sounds

- uncleanliness, which attracts rodents and flies

- unsightliness of barns, fences, or other enclosures

Obviously, the best way to avoid a nuisance complaint is to operate so as to diminish any objectionable features. Hauling away manure or having it removed on a regular basis, maintaining buildings and fences, and restricting breeding to behind closed doors not only eliminates the likelihood of a legal nuisance complaint, but also enhances the business' reputation.

Is a Horse Ever an Attractive Nuisance?

Generally speaking, dangerous or attractive property which is left unguarded and unprotected from the natural curiosity of a child is considered to be an "attractive nuisance." Children under the age of 14 are presumed to possess immature judgment and are unable to recognize apparent dangers. The fact that a child is a trespasser does not relieve the owner of responsibility.

A horse by itself is considered a "natural thing" and as such is not an attractive nuisance. The attractive nuisance is defined as an artificial condition that does not exist in nature. An example of where the attractive nuisance principle applies to horse-related activities might be if a horse and carriage are left on the street unattended. If a child is injured while playing on the carriage, the owner may be held liable for any injuries to the child. In this case, the horse itself is not the attractive nuisance. If the horse alone is involved, the doctrine of attractive nuisance should not apply.

Suppose, for example, that Kenny Fisher owns a small ranch not far from a residential area. Although there are many young children living in the area, there have been no problems with them in regard to the horses. However, Kenny noticed of late that a couple of them have been climbing over the fences and walking across the corner of an empty pasture to get to a recreation park. As part of his pasture rotation procedure, Kenny recently moved a young stallion to that pasture. While cutting across the pasture, a child tried to approach the young stallion and was injured. Kenny may be liable for the injuries to the child.

In determining if a landowner is liable for an attractive nuisance, the courts have deliberated the following points:

- Was the landowner aware that children were able to trespass close to the danger?

- What type of danger was it? And did it create a senseless risk of grave injury or death to children?

- Was the danger such that could be recognized by children?

- How crucial to the landowner is the continuance of the dangerous circumstances?

- How does the hardship imposed by getting rid of the danger relate to the chance of harm?

- Has the landowner practiced reasonable care in attempting to do away with the danger or to guard the children's safety?

Court cases where a horse has been considered an attractive nuisance have been rare. When considering this problem, courts have concentrated on the basic inclinations of the horse. This would mean that a gentle horse with no bad tendencies would not be considered a risk of causing serious injury, and thus, not an attractive nuisance.

WHEN CAN THE OWNER BE HELD LIABLE?

Liability is generally assigned to the person who causes injury to another person by an act of negligence or omission. In the horse business, the responsibility for injury begins the moment one takes control of a horse. The person in charge of the horse (who may or may not be the owner) is expected to know how to control that horse. Even so, the question of fault must be addressed in assigning liability.

When an owner knows that a horse has dangerous tendencies, he or she has a duty to make these tendencies known to anyone exposed to the horse. Where the horse's owner is not aware of the dangerous tendencies, there may not be any liability. Some states hold that the owners of domestic animals are not liable for injuries caused by those animals unless the owners are aware of some dangerous or vicious tendencies.

A determination of negligence is based on both the facts and the particular state law. Actions that may be deemed negligent in one circumstance may not be considered so in another. And the same actions may end in liability under the laws of one state but not under the laws of a neighboring state. The primary test for negligence is if the person's conduct in a specific situation is reasonable. If the party has exercised the same care that a reasonably prudent and careful person would use, then they are not likely to be held negligent. Not practicing this type of care may lead to the person being held liable for the damage that happens.

"Absolute" Liability

The possessor of a dangerous animal, whether domesticated or wild, will be held liable for injury caused by that animal no matter how the injury occurs. This is the "absolute" liability position, which holds that the possessor of the animal knows or should know of its dangerous tendencies. Again, if the animal is domesticated, as most horses are, it may be necessary to prove that the owner was aware of the danger. (Wild animals are always considered to be dangerous.)

Employee Negligence

Owners may also be held accountable in situations where an employee is found negligent. Cases have come up where both owner and employee have been found negligent in the handling of horses where that negligence has caused fatal accidents.

Sometimes it is not necessary to prove the owner was negligent. This is called *res ipsa loquitur,* which is Latin for "it speaks for itself," and is used in cases where the injury could only have happened as the result of someone's negligence. An example of such a case would be if a riding student fell off a school horse because a rotted stirrup leather broke and came off the saddle. This accident could only have been caused by the riding school's negligence, as equipment should always be checked for safety.

Transporting Horses

Whether it be for racing, breeding, showing, or simply relocating, almost every horse operation is involved to some extent in transporting horses. Regulations and responsibilities vary depending on whether the transportation involves private or commercial carriers. Owners should be familiar with these regulations.

All states have their own laws in regard to the hauling of horses. Included are the number of horses hauled, the size of the trailer, safety chains used, and paperwork required for entry into each state. It is a good idea to call the Department of Motor Vehicles, the highway patrol office, and the state veterinarian in each state traveled through, as well as the Federal Highway Administration or the U.S. Department of Transportation. Before calling, measure the height, length, and width of the rig and know its weight, as this information will most likely be requested. Each agency has its own regulation and this way it is possible to find out whether stops at weigh stations are required, and whether public rest areas can be used to unload horses for rest and exercise.

Each state has laws for travel within its boundaries. In some states, all trucks must stop at weigh stations. And other states require any vehicle with a commercial license plate, regardless of weight or use, to stop at weigh stations. Have driver's license and registration handy. Some states also inspect health papers, brands, or safety equipment. Safety requirements for horse trailers include: all lights in working order, break-away brake, and safety chains on tagalong and gooseneck trailers. Trailers weighing over 3,000 pounds require brakes on at least one axle. If weight if over 6,000 pounds, brakes are needed on both axles.

If a truck is required to enter a weigh station and does not, a state patrol officer can issue a citation. Fines for not stopping at weigh stations can be quite expensive and some states require fines be paid in cash, and this will probably mean points on the driver's license. Not having the driver's license, vehicle registration, and horse papers in order, or not adhering to the state's safety code, could cause the rig to be impounded. Knowing and complying with the laws can mean serious problems will be avoided.

Although the paperwork for horses being transported varies from one state to another, proof of a negative Coggins is always required within the last six months or year. In most cases, a health certificate issued within the last 30 days is required.

When a carrier is transporting the horses, find out what their insurance covers. If it is limited to certain types of illness or accidents, the owner will probably find it necessary to carry insurance as well.

Private Carriers

Anyone transporting horses for recreational purposes, with no intent to profit, with a vehicle (or combination of vehicles) weighing 10,000 pounds or less, is usually considered a private carrier. Although private carriers are not subject to federal regulations for transporting horses, they are still subject to liability.

Owners who use their own vehicles to transport other people's horses should consult with their insurance agents to determine the extent of their coverage in such situations. Normally, a trailer can be added as an extension to basic auto liability coverage. Owners may also want to add comprehensive and collision insurance to their policies if they do a lot of hauling.

If the majority of hauling involves someone else's horses, the owner may want to consider care, custody, and control insurance, which covers damages to another party's horse. *(See Chapter 9 for more information on insurance.)*

Commercial Carriers

Many horse business owners are unaware that operating a commercial stable, and/or hauling horses for sale, racing, training, showing or other purposes (with intent to profit) subjects them to federal regulations for commercial vehicles. If the vehicle (or combination of vehicles) used in transporting horses weighs 10,001 pounds or more, and if the person in charge of the vehicle receives some sort of compensation for hauling, the vehicle is generally considered a commercial carrier.

Responsibilities and duties of commercial carriers are spelled out by federal law. Carriers must stop and rest the horses for at least 5 consecutive hours after hauling them for 28 hours (although most carriers prefer to stop and rest the horses more often). The amount of hauling time may be extended to 36 hours by written request from the owner or person in custody of the horses (e.g. a trainer or someone leasing the horses).

A carrier who violates the "28 on, 5 off" rule can be held guilty of negligence. However, even if the hauling time limit is not exceeded, a carrier can be found guilty of negligence when injury to the horses results from improper transporting. This happened when a valuable mare was transported across the desert in the heat of the day and subsequently died from heat exhaustion.

When the owner accompanies the carrier, the carrier is not liable for injuries to the horses even if the time limit for hauling is exceeded: the owner is responsible for requesting that the horses be unloaded and rested. Thus, using a commercial carrier to transport a horse does not always relieve the animal's owner of responsibility for its care. Read any transport contract carefully to determine just what the carrier's responsibilities are. For example, feeding and watering the horses is the responsibility of the carrier for the duration of the shipment.

The risks and responsibilities of commercial carriers are high. For this reason, most states not only require commercial horse transporters to have commercial driver's licenses, but they require them to carry a minimum amount of insurance as well.

Collision With Vehicles

When damage or injury is caused by a collision between a horse and a vehicle, the horse owner is not automatically assumed to be at fault. The facts of each case determine whether there was negligence on the part of the horse owner, the owner of the vehicle, or a third party.

In one case, failure to reduce speed to avoid the collision caused the operator of the vehicle to be found negligent. In other cases, when collisions were caused by horses running loose on public highways, owners were not found negligent if something or someone beyond their control caused the horses to get loose.

Illegal Trespass

Horse owners are required by common law to keep their horses from running free on other people's land. Failure to keep their horses from running at large is considered illegal trespass and leaves horse owners open to lawsuits for damages caused by the loose horses. In some areas, the landowner may be allowed to take possession of the horses and keep them until restitution is made for the damages.

EQUINE LIABILITY LAWS

Equine liability laws came into existence because of the large number of lawsuits against horse businesses. The liability insurance premiums were so high that most businesses could not afford to carry the insurance, and there was a real danger of many being forced out of business. The horse industry was being threatened with economic damage.

Recently a large majority of states have enacted some form of equine liability statutes, and others are proceeding to adopt some form of these laws. Although the laws in each state are not the same, they are all intended to protect from liability those who provide the horses or sponsor the horse activity events. And they are intended to hold the participants in these events responsible for their own actions. Because of the inherent risks of equine activities, the sponsors, professionals, and horse providers all benefit from these laws as a protection from liability in the event of injury or death of participants. There are exceptions written into most of the laws that preclude deliberate wrongdoing, intentional negligence, providing defective tack or equipment, etc.

Relevant Court Cases

Washington was the first state to enact the Equine Liability Statute, and in 1993 the first case was heard in Washington's Court of Appeals. A rider who was injured falling off a horse filed a lawsuit against the previous owners claiming that they were "equine activity sponsors" under the Washington law. The claim was that they were liable for not making sure that the horse was suitable for the rider. The court found the former owners were not liable because the rider had accepted title to the horse.

In another lawsuit in Tennessee, a claim was filed for a minor child who was hurt at camp. The horse she was riding, as a part of an extra activity offered by the camp, pinned her leg to a tree. In order for the child to take part in this extra activity her parents had signed consent and release of liability forms. The case was dismissed under the Tennessee Equine Liability Act.

Complying With State Statutes

While most states call for warning signs to be posted and require signed release of liability forms, the wording of these signs and release forms differ from one state to the next. Other requirements may also need to be met. The state laws also vary in the protection offered to the horseperson and the riding stables.

It is important to use warning signs and release forms even if the state does not have a law limiting liability. And it is even more important to use these when the state statute does offer protection to the horse operation and the horseperson. In any case that protection is valid only when the requirements of the law have been met. Be sure to use the required wording for warning signs and releases.

These state statutes can benefit the horseperson and horse operations by reducing the number of lawsuits and thus lowering the cost of liability insurance.

GUARDING AGAINST LIABILITY
Contracts

The fact that a person has possession of another person's horses and has a contract with that person stating that he or she will assume all risks involved, does not necessarily absolve the owner from liability in case of injury or damage. In other words, a stable owner may be held responsible even with a contract stating that the horse's owner assumes all risks, if the injury or damage resulted because of the stable owner's negligence. It is not advisable to rely exclusively on a contract to provide liability protection. An owner of a horse operation also needs a good insurance program.

Releases

A Release and Hold Harmless Agreement is a common measure used to defer liability, and is essential for any operation offering a riding program. The release is a statement signed by the participant affirming that he or she is aware of the risks involved in all horse-related activities and that he or she will not hold the stable responsible should injury occur while at the stable. Minors need a parent or guardian to sign this release for them, as they cannot sign a binding contract.

Releases typically are required before trail rides, lessons, and other horse-related activities. In every state, it is an accepted fact that horse-related activities include some risk of injury.

Documentation is very important when there is an accident. Write down everything, including what, where, and how the accident happened, what horses and riders were involved, the names and addresses of any witnesses and even the weather and terrain conditions. This way the information is always available if a lawsuit is filed, even if it takes years for the case to go to trial. Horses may have been sold, witnesses may have moved, and memory may have faded, but the written record will not change.

When accidents have happened and lawsuits were filed, signed liability releases have been held up in court in a number of cases. To be effective, the releases must be extremely well written and must comply with the laws of the particular state. Here are some ideas regarding equine activity liability releases:

- Use a title for the release that will help make known what the person is signing. The title could be Release or Waiver of Liability, or Release and Hold Harmless Agreement.

- The wording of the release must be clear and easy to read. And the persons to be released from liability must be positively identified.

- Be sure to include in the release the fact that horse activities are dangerous and could cause the signer serious harm or even death.

- The part where signers waive any legal rights to bring a lawsuit is the most important part of the release, and must be carefully written to be effective.

- Use bold capital letters to draw attention to the most significant wording of the release.

- The signer should include full name, address, and phone number. Signatures of minors (persons under 18 years) are not legally binding, and only the parent or legal guardian can sign for them.

- Name the state under whose law the release is applicable.

- The release should mention when the parties will be bound by listing the activities to be engaged in.

- Check the applicable state law to determine if a special warning notice is required to be posted and included in the release.

- Include a statement of acknowledgment that the signer has read and understands the release. If required by state law, include a place for witnesses' signatures.

- Remember that having a release does not mean that insurance is not needed. (See Chapter 9 for more on insurance).

- It is a good idea to have an equine attorney draw up the release as each situation is different and has differing needs.

Having riders sign releases will not necessarily protect the stable owner. Any time negligence is found in a situation, the person(s) guilty of that negligence will be held responsible for any resulting injury. Therefore, it is also important that stable owners have a good liability insurance policy.

Stable owners should take measures to ensure that their operation is run in a manner that minimizes the likelihood of injury to participants. Riders should be required to wear protective headgear and the tack must be in good repair. Instructors should be well qualified and all activities monitored carefully. Only horses with histories of safe behavior should be kept at a public stable.

A special law applies to riding operations, in addition to the general negligence principle already discussed. Unless specifically stated to the contrary by the stable operator, the horses available for riding are considered safe and suitable for that purpose. This is known as an implied warranty or guarantee. The stable owner may not be liable for injury caused from riding a horse when the owner had no knowledge of the horse's unworthiness, unless it can be demonstrated that the owner should have known.

Other Recommendations for Avoiding Liability

The best way to avoid liability is to prevent injuries from happening. There are actions the owners can take to make their facilities safe for their horse business. The following recommendations can help in making the horse facility a safe place to operate:

Release and Hold Harmless Agreement

The Participant acknowledges the inherent risks which are involved in riding and working around horses. These risks may include, but are not limited to, damage to personal property, illness, bodily injury, trauma, or death resulting from a fall or while riding or being in close proximity to horses.

The Participant further understands that both horse and rider can be injured in the normal course of events while hacking, schooling, or competing, and therefore agrees to indemnify and hold harmless _____ Stable and its employees, and further release them from any liability or responsibility for any accident, injury, damage, or death to the Participant or any property or horse the Participant owns, or to any family member or spectator accompanying the Participant while on the premises of _____ Stable.

_____

Signature of Participant   Date

_____

Name (printed)

_____

Address

_____

Signature of Parent or Guardian (If Participant is under 18)

Fig. 8–2.

- Check all pasture fences and barn areas for any loose items or sharp edges, and make necessary repairs.

- Safeguard all windows from breakage by horses or people.

- Have adequate lighting to keep the facility well lit.

- Do not leave holes uncovered.

- Have snow and ice removed from driveways and parking areas.

- Make sure that electrical cords are placed so that people will not trip over them and they are out of the reach of horses.

- Have warning signs posted in appropriate areas. Also post facility rules and give a copy to all boarders.

- Dangerous horses should be kept away from visitors by placing them in distant pastures or secure stalls and posting warning signs.

- Have a message system in place for problems that occur.

- Keep a first aid kit in a place known to all.

- Have people wear protective helmets while riding.

- Have insurance in place and up to date.

- Never allow intoxicated people on the premises.

- Use contracts and written releases for horse transactions such as riding lessons, horse rentals, and horse training. Consider updating existing release forms.

- Have "No Trespassing" signs posted.

SUMMARY

Many aspects of running a horse business—including stabling, riding, and hauling—involve potential liability. By being aware of their legal responsibilities, horse business owners can avoid most legal trouble.

Another positive step that a horse business owner can take to protect the business is to purchase insurance. Chapter 9 discusses different types of insurance and how they protect the business owner in many instances.

9

INSURANCE CONSIDERATIONS

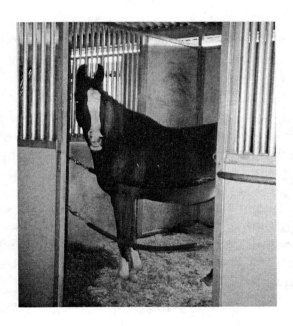

Fig. 9–1.

A good insurance policy transfers the risk of a major loss of horses or other property to an insurance company. Then, the business owner is not responsible for the financial loss.

Some factors that an owner should consider before buying insurance are:

- the financial stability of the business

- the value of the horses

- the level of risk involved in the activity each horse performs

- the level of personal involvement with the horses

- the likelihood of experiencing a covered loss while insured

Before making a decision on any insurance policy, it is best to anticipate all the potential situations in which the horses or the operation may be at risk.

CHOOSING A COMPANY

Arguably as important as choosing an insurance policy is choosing a company that can stand behind it. A phone call to the State Commissioner of Insurance will confirm that the company is licensed and will reveal any complaints from consumers. The insurance company should be well established, and the agent should be knowledgeable about the horse industry. This expertise is invaluable, because, as in any industry, there will be occasional fluctuations of values, and insurance premiums are based on current market conditions. Not only are there value fluctuations based on the horse industry as a whole, but it may be difficult to determine an individual horse's actual value.

For example, a racehorse that is running in claiming races may, at first glance, be valued at the claiming level of the horse's average race. However, the trainer may enter the horse in races below the horse's actual value in hopes of winning an easy purse. Conversely, the trainer may enter the horse in races above its actual value to prevent it from being claimed or because it has just been

---

A.M. Best

A.M. Best is a company that provides quantitative and qualitative evaluations of insurance companies. Their ratings are considered the industry standard for insurer financial performance.

Best's Ratings use traditional letter grades, from A++ (Superior) to F (In Liquidation). Best's Financial Performance Ratings are graded on a scale of 9 (Very Strong) to 1 (Poor).

A.M. Best can be found on the web at http://www.ambest.com. They can also be reached at (908) 439-2200.

Fig. 9–2.

claimed and the trainer has no choice. An insurance agent must be well informed to provide proper coverage in such situations.

Some points to consider when choosing an insurance agent or company:

1. Find someone who specializes in equine insurance or at least has some experience with horses.

2. Specify companies who specialize in horse insurance. The horse business needs will not be served by trying to make do with an ordinary homeowner's or business owner's insurance.

3. Check with the State Commissioner of Insurance to determine that the agent is licensed in the state of the horse operation, and that no complaints have been filed against the insurance company.

4. Do business only with companies rated "A" or higher A.M. Best. (The highest rating for an insurance company is A++9.)

5. When comparing insurance company quotations, remember not all insurance is the same. Be sure that limits are compared to limits, and deductibles to deductibles, etc.

CHOOSING A POLICY

There are three major divisions of insurance policies applicable to the horse industry: coverage for the facility, coverage for the horses, and coverage for people or property in connection with the facility or horses. When choosing a policy, the owner should assess the value of all major business assets. Once the policy is chosen, it should be reevaluated each year to make sure changes in the facility's assets or operations are still covered.

Property Insurance

Perhaps the most common type of insurance for a horse operation is coverage for the property. Not only is it necessary to protect the business from fire, theft, bad weather, and other disasters, but when there is a mortgage or other indebtedness on the property, the lienholder will likely require coverage to protect his or her investment. Property insurance covers all types of farm property, including barns, equipment, vehicles, livestock, tack, etc.

Most homeowner's policies cover damages to backyard stables as long as they are included in the policy. If someone else's horses are boarded on the homeowner's property, the homeowner's policy usually covers any losses for stolen saddles or items destroyed by fire. However, for those business owners operating larger equine facilities, simple homeowner's insurance will not provide adequate coverage.

Property insurance choices include:

• Coverage for spoilage of medicines due to power outage.

- Replacement costs guaranteed on the living quarters occupied by the owner.

- Coverage for the computers, including software and all horse operations records.

- All buildings on the premises including barns, sheds, stables, arenas, offices, and mobile homes.

- Coverage for all machinery, including vehicles, tractors, manure spreaders, etc.

- Replacement cost of tack and equipment.

- Broad perils policy on horses that protects against drowning, electrocution, attacks by wild animals or dogs, accidental shooting, as well as the usual theft, fire, or lightning.

General Liability

Because of the added exposure of commercial operations (breeding, training, boarding, riding, etc.), these establishments need to carefully consider liability insurance. This type of insurance provides coverage for accident and bodily injury resulting from being around horses.

Racehorse trainers usually arrange for liability insurance for their charges while the horses are at the racetrack or training facility, and bill the horse's owner for the premiums. Or, the racehorse owner may wish to make the arrangements. For boarding, breeding, and riding operations, requiring horse owners and riders to sign a written release (holding the operation harmless) should be part of the contract and should always be implemented. However, releases will not stand up in court in cases of negligence. To fully protect the operation's assets, a liability policy is recommended.

The value of the facility and animals determine how much liability insurance is needed. Settlements of lawsuits are typically based on the defendant's assets and ability to pay. The more assets, the more liability insurance needed. Where the operation is located is also important, as laws vary in different regions. If the assets total over $1 million (such as a racetrack), a commercial umbrella policy may be added. This policy normally covers assets in excess of $1 million, usually up to $5 million. An insurance policy should be reevaluated each year to make sure any changes in the farm's assets or operations are still covered.

Care, Custody, and Control

Public horse centers that take care of privately owned animals, such as boarding, breeding, or training stables, might want to carry what is known as Care, Custody, and Control insurance. This type of insurance covers damages to horses that the center does not own. In the event of injury or death of those horses (for example, during hauling), the insurance company may reimburse the horse owner for veterinary bills or for the value of the horse on a case-by-case basis. If neither party appears to be at fault, the insurance company will probably pay. The insurance company will usually pay if the horse operation was negligent and does not deny negligence. If the horse operation denies negligence, but is proven negligent in a court of law, then the insurance company will be financially responsible for any damages awarded to the horse owner.

Care, Custody, and Control insurance covers both death and injury. However, it does not cover loss of use. Under this policy, a dollar value per horse must be established.

Horse Mortality

A basic horse mortality insurance policy covers the life of the horse. Also, some companies may be willing to add extra coverage to the mortality policy for loss of use or medical expenses.

The insurance company may require a veterinarian's

statement of the horse's health as well as a statement from the owner regarding its age, identification, and value. To avoid problems should a loss occur, closely following these factors will usually fulfill the requirements of an insurance policy:

- Only healthy animals can be covered. All pre-existing conditions are to be disclosed.

- All insured horses must be given adequate medical care, and notice of any illness must be given to the insurance company.

- The insurance company must give permission before performing non-emergency surgery on a horse. When emergency surgery is performed, permission is not necessary because of the time constraints, but notification must be made in a reasonable amount of time.

- Permission from the insurance company is required to perform a castration. Consent is also required to euthanize an insured horse suffering from illness or disease, but permission is not needed in emergency circumstances where the horse is suffering and a veterinarian states that it is necessary. In all cases an autopsy must be performed on the horse.

- Nerving an animal without notice or consent will result in loss of coverage.

- Medication must be given by a qualified veterinarian or experienced person under direction of a qualified veterinarian.

- When a horse is entered in a claiming race the amount of coverage will be reduced.

Insurance rates vary for every breed and within the breed for different classes of horses. Performance horses are usually the least expensive to insure for mortality because they are generally kept in good physical condition. Halter horses, however, are more expensive to insure because they can look good but actually be in very poor physical condition. Whether to purchase mortality

Basic Mortality Insurance Rates		
FOALS	24 hours – 30 days old	5.00%
	31 days or older	3.85%
YEARLINGS	Effective before November 1	2.85%
	Effective after November 1	**Adult rate by use**
AGES 2 – 14 (RACING)	Colts	4.75%
	Fillies	4.50%
	Geldings	6.30%
	Hurdlers/Steeplechasers	9.00%
AGES 2 – 14 (BREEDING)	Stallions and Mares	3.25%
	Stallions: Inability to cover due to accident or illness	50.00%
OLDER HORSES	15 years old	4.75%
	16 years old	6.75%
	17 years old	8.75%
	18 years old	10.75%
	19 years old	13.75%
	20 years old	16.95%

Fig. 9–3. These rates are for basic morality insurance for one Thoroughbred insured for less than $500,000.

insurance depends on the operation's financial resources and the horses to be covered. There may be no reason to insure horses if the business is able to afford the losses.

An owner could misunderstand the amount of mortality insurance being purchased. Misunderstandings arise with failure to understand the difference between an "actual cash value" and an "agreed value" policy.

To illustrate the differences between these policies, let's assume a claim on a $10,000 mortality insurance policy issued on the life of a horse. The horse owner properly submitted the claim on time, the loss was a covered loss, and the insurance company agreed to pay the claim as the owner had purchased an "agreed value" policy for $10,000.

A similar claim is made on a racehorse also covered by a $10,000 mortality policy. However, this time the policy is an "actual cash value" or fair market value policy.

The horse owner receives only $8,500 for the horse. Where "agreed value" policies are for an agreed-upon amount the "actual cash value" policies are for the fair market value of the horse around the time of death, which the insurance company may or may not calculate to be the insured amount.

Full Mortality

All Risk of Mortality or Full Mortality insurance reimburses the full value of a horse that is stolen or dies from accidents involving fire, transportation, shooting or bone breakage, natural disaster, and illness. Largely because purchasing full mortality enables owners to tack on riders for health coverage, it is the most popular policy.

Full mortality insurance is usually not available for horses more than 15 years of age, and many insurance companies will not cover high risk activities, like racing. There restrictions include non-coverage of death due to surgery when it is not to save the horse's life, death caused by negligence or complications from nerving procedures, and death from injections not given by a veterinarian.

Riders or endorsements for surgical and major medical coverage can usually be added to full or limited mortality insurance policies.

Surgical and Major Medical

Surgical insurance typically covers up to $5,000, including anesthesia, plus 35% of the combined cost of anesthesia and surgery in x-rays, hospitalization, lab tests, and medications. This insurance will not cover horses with a pre-existing health condition. Most will not cover racehorses. It does not pay for nonsurgical costs, castration, cosmetic surgery, performance-enhancing procedures, or autopsies. Coverage usually ends at age 16.

Major Medical insurance covers non-surgical treatments as well as everything surgical policies cover. This policy therefore includes diagnostic tests, non-surgical illnesses, and certain other medical care given to the horse by a licensed veterinarian.

In addition to the restrictions carried by the surgical policies, this insurance has a restriction for voluntary surgery and well care treatments, as well as congenital birth defects

Both Surgical and Major Medical insurance are generally economical to purchase and are usually a good bargain. Like health insurance for humans, most of these policies specify a deductible amount as well as the claim limit of $5,000.

Loss of Use

An endorsement for loss of use can be purchased as additional coverage on the mortality policy, or it may be offered as separate coverage. The horse must be totally disabled for the owner to collect, and it is relatively expensive coverage. The insurance company is, in effect, buying the horse from the owner. If an owner wishes to collect the compensation, he or she must be prepared to relinquish the horse. If the horse has an important performance career (and is not a pet), this coverage may be a wise choice as the insurance company will pay approximately 60% of the horse's worth in the event it becomes totally disabled.

Health Maintenance Programs

A health maintenance program is a fixed-price program that supplies preventative care for horses. The program usually calls for a prepayment to cover a predetermined set of procedures for each horse. It can offer the horse owner savings and convenience because routine services are discounted. Some plans even offer discounts on farm calls and veterinary services.

It is not all about cost savings. Another benefit of a good health-care program is the veterinarian becomes familiar with the horses because they are examined at regular intervals. By knowing the individual horse's medical history, the veterinarian is better able to make accurate diagnoses. This way potential health problems can be caught and treated before they get out of hand.

Some of these plans cover just the basic procedures and others are more complete. The following is an example of what a $160 per year plan may offer for one horse.

- physical and dental examinations twice a year

- deworming twice a year, and two paste dewormers to be used on the horse by the owners between vet visits

- farm calls at no charge

- twice a year vaccinations

- no charge counsel on minor health questions

A less expensive plan may offer the two exams and the dewormings, but excludes some of the immunizations and charges half price on the farm calls. This plan may cost $140 for the first horse and $110 for each additional horse.

A more comprehensive plan may cover:

- physical and dental examinations twice a year

- deworming quarterly

- twice a year vaccinations

- floating of teeth (with sedation when called for)

- cleaning of sheaths for all stallions and geldings

- testing for parasite eggs

Because most of the horse owners in this plan trailer their horses to the veterinarian's clinic, farm calls are not included. The annual fee for this program may be in the neighborhood of $210 for mares and $230 for stallions and geldings. These same services on an individual basis would cost the horse owners as much as 40% more. And savings opportunities for participants may extend beyond preventative care. A program may give a discount on out-of-plan services and owners of several horses may benefit from discounts for multiple horses.

Worker's Compensation

For horse operations that have employees, this type of insurance may be mandatory. However, some states exempt farm labor. Business owners should call their state's Department of Labor or Worker's Compensation Commission to learn more about the requirements regarding this insurance.

Who is considered an employee for Worker's Compensation purposes? Usually this is construed to mean every person in the service of another, whether or not the classification of employee is used—anyone under contract of hire, written or unwritten, including minors who work for an employer. Again, household workers and farm workers may be exempt.

This type of insurance is normally inexpensive, as well as being a good form of protection in the event that an employee sustains personal injury while at the place of employment. The employer may also elect to be covered by this type of insurance. Some states automatically cover corporate officers, but partners and sole proprietors may need to elect the coverage.

Special Event

If the horse operation holds shows, open houses, seminars, or clinics where an unusually large number of persons will be on the property, the owner may opt to invest in insurance to cover this event. This special coverage that can easily be attached to the existing liability insurance, and can be in place for a day or a week as needed.

Other Insurance

Depending upon the operation's needs, special types of insurance may be considered, such as Group Health Coverage, Breeding Stallion Infertility, Broodmare Barrenness, Colic Surgery Reimbursement, Extended Perils, or Professional Errors and Omissions Liability insurance.

DENIAL OF COVERAGE

Even if premiums have been dutifully paid, insurance companies can deny coverage if the owner gives the company false information, or if owners fail to notify the company or meet additional policy requirements. For instance, if a horse is to undergo a routine surgery such as castration, the insurance company may require that notice is given, or may even require an additional charge to cover the risk of putting the horse under an anesthetic. Owners should read insurance policies carefully, and should be aware of any special requirements that could result in loss of coverage before committing to a policy.

MISCONCEPTIONS ABOUT EQUINE INSURANCE

For some time now there have been misconceptions in the equine industry about horse-related insurance. Instead of reading their insurance policies, horsepeople quite often rely on myths. Thus they fail to observe the policy conditions and make expensive errors, or they may find out too late that the policy does not cover the current problem.

It is important to examine the misconceptions that plague such a significant and costly purchase.

Liability insurance is no longer needed on the horse operation because the state has enacted an equine-activity law. Although liabilities in the horse industry changed a great deal in the 1990s, and the majority of states have passed laws designed to limit or control liabilities in the horse industry, none of these laws is a "zero-liability" law. Horse business owners still need to contend with liability, and the need for insurance remains.

All liabilities originating from the owner's horse business are covered by the homeowner's policy. Liabilities that arise as a result of injury to parties involved in business activities are almost certain to be excluded from a homeowner's policy, because this type of policy will not cover businesses.

Adding an umbrella policy to the homeowner's insurance will create coverage for horse business activities. Adding an umbrella will not change the primary function of an insurance policy.

When Does an Insurance Company Require Notification?

Most equine insurance companies require notification under the following circumstances:

- upon detection of injury
- upon diagnosis of illness or disease
- before surgery of any kind
- when there is a change in use of the horse
- when there is a change in ownership of the horse
- before the horse is transported out of the country, or out of the range covered by the policy
- when there is a change in the value of the horse

Fig. 9–4. Before committing to any insurance policy, owners should know when the company requires notification to ensure coverage.

Since the homeowner's policy does not cover business activities, it is almost certain the umbrella will not either. This kind of policy is meant to increase the coverage of an existing insurance policy.

Insurance is not needed because everyone signs a release of liability. Even though they sign a release or waiver of liability, people can still sue. Having insurance will put the burden of the legal fees on the insurance company who will handle the defense for the insured, and pay the claim or judgement up to a specified amount. So having a waiver or release of liability does not do away with the necessity for good insurance coverage.

The owner's equine business liability insurance will covers when the owner is accused of negligently caring for a horse placed under his/her control. Accidents and injuries to people are covered by a standard equine commercial liability policy, but not horses. This is because horses are treated as personal property. To cover this type of risk, the owner might want to add "care, custody, and control" insurance to the commercial liability.

Insurance companies will pay the policy limits on a valid

claim in the death of a horse. An insurance company could be justified in paying less than the policy limits. The fair market value of the horse around the time of death is all that actual cash value policies are required to pay.

The time to call the mortality insurance carrier is after the horse has died. If the horseowner does not call the insurance company immediately upon the horse's injury or illness, the insurance company most likely not pay on the death claim.

The owner can just call the insurance agent who sold the horse mortality policy in the case of the horse's death. Most likely the insurance agent is not the person to call. The owner should check the insurance policy for the name and phone number of the designated party.

The true value of the horse does not need to be considered when purchasing mortality insurance, as any amount will do. The fair market value of the horse should determine the amount of mortality insurance purchased.

It does not matter that a horse went lame after the equine mortality insurance was purchased, the policy can be renewed without a veterinary examination. While some may allow automatic renewals, a veterinary certificate may be required by many insurance companies.

With a loss-of-use policy, 100% of the horse's value can be recovered when the horse is sold. The fact that the horse is disabled will not mean that insurance monies can be collected. The loss-of-use policies are designed to pay 100% of the value of a horse only when it can be proven that the horse is permanently and totally unable to perform its intended use. This may require the opinion of two veterinarians. A temporary soreness condition will not make the horse a candidate for payment under a loss-of-use policy. When a horse qualifies for payment because of loss-of-use, the insurance company will most likely ask the owner to surrender the horse to them.

Workers Compensation Insurance is not needed because it covers the same thing as the owner's equine business liability insurance policy. Workers' Compensation covers injuries to employees on the job who are usually not covered by business liability insurance.

It is always better to buy cheaper insurance. Cheaper insurance may mean less coverage. It is smart to shop around and compare insurance, making sure that the policies being compared have the same coverage. Also make sure that the chosen company is financially sound and has a good reputation.

Major medical and surgical insurance pays all expenses involved in keeping the owner's horse. This type of insurance is designed to cover surgery and other expenses associated with serious illness and costly care of a horse, and usually has a policy limit of $5,000. If the veterinary expenses exceed the limit, the owner is responsible for paying the excess.

The insurance policy the horse association purchased to cover their special event insures them against claims by spectators and participants. Usually event liability insurance only covers injury, damage, or death claims brought by spectators. It most likely will not cover claims brought by event participants unless it specifically states in the policy that it will.

SUMMARY

Before choosing an insurance policy, business owners should make sure it is appropriate for the type and size of operation they are running. They should analyze their financial situation, the value of the animals, the degree of personal involvement in their business, and the risk of experiencing a loss. Discussing these factors with an insurance agent (or better yet, several insurance agents), and having the business' attorney review a potential policy will help owners to find the best coverage for their facility.

10

HORSE RECORDS

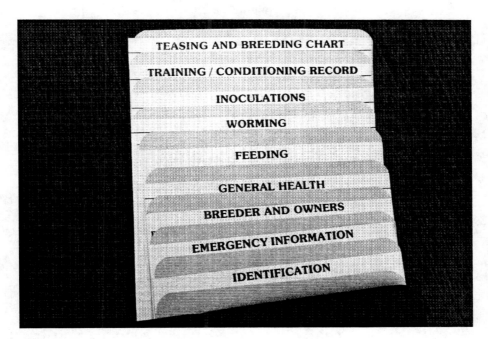

Fig. 10–1.

In any business, keeping detailed and accurate records not only simplifies operations, but helps to demonstrate a profit motive to the IRS. Record keeping may not be the most exciting job on the farm, but running a successful horse operation requires

233

organization and attention to detail.

Business records that should be kept:

- advertising and promotion of the business
- daily business activities
- health care records (deworming, vaccination, shoeing schedules, etc.)
- identification and location of horses
- insurance policy for the business
- outside horse information
- race/show records
- registration certificates, stallion reports, etc.
- sales lists
- special information
- training and conditioning
- winnings

Fig. 10–2. Keeping accurate records for all aspects of the business is very important.

HEALTH CARE REMINDERS

Hanging charts up in the barn that list each horse and its required inoculations, dewormings, and shoeing information can provide good daily health care reminders. One look at this chart will show which horses need what care on what particular day. The same type of chart can also be established for teasing, breeding, and foaling schedules. If such a chart is used, it is essential that it be updated regularly, as incorrect or outdated information may create problems.

TRAINING & CONDITIONING RECORDS

Racehorse training and other performance facilities should also keep records of each horse's daily work routine. For example, which horses are walking, cantering, galloping, or breezing on any particular day can be written on a wall chart or can be recorded on individual stall cards. These records are useful for determining what tack or warm-up a horse needs that morning. They may help the trainer chart a horse's progress to determine when a horse is ready to compete. Notes from exercise riders and grooms about the horse's attitude or performance will help a trainer determine the best course of action for the rest of the day, week, or month. And notes about jockeys' comments can help decide the strategy for the next race.

To enter a horse in a race, the trainer must know in which races a horse has run, the amount of money won, and the weight allowance. Also, it is important to know the competition—many races are won using the Condition Book. Both racehorse trainers and owners might use records to track the expenses and earnings of each racehorse, showing which ones are earning their keep and which are not.

DAILY LOG BOOK

Regardless of the size of the operation, a daily report or log should be kept of important events as they occur, and should include the following:

- breeding dates

- foals born

- vaccinations and medical treatments

- shoeing and deworming schedules

- workouts/training accomplished

- shows/races attended

- unusual events or accidents

This daily log book can easily be kept in the form of a loose leaf notebook or on a calendar. Periodically the information from this daily log can be transferred to each horse's permanent record or to the appropriate business file.

IDENTIFICATION

The larger the operation, the more effort it takes to keep track of the horses. At a small operation it should be easy to identify each horse simply by appearance. But on farms where hundreds of horses are on the property, an alternative form of identification is necessary.

Pins and Tags

Location maps are commonly used on breeding farms where a large number of mares arrive for the breeding season. These maps allow the business owner to group horses under a common color to indicate the specific area of the farm or ranch where they will be kept. Each horse is represented by a pin which is flagged a certain color. When a horse is moved to a new location, the pin representing that horse is moved also.

An outside mare is easily tagged with a halter or neck strap tag. These tags give the mare's identification, information about her breeding status, the stallion to which she is to be bred, and vaccination and deworming dates. A newborn foal should be carefully tagged to prevent confusion in regard to the dam. Colored tags can be used on the mane or tail to denote whether the foal is a colt or filly.

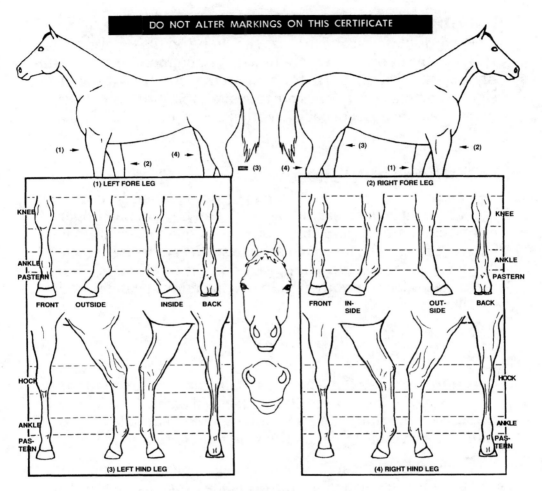

DO NOT ALTER MARKINGS ON THIS CERTIFICATE

CERTIFICATE EXPLANATION

THIS CERTIFICATE OF REGISTRATION IS ISSUED UNDER ASSOCIATION REGULATIONS WHICH ARE FULLY EXPLAINED IN THE OFFICIAL HANDBOOK.

ANY HORSE RECEIVING A REGISTRATION NUMBER AND RECEIVING THIS CERTIFICATE SHALL BE ELIGIBLE FOR BREEDING AND PERFORMING IN RECOGNIZED EVENTS.

AMERICAN QUARTER HORSE ASSOCIATION

AMARILLO, TEXAS 79168

Fig. 10–3. The signalment record used by the American Quarter Horse Association.

Signalments

Records of physical markings should be on file for every horse in the stable or on the farm or ranch. A signalment record is simply an outline of the horse from different viewpoints (back, front, side). The horse's markings are drawn on this outline. Accompanying the drawing is usually a written description of the horse.

Hair Patterns and Chestnuts

Hair patterns and chestnuts can be used to identify horses, although first it is necessary to record them. Like human fingerprints, hair patterns and chestnuts are unique to each individual horse. Photographs taken of each chestnut can be used to identify the horse. Likewise, the hair patterns on the forehead of a horse can be recorded by photographing them or drawing them on the signalment.

Brands

Hot iron brands have been used for many years to identify livestock, including horses. Racehorses have traditionally been tattooed on the upper lip for positive identification. Both of these methods are subject to alteration and tend to fade with time.

A more desirable method of branding is freeze marking. Here, an iron is submerged in a liquid nitrogen bath that has a temperature of -320°F. The iron is then applied to an area of the horse (generally the neck) which has been clipped and washed with alcohol. It is applied for 8 – 30 seconds, depending on the color of the horse's coat. Freeze marking gray horses requires the longest time because the hair must not grow back at all—the area where the brand is must be dark to be visible. On darker horses the hair grows back, but the pigment is destroyed, which makes the branded area white. The marks are symbols that usually represent the horse's registration number. Because each symbol represents a number, it is virtually impossible to alter this type of brand without making it extremely obvious.

Microchip Implants

The newest form of identifying horses is through a tiny microchip implanted in the horse's neck. Each microchip is encoded with an identification number, read using a hand held scanner. Held alongside the horse's neck, the scanner uses a common low-power radio signal, which can penetrate the neck, to read the ID number.

Along with the microchip, a capacitor and an antenna coil are needed to transmit the code to the scanner. These three elements are encased in a glass shell (about the size of a grain of rice), and the whole package is called a "transponder." Because the outer shell is glass, it would seem that the transponder would migrate once injected. However, the glass is sheathed in a polypropylene shell that begins to bond with the horse's surrounding connective tissue within 24 hours of injection, holding the transponder in place. The transponder remains inactive except when energized by the scanner's radio beam. Because it carries no battery, the transponder never wears out.

The transponder and needle come pre-packaged and pre-sterilized and must be inserted by a veterinarian or a qualified technician, in much the same manner as a vaccination. The chip is placed halfway between the poll and the withers on the horse's neck, approximately 1 inch below where the mane begins. This area must be shaved and scrubbed with a betadine solution before the transponder is inserted. Using a needle syringe, the veterinarian inserts the chip approximately $3/4$ inch deep into the horse's neck. Studies conducted by the manufacturing companies and the registry organizations report that there have been no complications due to the use of these microchips.

Compared to the other methods of identification, the microchip is more humane, lasts longer (approximate life is 75 years), and cannot be altered or scrambled. It is also fairly cost-efficient. The microchip, the veterinarian fee, and the cost of lifetime registration will total about $50 per horse.

More than 150,000 horses worldwide have been implanted with these transponders. The devices are manufactured by several different companies—including Avid and Destron/IDI—and are available from veterinarians. There are also organizations that register and keep track of identified animals through a national (or international) database. These organizations include Electronic ID, Inc. and The National Microchip Horse Registry.

Among the registries that accept this method of identification are the American Paint Horse Association, Tennessee Walking Horse Breeders and Exhibitors Association, Belgian Draft Horse Corporation, and American Suffolk Horse Association. The Jockey Club has not yet approved electronic identification as an alternative to lip tattoos for Thoroughbred racehorses.

Blood Typing/DNA Testing

Blood typing is a tried and true method of identifying horses and has been widely adopted by the major breed registries. Some registries require only that the stallion be blood typed; others require that the mare also have her blood type on file. As advancements in DNA testing continue, however, it is expected that this nearly 100% accurate method will supplant blood typing.

Photographs

Color photographs provide an accurate and precise method of identification. Although photographs may be taken from every angle, they should at least show the following:

- a front view of legs, body, and head, including face markings

- both the left and right side views, including legs

- rear lower legs, including heels

Care should be taken to get sharp, detailed photographs.

BREED REGISTRATION

Each breed registry has its own rules and standards for registration. Regulations concerning blood typing, transfer of ownership, embryo transfer, and artificial insemination vary from breed to breed. Owners should be acquainted with the registry rules for all breeds with which they may be involved.

Application

Registration begins with the application, which is a permanent record and needs to be completed with care. At the time of breeding, the mare's owner (known as the breeder) and the stallion's owner attest to the fact that the mare was bred to the stallion on a certain date or dates by signing a breeding certificate, or in some cases, the actual application.

The bulk of the application is usually completed by the mare's owner at the time of foaling. There is usually space on the application for several name choices. A description of the horse is also important. This usually includes a signalment of the horse and a written description of sex, color, and markings.

Stallion Report

Many registries require a stallion report be submitted by a specified date. This report lists the mares the stallion has bred during the year and the dates they were bred. It also shows the owner, location, and registration number of the stallion, and the owners and registration numbers of the mares. This report must be submitted to the registry before any foals can be registered.

Certificate of Registration

Once the application process is complete, a certificate of registration is issued to the owner of the registered horse. Registries are usually very careful and applications are sometimes delayed for missing or incorrect information. Examples of these reasons are:

- lack of blood typing of the stallion (and in some cases the mare)

- lack of a stallion report

- breeding service dates on the application do not agree with dates on the stallion report

- incomplete signalment

Other Forms

When a mare is sold in foal, the seller or breeder completes a transfer form for some registries, allowing the new mare owner to register that foal.

Most breed registries also require castration reports for stallions that have been castrated and mares that have been spayed. The existing registration certificate is usually returned with this report and a new one issued.

To report a horse's death to the registry, a death report must be completed stating the date of death. The registration certificate should be returned so it can be canceled.

In most cases, lease agreements are required to be recorded with breed registries. This is to ensure that the lessee can register foals from the leased horse, or meet the requirements for showing the leased horse, if that is the intent.

FALSE REGISTRATION PAPERS

Problems with registration papers do not occur often in the horse business, but they do happen. Because of this horse owners need to be aware of what can happen by mistake, carelessness or from intentional wrongdoing.

It is conceivable that even an honest and painstaking horse breeder could confuse the papers on a horse. Perhaps the foals have swapped mares soon after birth. This is generally the reason for faulty registration papers. But a mix-up could also happen when a group of young horses are taken to a sale together and the papers get shuffled. It is possible that the mistake will never be found, but when it is, honest sellers will do everything in their power to set things straight.

DNA testing can be used to determine parentage in cases where it is suspected that papers have been switched from one horse to another. There was the case where a couple of young racing fillies were prevented from being registered because this type of test disproved the parentage on the registration papers. It was determined that the foals had switched dams soon after birth. In this case, the mix-up was discovered and straightened out.

DNA testing can help to expose fraud as well as genuine mistakes in the registration of horses. But it can not prevent misrepresentation from taking place. There will always be those unethical sellers who will try to con innocent buyers.

Registration papers may be switched deliberately to increase a horse's selling price. This typically happens when a number of horses are sold to a killer operation. Because the killers are not concerned with the horse's papers, the seller can keep them. A dishonest trader may acquire a supply of registration papers in this manner. Then it is just a matter of finding and purchasing horses that are unregistered who closely fit the description on the papers. These horses are then sold with the papers and the buyers believe they have a registered horse. Therefore, it is important to be very careful to inspect registration papers to see that the markings on the horse match the markings on the papers.

This type of paper switching usually involves medium caliber horses, but there have been instances where quite valuable horses were involved in fraud concerning registration papers. There was one case where breeders, who were standing several stallions at stud, had a well-known Quarter Racing Horse that was sterile. Foals were being registered as having been sired by this horse and their owners being charged his higher stud fee when actually the mares had been bred to other stallions. Some 50 foals were registered to this stallion before it was discovered that he was sterile. As a result of this duplicity, the breeders were subject to fines, sanctions, suspensions, and law suits.

False registration papers can hurt the integrity of the registration procedure. Because of this, either blood typing or DNA testing is required by most breed registries for verification of parentage.

The best bet is to purchase horses with a brand which must appear on the registration papers. This makes it almost impossible to transfer papers from one horse to another.

BRAND INSPECTIONS

Most states in the western part of the United States have brand inspection services. This service is a registration system where the horse is identified, its markings recorded, and its title verified. Where a title does not exist, one is created in the name of the owner.

The title is called a brand inspection card, or more commonly, a "hauling card." These cards are generally small and have on them a complete description of the horse, including name, registration number, sex, foaling date, brand, and markings. Some have photographs of the horse and list additional features that may help to identify it. Whenever the horse is transported for any reason, this card must accompany the animal. When the horse is sold, the new owner pays a fee to transfer title, just as a person would transfer title to a car.

A horse does not need a brand to have a brand inspection. In that case, the inspector would use breed registration papers, veterinary records, bills of sale, photographs and health certificates.

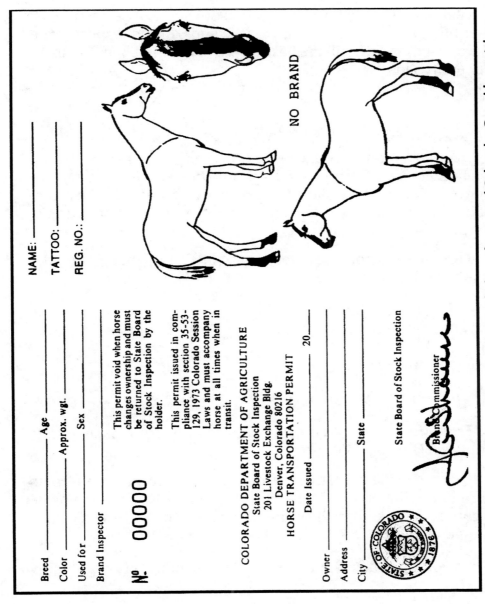

NAME: _____

TATTOO: _____

REG. NO.: _____

NO BRAND

Breed _____ Age _____

Color _____ Approx. wgt. _____

Used for _____ Sex _____

Brand Inspector _____

N⁰ 00000

This permit void when horse changes ownership and must be returned to State Board of Stock Inspection by the holder.

This permit issued in compliance with section 35-53-129, 1973 Colorado Session Laws and must accompany horse at all times when in transit.

COLORADO DEPARTMENT OF AGRICULTURE
State Board of Stock Inspection
201 Livestock Exchange Bldg.
Denver, Colorado 80216
HORSE TRANSPORTATION PERMIT

Date Issued _____ 20 _____

Owner _____

Address _____

City _____ State _____

State Board of Stock Inspection

Brand Commissioner

Fig. 10–4. A brand inspection card, or "hauling card" from the state of Colorado. One side contains owner information and the other side records the horse's markings, brand, and identifying marks.

All horses should be marked with some type of permanent identification, such as hot or freeze brands. Brand inspectors believe that these are still the best way to avoid theft because they are easily seen.

PERMANENT RECORDS

All information—from when a horse gets a vaccination, to when there is a change in feed—should be recorded in a permanent file. Keeping this file up to date allows for ease in the process of buying and selling. It also allows the owner to find out the status of each horse at a glance.

Permanent records for breeding stallions and mares should also include:

- semen evaluations

- fertility history/current fertility status

- breeding/foaling dates

- reproductive examinations/treatments

Entering teasing and breeding information from the daily log book will keep this file current.

Every new foal born on the ranch or farm should have its own permanent file as soon as it is weaned. From birth to weaning, its records can be kept in the same file as the dam's. These records should include:

- a complete description of the foal, including photographs

- foaling date

- vaccination, deworming, and medical treatments

Permanent File

Items to be kept in this file include:

- advertising and promotional material (if the horse is for sale or lease)
- bill of sale
- veterinary record, including deworming and vaccination schedules
- dental care history and maintenance schedule
- depreciation schedule (if applicable)
- habits or vices
- identification (photos, signalment, etc.)
- insurance policy on the horse
- pedigree
- race/show record
- registration certificate
- shoeing history and schedule
- special feeding requirements
- training and conditioning record
- UCC-1 Form (if applicable)

Fig. 10–5. A permanent file should include all information pertaining to the horse.

OUTSIDE HORSES

An operation that takes in horses for breeding, training, or showing should maintain a file on each outside horse. This file should contain the horse's arrival date, inoculations and general health records, shoeing records, special feeding requirements, and breeding or training status. In addition to the above records, it is a good idea to have on file the telephone numbers of the veterinarian, farrier, and insurance agent for each outside horse.

SUMMARY

Once a good system of record keeping is in place, it takes minimal time and effort to keep health care, training, insurance, and other records current. Remember, a good record keeping system saves much energy and expense, enhances a business' professional reputation, and helps to prove a profit motive to the Internal Revenue Service.

11

COMPUTER & SOFTWARE ASSISTANCE

Fig. 11–1.

Acquiring a computer system to help manage a business is nearly essential. Keep in mind that choosing the right software is as important as choosing the computer. The size and type of operation should be considered when deciding what brand of software and computer system to purchase.

A computer will likely pay for itself in cost effectiveness. Even a small operation that anticipates growth would benefit from the help of a computer system. And operations like breeding farms might need a specific record keeping program.

When the horse operation has a computer all the business records are easily accessible. There is no more searching in drawers and boxes for items such as client information, health records, breeding dates, veterinary records, exercise programs, billing invoices, show and race information, and feeding and deworming schedules. All of this date is available with the touch of a finger. And a paper copy of all records can be printed almost as quickly.

In addition to financial and horse care programs available for use with the computer, the horse business can take advantage of the many services offered on the internet. This is a great way to learn about horse subjects of all kinds. It is possible to determine the results of shows and races, contact breed organizations and registries, find out the schedules of equine events, and purchase needed books and videos. The computer has already become an invaluable tool for many in the horse industry, providing an easy and time saving way to manage all those records and also a research tool for all aspects of business administration as well.

CHOOSING THE RIGHT SOFTWARE

Software refers to the programmed information that enables the computer to perform its many tasks. In the late 1970s, computer software manufacturers began to work directly with individuals in the horse industry to meet specific business needs. Today, there are a large number of software programs that cover many aspects of horse and farm management. These software programs include record keeping systems for racing, boarding, breeding, and showing operations.

The best software program is one that is advanced enough to perform the necessary tasks, yet not so complex as to be cumbersome.

Horse business owners want a "user friendly" system that relieves some of the workload and provides accuracy and timeliness in record keeping.

Before purchasing software, determine why it is needed. Will it be used to keep financial records? Will it be used to keep breeding, racing/showing, and training information? Or is it exclusively to keep health records?

There are many kinds of software systems for a horse business to choose from. For a small operation with just a few horses, software is available for around $50. Software for a large horse business will be quite a bit more expensive. Where the horse business is in the market for a computer as well as software, prices could average thousands of dollars.

Many software companies have sites on the world wide which offers a trial version of their product, either via download or snail mail on diskette or CD.

Software Options

Some software packages offer the option to add various modules to the basic system. These modules might include breeding, training, racing, and showing records, a billing module, a pedigree generator, teasing charts, race manager module, and complete accounting packages to handle general ledger, payroll, accounts receivable, and accounts payable. Many of these programs are updated periodically (sometimes annually), and the manufacturers give previous customers a discount on the update.

Applications included in most software packages are:

1. A horse management module for keeping general horse records. This module allows the business owner to list horses or clients in a systematic way for easy retrieval. Some packages offer pedigrees generated by this application.

251

2. A breeding records module for keeping broodmare and stallion records. This module usually includes a variety of breeding reports, including stallion and mare performance reports, broodmare teasing charts, broodmare calendars, and stallion reports. Some packages print out registration applications for newborn foals.

3. Horse health or medical records, including vaccinations, physical exams, surgery, lab work, hoof care, deworming, and dental care. Each horse's record can be displayed or printed out as needed. Also, reminders for routine deworming or farrier care may be called up on the screen or printed out when desired.

4. Inventory files for keeping track of supplies, equipment, and bulk items. Also, horse files may list horses by name and their genealogical records. An inventory of insurance policies and vehicle records could be kept this way, as well as client lists.

5. Boarding and training records keep track of horses that are being boarded or trained and the fees charged. A printed report can be generated for billing.

6. Billing and accounts receivable applications may be included for printing invoices for services rendered. An aging report can be printed to show customer activity at any time.

7. Race or show results and expenses are kept on the individual horse's performance record, indicating purse money or points accumulated and expenses incurred.

8. Sales of horses application creates sales reports and fact sheets.

9. Check register and expense records system may also be offered, with expenses being automatically posted to preset tax categories.

10. A general ledger module may be included in some packages that interfaces with the billing and check register and expense records.

11. Payroll accounting, which generates checks, reports, and records for payroll, as well as W-2 forms. This module also interfaces with the general ledger module.

COMPUTER TERMS

The **hardware** is the physical machine, made up of the monitor, speakers, keyboard, circuit boards, floppy diskette drive, compact disc drive (CD-ROM), hard disk drives (internal and/or external), and printer.

When a business owner buys software, it usually comes on floppy diskettes or a CD. Guided by the computer, the business owner "installs" information from the disc onto the internal hard drive. The hard drive is where all software programs and documents are stored. Even so, some programs require the compact disc to be in the CD-ROM drive while running the program.

The **operating system** runs the software once it is installed on the hard disk. Most computers are either IBM-compatible, the majority of which use Windows; or Macintosh, which have their own operating system. Most software is written for these formats.

Some of the more complex software packages have made **RAM** (random access memory) more significant. Basic programs may require 8 megabytes (MB) of RAM; complex programs may require 32 MB, and recommend 48 – 64 MB.

The **processor** determines how fast the computer processes information. It is best to purchase a computer with the fastest processor you can afford. Most computers sold today have processors of 500 – 1200 megahertz (MHz).

Programs that are installed on the computer and documents stored there, take up space on the hard disk, which is something that needs to be considered. Just a few years ago anything more than 100 megabytes was believed to be a lot of storage space. Today 20 - 30 gigabytes and more is considered average. In choosing a computer it is important to make certain the hard disk has enough free space for whatever software programs are chosen.

External hard drives are also available. An external hard drive can be purchased separately from the computer system as the need for more space grows.

Floppy diskettes are sometimes used to physically transport information. For example, you can copy your farm's logo onto a floppy and take it to the printers to create letterhead stationary, envelopes, and business cards. Floppy diskettes are also sometimes used to store files separately from the computer for safekeeping (to prevent loss of valuable information because of a computer breakdown, theft, lightening storm, etc.). This process is called backing up, and it is best to perform this task daily, or weekly at least.

Removable hard drives are an alternative file transport and backup system to floppies. They come with a drive, software to run the drive, and usually several disks. The user plugs the drive into the computer, installs the software, and then inserts the removable disk into the drive. Removable hard drives combine the roominess of external hard drives with the convenience of transporting the disk safely. Removable hard disks may hold 40 – 500 MB of information, whereas floppies hold only 1.4 MB. It is safe to carry the disk in a briefcase, mail it across the country, or store it for long periods. These disks make backing up or sending promotional photos of your stallion a quick and easy task. Some popular brands of removable hard drives are Zip™, Jazz®, and Syquest®.

CHOOSING THE RIGHT COMPUTER

Changes in the computer industry have led to machines that are faster, more useful, and more affordable. Today's personal computers can handle almost any software and are easy to operate, even for those business owners with little or no computer experience. It is usually best to choose the software that is best for the business, then buy the machine to run it.

Computers are usually sold with five basic components: the central processing unit, which holds the circuit boards and disk drives; a keyboard; a mouse; speakers for sound; and a monitor. The operating system is pre-loaded on the computer's hard drive. Sometimes the monitor is sold separately. A printer, which is needed to get full use of the system, is usually sold separately. Most printers are laser jet or inkjet/bubble jet.

Advances in the computer industry are happening so fast that it is impossible to keep up. However, some things about computers have not changed. They still need to be protected from electrical surges (lightening storms) and dust. If the computer must be kept in the barn, it should be in a clean office. The computer should be well ventilated: find the ventilation slots and do not block that area. Computers can withstand all but extreme heat and cold—generally, if the user can stand the temperature, so can the computer.

ONLINE SERVICES

To access online services a horse business needs a computer with a modem, an internet service provider (ISP), and a program that automates the service. All computers sold today come with an internal fax/modem. An ISP is a business that sells permission to use their server, via the phone lines. As for software, several companies allow their browser and e-mail software to be installed on new computers for free. To connect, the user tells the computer to call a local telephone number provided by the ISP (using the modem), then the user "logs on" to that server using a password.

On this "information superhighway," the business owner can send and receive e-mail to and from anyone around the world; read electronic bulletin boards and newsgroups for information on subjects like breeding, training, equine health, and racing; and participate in worldwide conferences on these subjects as well. The horse business owner can go to a web page featuring a stallion in which he or she is interested, buy tack online, or discover who has hay for sale.

Commercial Services

CompuServe, Prodigy, and America Online are three of the many commercial companies that charge their own rates and provide their own internet services. For a set fee, the farm owner uses the company's software, and their phone lines, to log onto their server. They provide e-mail, web access, and newsgroups. These services are newbie-friendly and good for people who are just getting started with computers.

The Internet

The Internet started as computer links among universities and libraries. Most users were researchers, professors, and students. Now, however, the Internet is a huge worldwide network of people from all walks of life: government officials, rock stars, and horse business owners can all find relevant forums on the Internet. In fact, the Internet is especially popular among horsepeople because horsepeople tend to live in rural areas, away from convenient shopping and libraries. The internet and the world wide web offer a convenient and inexpensive way to buy and sell horses and horse-related products, and to stay current with industry trends.

Today almost every product, advertisement, and the cover of any magazine carries the "http://www.the business.com" that denotes a web page. This is the electronic address, called a URL, for a specific web site on the world wide web.

It is no longer necessary to call an 800 number or to order information by mail. Equine products and services can be viewed instantly on the internet. Many people worry about the security of online shopping. But in reality, it is much more likely that a credit card number will be intercepted while using a phone or fax than online via a secure server. That is not to say that it never happens, but after all, credit card fraud existed before the Internet.

Fees for Online Services

Once on the Internet, the exchange of information is free. However, access to the Internet requires a subscription to an ISP or commercial internet service. The service charges a subscription fee and/or connection fees.

Fees for online services may be a flat monthly rate, an hourly rate, or the service may have variable fees based on the time called (just like a cellular phone bill). The service provides all of the information necessary to get started, including a password and an e-mail address. They may provide a program to automate the service, or they may sell one, or they may suggest one.

The best way to save time and money while using an online service is to 1) log on, 2) "download" all e-mail and new files in any forum that looks interesting, 3) log off, 4) read the e-mail and files, 5) write any responses, and then 6) log back on to "upload" the written responses. In this way, as little time as possible is spent actually using the service and clogging up the phone line. All downloaded files can be sifted through on the user's computer, to be saved or deleted at the user's convenience.

Database Services

Another form of the online service is provided by companies that offer pedigree and other database services. For example, Bloodstock Research Information Systems, Inc. compiles pedigree and racing statistics related to the Thoroughbred industry. The American Quarter Horse Association also has an online service for similar statistics relating to the Quarter Horse industry. Horse business owners can use their computers to call the service's computer (for a fee) and download race records, daily racing forms, pedigrees, and sales histories. The databases are very comprehensive and are used by breeders, farm owners, racehorse owners, trainers, jockey agents, and handicappers.

SUMMARY

Computers and specialized software packages allow accurate record keeping and information retrieval in a timely manner. Records can be called up instantly on the computer screen and printed out. Using online services, the owner can access data and information from all over the world. The computer will conveniently sort this data and provide organized lists of information as needed.

Perhaps the greatest advantage of computerizing a horse operation is that records are all in one place, rather than scattered around on various slips of paper or in unmarked notebooks. Having everything organized in a computer lends a professional air to the business, and makes everything much easier at tax time.

12

UNDERSTANDING ACCOUNTING & TAXATION

Fig. 12–1.

Sometimes the most challenging and confusing areas of business management are financial record keeping and tax returns. This chapter offers understandable explanations of financial principles relevant to a horse business, such as methods of accounting, what constitutes income and expense, and how to figure depreciation. Special tax cases, such as capital gains, installment sales, and loss of property are discussed as well.

While this chapter explores many financial routes, it cannot cover every one. Inevitably, owners will have very specific questions that cannot be answered by this book. Then, it is best to seek out an accountant or tax attorney. It cannot be emphasized enough that proper financial records and accurate tax returns are instrumental in proving profit motive to the IRS and thereby avoiding penalties.

RECORDING TRANSACTIONS

One of the first things a business owner should do is to obtain the proper documentation necessary to open a checking account in the name of the business. *(See Chapter 1 for information on business names.)* Depositing all business-related income to this account and paying all expenses by check out of this account will simplify financial records considerably.

All income should be identified when deposited in the account, and any paperwork pertaining to that income should be kept in a monthly file. Similarly, every check written should be recorded on the check stub in the business checkbook. Using deposit receipts and check stubs, it is a fairly simple matter to create a spreadsheet, either on a computer or by hand, and itemize income and expenses. Doing this on a month-to-month basis prevents loose ends at tax time. *(See Figures 12–2 and 12–3 for examples of a monthly income record and a monthly expenses record.)*

Accounting books are available that are set up for recording income and expenses along with a monthly summary. Spreadsheet programs are available as well. Most accounting software organizes the records and allows for a monthly (and yearly) printout of income and expenses in the form of an income statement. *(See Chapter 11 for more information on software for horse businesses.)*

		INCOME			
Month of _____		cash method			
Date of deposit	Check number	Received from	Account number	Amount	
Total income this month				$	

Fig. 12–2. An example of a spreadsheet used to keep a monthly income record.

261

| EXPENSES | | | | | | |
| Month of _____ | | cash method | | | | |
Date of payment	Check number	Payee	Item and quantity	Account number	Amount	
Total expenses this month					$	

Fig. 12–3. An example of a spreadsheet used to keep a monthly expenses record.

Entries can be made to the spreadsheet at the end of each month from the checkbook. Then income and expenses are recorded by category on different pages, using as many columns as needed. When all entries for the month have been made, all columns are totaled and a summary of income and expense taken from these totals.

METHODS OF ACCOUNTING

There are two methods of accounting that businesses which involve horses can use—cash or accrual. Years ago the IRS granted farmers and ranchers the right to use the cash method, which is the simplest and most flexible accounting method.

Who Is a Farmer?

The business of farming includes cultivating, operating, or managing a farm for profit as an owner or tenant. According to the IRS, any activity involving feeding, caring for, training, and managing horses is normally classified as a farming business. A farm can be a sole proprietorship, partnership, or corporation.

Cash Method

Regular corporations with gross receipts under $1 million, subchapter S corporations, partnerships, and sole proprietorships can use either the cash or accrual method of accounting. Many people in the horse business choose the cash method because it is straightforward and allows more financial flexibility.

Using the cash method of accounting means that income is recorded when received and expenses are recorded when paid. For example, a business owner sells a horse on December 29 and does not receive payment until January 3 of the next year. Using the cash method, the income would be recognized when received—

January 3. If this business owner makes a major feed purchase on December 30, but does not pay the feed store owner until January 2, the expense would be recorded when paid—January 2.

This method of accounting is beneficial to new horse businesses because it allows the owner more flexibility in planning income and deductions. This flexibility is advantageous when a horse business is trying to show two profit years in seven.

Accrual Method

Most regular corporations with gross receipts over $1 million, partnerships that have a corporation as a partner, and tax shelters will use the accrual method of accounting. Using the accrual method, income is recorded when it is earned and expenses recorded when they are incurred.

Using the examples above, a business owner sells a horse on December 29 and does not receive payment until January 3 of the next year. With the accrual method, the income is recorded on December 29. If a major purchase of feed is made on December 30, but the payment is not made until January 2, the purchase would be recorded as a December expense.

Horse-related businesses that deal with inventory (such as tack or feed stores) must use the accrual method. It should also be noted that tack and feed stores are *not* considered agricultural, even though they are agricultural-related. Thus, their inventory is considered non-farm property and subject to different tax guides than the property discussed in this chapter. Because the accrual method requires the extra work of using inventory to determine gross income, most horse businesses do not use this method.

A business entity chooses the method of accounting when the first tax return is filed. And the tax return must be filed using the same method used for the tax records. If, after the first tax return is filed, the owner wants to change the accounting method, he or she must first get consent from the IRS.

INCOME

The primary source of income for a horse business is money received for products or services. In addition, purse money and prize money is considered income. There is also special income, such as capital gains and insurance proceeds (discussed later), and forgiveness and cancellation of a debt. (When money is borrowed, not repaid, and subsequently forgiven, the amount of the forgiveness is considered to be income to the recipient.)

What Is Income?

- Money received from the sale of raised horses
- Money received from the sale of horses purchased for resale
- Money received from the sale of horses used for breeding or sport
- Fees for boarding, breeding, training, leasing, and riding instruction
- Purse money or prize money
- Forgiveness and cancellation of a debt
- Insurance proceeds

Fig. 12–4. Examples of items that should be recorded as income.

Billing for Services

Money taken in for boarding, breeding, training, leasing, and riding instruction should be recorded as income. However, billing customers and recording their payments requires extra record keeping. Whether done by hand or on a computer, a separate income record or journal (called an "accounts receivable" file when using the accrual method) should be kept for this purpose. A simple system is to keep copies of customer invoices in a file marked "unpaid." When payment is received and deposited in the bank, the payment is recorded and the invoice transferred to the "paid" file. This system allows the owner to know, at a glance through the file, those customers who have not paid their bills. The system can be kept by recording the invoices as they are prepared and the payments as they are received.

EXPENSES

A horse business incurs various types of expenses. Examples of ordinary operating expenses include feed, veterinary services, and farm labor. These expenses should be differentiated from the owner's personal expenses, such as clothing, home rent, or maintaining a vehicle for personal use. There are also capital expenditures for those items which, while they are business expenses, are not ordinary. These items might include the cost of building a new barn or arena. These three categories of expenses—operating, personal, and capital—are discussed in detail in the following sections.

Keeping invoices and other bills separate from personal records is a must. A file of all canceled checks, receipts, bills, and bookkeeping records should be kept for at least six years. When a capital expenditure is made, a copy of the bill of sale or other paperwork must be retained indefinitely.

Operating Expenses

Ordinary and necessary expenses of operating a horse business can be recorded on a monthly expense record (categorized as "accounts payable" under the accrual method) and generally include products or services that are purchased or paid for on a regular basis. These expenses can be deducted from the business' *gross* (total) income. The balance is *net* income (profit) or loss.

Expenses directly related to business meetings of employees, and the cost of food and beverages for employees, are deductible. For these expenses to be allowed as business deductions, corroborating records must be kept to show the amount of the expense, the time and place, the business purpose, and the business relationship to the persons involved.

Only 50% of the cost of business meals or entertainment is deductible as a business expense. For either meals or entertainment expenses to be deductible, they must relate to the business and directly precede or follow a business discussion. Business must actually be conducted,

How Long to Keep Records?	
Tax returns	Permanently up to at least 10 years
Cancelled checks, bank statements, other banking or borrowing cards	6 years or 2 years after the tax is paid, whichever is later
Paid bills, receipts for deductible items, including interest, donations, and all business deductions, records showing cost and sale price of horses, and copies of registration papers, medical records, and veterinary bills	3 years or 2 years after the tax is paid, whichever is later
Records relating to retirement plan contributions or withdrawals	Permanently or until 3 years after all funds are withdrawn and reported on tax returns
Records relating to cost of real estate and improvements to the real estate	Permanently or until 3 years after the sale of related property and the sales reported on tax returns
Records relating to purchases of securities, including mutual funds	Permanently or until 3 years after the sale of the securities and the sale reported on tax returns
Mortgage loan documents	Permanently or until 3 years after the loan is paid off

Fig. 12–21. This chart shows how long to store business-related documents.

and the principal reason for the entertainment or business meal must be the transaction of business. (There has been controversy over whether expenses incurred by racehorse owners at the track are deductible as business expenses because of the strong entertainment element.)

267

Travel expenses incurred in connection with the horse business such as transportation costs, lodging, tolls, telephone charges, and tips are deductible. However, no lavish or extravagant expenses will be allowed, and the cost of taking a spouse along on a business trip is usually not deductible.

Labor expense includes wages paid to regular farm workers, including children of the owner. (In the case of children, the wages must be reasonable for services performed.) Wages paid for performing ordinary repairs and maintenance work are deductible. However, when wages are paid to construct buildings or make major repairs, then the labor cost is considered a capital expenditure and cannot be deducted as a current expense.

Interest on horse business indebtedness (such as horse loans, equipment loans, lines of credit, and other notes) is ordinarily fully deductible as a business expense.

Personal Expenses

While some personal expenses may be used as itemized deductions on the personal tax return, no personal expenses can be deducted as business expenses. In cases where an expense is both business and personal, there must be an allocation on a reasonable basis.

For example, where electricity and water are used for the personal residence and for the horse business on the same property, it would be best to have separate meters. Where this is not possible, some method of allocation should be used. The allocation must be reasonable and substantiated by facts. Other items that may have both a personal and a business application are automobile expenses, rent, fuel, interest, and taxes.

BUSINESS EXPENSES	
Operating Expenses (deducted directly from business income)	**Capital Expenditures** (deducted as depreciation or expensed)

• Advertising
• Boarding fees
• Breeding fees
• Business-related subscriptions
• Commissions
• Depreciation
• Entry fees
• Farrier services
• Feed purchases
• Fertilizer and lime
• Insurance premiums for fire, storm, theft, and accident losses
• Labor
• Professional fees
• Rent
• Repairs and maintenance
• Riding attire
• Stable supplies
• Taxes and interest
• Telephone and utilities
• Training fees
• Transportation
• Travel/entertainment
• Veterinary services
	• Breeding equipment:
	    artificial insemination devices
	    embryo transfer devices
	    foal monitoring devices
	    laboratory equipment
	    teasing pens or chutes
	• Buildings (barns, arenas)
	• Costs of material and labor related to the construction or installation of any of these items
	• Farm equipment, tractors, and other machinery
	• Fences
	• Trucks, cars, vans and horse trailers
	• Major improvements to buildings
	• Major machinery overhaul
	• Purchased horses
	• Training/therapeutic equipment:
	    tack
	    hot walking machines
	    infrared cameras
	    jog/racing bikes
	    jump courses
	    swimming pools (for horses)

PERSONAL EXPENSES	
(not deductible from business income)	
• Clothing • Consumer interest • Personal taxes • Home rent	• Household costs/Food • Life insurance premiums • Maintaining a horse or automobile for personal use

Fig. 12–5. Examples of various expenses that a horse business might incur, versus personal expenses which are not deductible from business income.

269

Limits for Health Insurance Deduction

Taxable Year Beginning In	Applicable Percentage
1998 – 2002	45%
2003	50%
2004	60%
2005	70%
2006 and thereafter	80%

Fig. 12–6. The limits for the health insurance deduction for the self-employed.

Self-Employed Health Insurance Deduction

Sole proprietors (and general partners, limited partners receiving a guaranteed payment, and an employee of an S corporation who owns more than 2% of the stock of that corporation) can deduct a portion of their health insurance for themselves and their families. This deduction is not an itemized deduction nor is it deducted from the business income, but is subtracted from the total income of the taxpayer on the front of Form 1040. The limits for this deduction are found in Figure 12–6.

Capital Expenditures

Money paid for the acquisition or improvement of property having a useful life of more than one year is generally considered a capital expenditure. There is no monetary limit for capital expenditures. However, many businesses set a dollar amount under which the item is deducted from ordinary income as an operating expense. An item which is over the set amount is listed as a capital expenditure, or "capitalized." For example, building an indoor arena would be considered a capital expenditure. Repairs to property are capitalized if they extend the life or increase the value of the property. If the repairs merely sustain the property's value and life expectancy, they are expensed.

Capital expenditures are not expensed (fully deducted from ordinary income in the year of purchase); they must be deducted over time through depreciation (unless they are expensed as section 179 deductions, which is discussed after depreciation).

DEPRECIATION

Depreciation is a means of recovering the cost of horses or other business property having a useful life of more than one year. This cost recovery is done by deducting a certain percentage of the original cost (or other basis) of the business property from gross business income each year for a specified number of years. (As mentioned above, a business may recover the entire cost of depreciable property in the year of purchase by taking a section 179 deduction, but there are limits to this option.)

Instead of deducting the full cost of all property used in the business as a current expense, the tax laws (Internal Revenue Code) require businesses to spread the cost recovery over a number of years, according to the type of property. Although it may be more desirable for the business to expense the cost in the year placed in service, the concept behind depreciation is that the property will lose its value over time due to wear and tear, and that businesses can get back the property's cost by taking annual deductions for depreciation while the property is in use.

Depreciation deductions can be taken by each new owner; in other words, property can be depreciated in full a countless number of times (only once per owner per business) as long as the property meets certain criteria.

Criteria for Depreciable Property

Depreciable property must meet the following qualifications:

- It must have a useful life of more than one year.

- It must be held for use in a trade or business or for production of income.

- It must be something that can be worn out, used up, or loses value from natural causes.

Depreciation applies to purchased property placed in service in a business. For example, horses bought and used in a business for draft, breeding, or sport may be depreciated. Property that is inherited, received as a gift, or received in a tax-free exchange may also be depreciated.

Depreciation begins when the horse is placed in service, and not before. Property is considered placed in service when it is ready and available for a specified function. Therefore, young horses acquired for draft, breeding, or sport cannot be depreciated until they have reached the age when they can perform their intended activity.

Property which has no determinable useful life, such as land, cannot be depreciated. Property which has a useful life of less than one year (for example, small tools and equipment) cannot be depreciated, nor can property held primarily for sale to customers (for example, a horse held for resale). Also, raised horses cannot be depreciated because their upkeep costs have already been deducted as operating expenses.

Basis for Depreciation

Before getting any further into depreciation, it is necessary to understand the basis for depreciation. *Basis refers to the value of the property for tax purposes, which is not necessarily the property's true value.* For instance, a raised horse may have a basis of zero. However, if the same horse is purchased for $1,000, the new owner's basis in the animal would be $1,000. If the same horse is subsequently exchanged, or purchased and held for resale, the basis may be different again. Consequently, an owner (or IRS agent) cannot always determine the value of each horse just by reading the accounting books.

The original basis for tax purposes, or depreciation, can be any of the following:

- cost
- transferred basis
- fair market value
- substituted basis

Cost is the most common basis and represents the original investment in the horse or other property. For example, with a purchased horse, the cost basis is what the owner paid for the animal. (Again, with a raised horse the basis is zero because its cost has already been deducted as an operating expense.)

The basis can also be the horse's fair market value on the date received (by the new owner). Fair market value is an estimate from an appraiser of what the property could sell for that day on the open market. While fair market value is not always the basis for

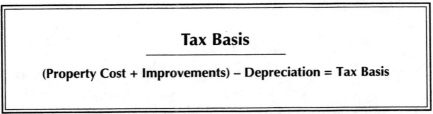

Tax Basis

(Property Cost + Improvements) – Depreciation = Tax Basis

Fig. 12–7. A formula for calculating tax basis for purchased or exchanged property.

depreciation, it is the most accurate measurement of the horse's true value. For instance, raised horses and horses that have already been depreciated to the full extent have a zero cost basis, but may still have a fair market value of $10,000.

Transferred basis is the basis of the horse in the hands of the transferrer at the time of transfer. If a horse or other property is transferred from personal use to business use, depreciation is based on whichever basis is the lowest—original cost or fair market value at the time of transfer to the business. For instance, a gelding was purchased for personal use at a price of $3,000. When the horse was placed in business two years later as a school horse, it was appraised at $2,500. Because the $2,500 was the lower of the two values, that was the basis for depreciation.

Substituted basis is determined by reference to the basis of the other property held and exchanged. For example, no gains or losses resulting from exchanges of like-kind property are recognized. In exchanges of this type, the basis in the old property becomes the basis in the new property. This new basis is known as the substituted basis. *(See the section entitled "Exchanges of Property" for additional information on tax-free exchanges of like-kind property.)*

When depreciating or figuring gain or loss from a sale for income tax purposes, adjustments must be made to the original basis to reflect increases (additions) and decreases (depreciation) on the property. This "adjusted" basis is referred to as tax basis.

Tax Basis

Tax basis is an adjusted measure of depreciable property's value. It is the property's original cost, plus improvements, minus depreciation. Additions or permanent improvements to the property increase the tax basis. Ordinary depreciation, section 179 deductions (discussed later), and casualty losses (losses from fire, theft, flooding, etc.) decrease the tax basis.

While business owners must know the original basis of property in order to calculate depreciation, they must also know the depreciation taken before they can calculate tax basis.

How to Figure Depreciation

As explained above, when property is depreciated, a certain percentage of the cost or other basis is deducted from the gross income of the business. A deduction is made each year until the entire basis is recovered, or until the property is disposed of, whichever comes first.

Depreciation may not be taken retroactively, or in excess of the allowable amount for a particular year. In other words, if the owner fails to take depreciation in the first year, that amount cannot be added to the depreciation for the second year. However, unclaimed depreciation can be claimed on an amended return if it is filed within three years of the date the original return was filed, or within two years of the time the tax was (incorrectly) paid, whichever is later. *Even if allowable depreciation is not claimed that year, the basis of the property must still be reduced as if it had been claimed.*

If property is used for both personal and business purposes, the business part can be depreciated. For example, if a truck is kept partly for the horse business and partly for personal use, a depreciation deduction can be made for the percentage of time it is used for business. Also, if part of the home is set aside for business use, the business portion may be depreciated.

It is important to keep a schedule for all depreciable property, and the amounts of depreciation taken. Owners should document the purpose for which the horse (or other property) was purchased and the primary use of the property as part of their depreciation records. These records do not need to be complicated. In fact, simple ones often prove best.

Modified Accelerated Cost Recovery System

Farm property placed in service after December 31, 1986 is depreciated under the Modified Accelerated Cost Recovery System (MACRS) using the General Depreciation System (GDS) or

Description of Property	Year in Service	Cost or Other Basis	Section 179 Deduction	Depreciation Prior Years
Broodmare	eighth year	$2,000.00	–	$1,858.00
Wood Fence	fifth year	$6,540.00	–	$3,736.00
Stallion	third year	$8,000.00	$3,000.00	$1,492.00
Pickup	first year	$16,180.00	–	–
Horse Barn	first year	$10,500.00	–	–
Horse Trailer	first year	$1,950.00	$1,950.00	–

Fig. 12–8. An example of entries that might be included on a yearly depreciation

the Alternative Depreciation System (ADS). Unless ADS is specifically required by law or elected by the taxpayer, GDS is the preferred system because it allows the taxpayer to recover more of the property's cost over a shorter period.

Under each system, different items of property are assigned different property life classes, which determine the recovery period, or number of years over which the cost, or tax basis of the property is recovered. Although there are eight recovery periods under GDS, only four of them include property relevant to a horse business—the 3-, 5-, 7-, and 20-year recovery periods. Qualifying property that the IRS does not include in any particular category is usually put in the 7-year recovery period. *(See Figure 12–9.)*

Residential rental property or nonresidential real property placed in service after December 31, 1986 must be depreciated using longer recovery periods. For example, employee housing on a farm is considered residential rental property. The recovery period for this would be 27.5 years using the straight line method and the mid-month convention (discussed in the following sections). The farm office in the home must be depreciated as nonresidential real property over 39 years, also using the straight line method and the mid-month convention. Business owners should consult with a

Basis for Depreciation	Method and Convention	Recovery Period	Rate or Percentage	Depreciation Deduction This Year
$2,000.00	Str. line/half-year	7 years	7.140%	$142.00
$6,540.00	150%/half-year	7 years	12.248%	$801.00
$5,000.00	150%/half-year	7 years	15.033%	$752.00
$16,180.00	150%/half-year	5 years	15.000%	$2,427.00
$10,500.00	Str. line/half-year	20 years	2.500%	$263.00
–	–	–	–	–

schedule for a breeding farm.

tax advisor for help in determining depreciation for residential rental or nonresidential real property.

Farm property can be broken down into personal property and real property. *Personal property* includes most property involved in a horse business, such as horses, tractors, and feed bins. *Real property* generally refers to buildings and land, or improvements upon the land.

There are two methods of depreciating farm property under the General Depreciation System:

1. 150% declining balance method over a GDS recovery period

2. Straight line method over a GDS recovery period

The same method of depreciation must be used for all deductions for a particular item of property. However, the owner may choose to use a different method for other items of property placed in service in other years. Along with each method, the taxpayer must also apply a half-year, mid-quarter, or mid-month convention, depending on the type of property and when it is placed in service. The following sections discuss how and when to use these methods and conventions.

Recovery Periods Under MACRS/GDS	
3-YEAR PROPERTY	• Racehorses more than 2 years old when placed in service* • Other horses more than 12 years old when placed in service
5-YEAR PROPERTY	• Heavy farm trucks • Automobiles and light, general-purpose trucks** • Horse trailers and vans • Computers and peripheral equipment, office equipment, and research or experimentation property
7-YEAR PROPERTY	• Office furniture and fixtures • Farm machinery, equipment, and fences • Other horses 12 years old or less when placed in service • Feed and grain bins
20-YEAR PROPERTY	• Horse barns, stables, and other nonresidential buildings

Fig. 12–9. The above recovery periods apply when using the 150% declining balance method or the straight line method under GDS.

* Although January 1st marks the traditional birthdate of horses, for the IRS, "more than" 2 years old means 24 months and one day after the horse's *actual foaling date.*

** For any depreciation deductions to be allowed, vehicles must be used more than 50% of the time for business purposes. Consult an accountant for other limits on vehicle deductions.

150% Declining Balance Method

Under this method, which may seem more complicated than the straight line method, more cost is recovered in a shorter amount of time. The IRS provides tables of the percentages needed to calculate depreciation for all recovery periods. Find the correct recovery period and the year, then multiply the correlating percentage by the basis of the property to determine the amount of depreciation. *(See Figure 12–10 for IRS percentage tables for calculating depreciation using the 150% declining balance method.)*

In essence, the 150% declining balance method allows for larger depreciation deductions in the beginning and less at the end for qualifying property, thus the name "declining balance." *(See Figure 12–13 for an example.)* The advantage of deducting more in the beginning is that more cost is recaptured earlier for property that may have a relatively short life, such as a racehorse.

Straight Line Method

Although it sounds simpler than the 150% declining balance method, the straight line method is a slower means of recovering the cost of business property. Under the straight line method, the basis of the property is deducted in equal amounts over the property's useful life.

When using the straight line method, depreciation for each year is the same as if the cost of the property were simply divided by the number of years over which it may be depreciated. To figure the actual depreciation for each year, multiply the cost, or other basis of the property by the percentage listed next to each year. *(See Figure 12–12 for IRS percentage tables for calculating depreciation using the straight line method.)*

If business owners want to use the straight line method instead of the 150% declining balance method, they must make an election to do so on their tax return. Owners should keep in mind that when one item of property is depreciated using the

		IRS Percentage Tables for Depreciation of Farm Property (Using the 150% Declining Balance Method and the Half-Year Convention)		
YEAR	3-YEAR PROPERTY	5-YEAR PROPERTY	7-YEAR PROPERTY	20-YEAR PROPERTY
1	25.00%	15.00%	10.715%	3.750%
2	37.50%	25.50%	19.134%	7.219%
3	25.00%	17.85%	15.033%	6.667%
4	12.50%	16.66%	12.248%	6.177%
5		16.66%	12.248%	5.713%
6		8.33%	12.248%	5.285%
7			12.248%	4.888%
8			6.126%	4.522%
9				4.462%
10 ↓ 21				4.461% ↓ 2.231%

Fig. 12–10. The IRS provides percentages used for the 150% declining balance method to simplify calculation of depreciation. Multiply the property's basis by the percentage listed next to each year to find the depreciation for that year. This table can also be found in IRS Publication 534.

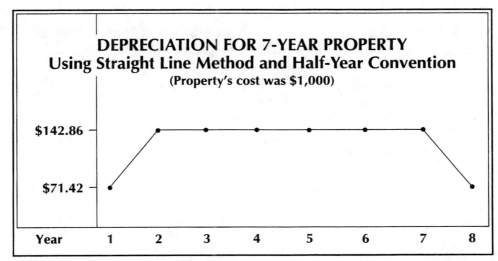

Fig. 12–11. Using the straight line method, depreciation is taken in equal amounts for each year of the recovery period (except in first and last years).

straight line method, all property in the same class (placed in service in that tax year) must also be depreciated using the straight line method.

Half-Year Convention

Under the half-year convention, all property placed in service or disposed of during the year is considered placed in service, or disposed of, on July 1. Because July 1 is halfway through the year, this is referred to as the half-year convention. Thus, depreciation in the first year (year placed in service) and the last year (year disposed of) is actually based on 6 months instead of 12. That is why it takes 4 calendar years to depreciate 3-year property, although its depreciation is still based on 36 months.

To figure depreciation using the half-year convention, simply use the appropriate tables for this convention, either Figure 12–10 or Figure 12–12. The tables take into consideration the half-year calculations for the first and last year of service when using the 150% declining balance method or the straight line method.

IRS Percentage Tables for Depreciation of Farm Property				
(Using the Straight Line Method and the Half-Year Convention)				
YEAR	**3-YEAR PROPERTY**	**5-YEAR PROPERTY**	**7-YEAR PROPERTY**	**20-YEAR PROPERTY**
1	16.67%	10.00%	7.14%	2.50%
2	33.33%	20.00%	14.29%	5.00%
3	33.33%	20.00%	14.29%	5.00%
4	16.67%	20.00%	14.29%	5.00%
5		20.00%	14.29%	5.00%
6		10.00%	14.29%	5.00%
7			14.29%	5.00%
8			7.14%	5.00%
9				5.00%
10				5.00%
↓				↓
21				2.50%

Fig. 12–12. The IRS provides percentages used for the straight line method to simplify calculation of depreciation for farm property. Multiply the property's basis by the percentage listed next to each year to find depreciation for that year. This table can also be found in IRS Publication 534.

Mid-Quarter Convention

When 40% or more of total depreciable assets placed in service in a year are placed during the last three months of a year, the mid-quarter convention must be used instead of the half-year convention. Using the mid-quarter convention, all property placed in service during any quarter of a tax year is treated as being placed in service at the midpoint of the quarter. This convention may be used with either the 150% declining balance method or the straight line method.

The following example illustrates when the mid-quarter convention would be used: a breeder purchases a new broodmare barn (and has it erected and placed in service) in December, at a cost of $150,000. The only other assets purchased during that year were a broodmare in March for $5,000 and a horse trailer for $10,000 in July. Because more than 40% of the depreciable assets were purchased and placed in service during the last three months of the year, the mid-quarter convention must be used for all assets placed in service during that year. To calculate depreciation for the barn, the mid-quarter table for the last quarter would be used; for the broodmare, the mid-quarter table for the first quarter; and for the horse trailer, the mid-quarter table for the third quarter. The appropriate tables can be found in IRS Publication 534.

Mid-Month Convention

Under the mid-month convention, property placed in service or disposed of in any month is considered placed in service or disposed of at the midpoint of the month. This convention must be used with the straight line method for residential rental and non-residential real property. For example, if the property is placed in service in July, it will qualify for depreciation for half of July and all of August, September, October, November, and December of that year. In other words, it is in service for 5.5 months (out of 12).

Tables provided by the IRS (in Publication 534) allow for the month placed in service, and percentages are provided for each

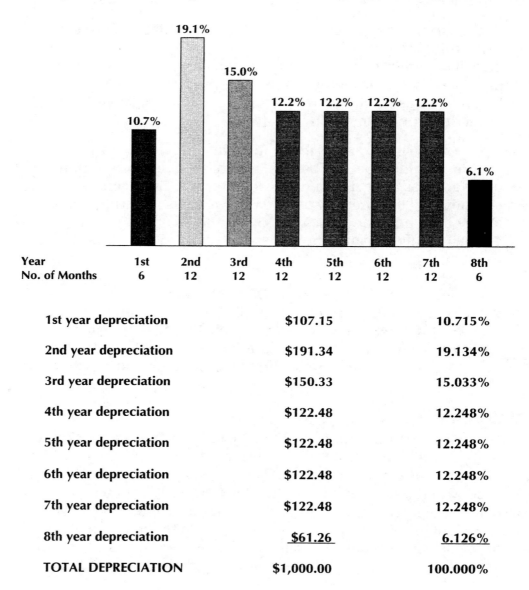

DEPRECIATION FOR 7-YEAR PROPERTY
Using 150% Declining Balance Method and Half-Year Convention

Year	1st	2nd	3rd	4th	5th	6th	7th	8th
No. of Months	6	12	12	12	12	12	12	6

1st year depreciation	$107.15	10.715%
2nd year depreciation	$191.34	19.134%
3rd year depreciation	$150.33	15.033%
4th year depreciation	$122.48	12.248%
5th year depreciation	$122.48	12.248%
6th year depreciation	$122.48	12.248%
7th year depreciation	$122.48	12.248%
8th year depreciation	$61.26	6.126%
TOTAL DEPRECIATION	$1,000.00	100.000%

Fig. 12–13. The depreciation of property that cost $1,000.

284

month during the tax year. The depreciable basis of the property is then multiplied by this percentage. The resulting amount is the depreciation to be taken in that year.

Changing Depreciation Schedules

When the use of property changes its recovery period, the depreciation schedule must be changed also. For example, if a horse is retired from racing to breeding before the end of the recovery period (three years), the recovery period must be altered to fit the new breeding status (seven years). The balance between the original basis and the amount of depreciation taken under the old period is now recoverable over the new period.

However, owners do not need to change depreciation schedules in mid-schedule whenever depreciation laws change. They should continue with the same depreciation method that was in effect when the horse (or other property) was placed in service. Only property placed in service *after* a new law has taken effect must be depreciated using a new method.

IRS Publication 534 contains additional information to help taxpayers calculate depreciation deductions.

Section 179 Deduction

The only way business owners can recover the entire cost of depreciable business property in the year it is purchased is through a section 179 deduction. Introduced as a tax incentive, section 179 deductions allow business owners to buy now, deduct in full, and pay less income tax. However, due to the limitations on this type of deduction, property that does not qualify must still be depreciated in the normal manner.

Sometimes section 179 deductions are referred to as "expensing" because cost is recovered in the same manner as it would be for ordinary expenses—in the year of purchase. The election to expense depreciable property is limited to personal property that is purchased. (Real property or property taken in trade does not qualify.) Also, a section 179 deduction can only be taken in the tax year the property is placed in service.

To elect a section 179 deduction, the business must show a profit before any depreciation is taken. The IRS limits section 179 deductions to the total amount of taxable income from the business during the tax year. If an operation has no taxable income, no section 179 deduction is allowed. (Taxable income is figured before taking deductions for the cost of any section 179 property.)

As some horse operations are not profitable during the start-up years, they may not be able to use section 179 deductions at first. Or, they may choose not to use the deduction, even when they have enough income, because they are trying to show two profit years in seven. For businesses that do show adequate income and are not concerned about showing a profit year, the owners can take advantage of this opportunity to recover the cost of business property immediately *and* reduce their taxable income.

Because section 179 deductions are not allowed when there is no taxable income, businesses operating at a loss may carry over the cost of section 179 property and expense it in a subsequent profit year. For instance, a stable purchases two 6-year-old broodmares during the year for a total cost of $10,000. Before they figure depreciation, the stable is showing a $2,000 loss for that year. Because they have no taxable income, they cannot elect a section 179 deduction this year. However, the $10,000 can be carried over and expensed in the next profit year.

There is another limitation on section 179 deductions: they may only total up to a set limit per year. Furthermore, deductions may not exceed the cost of the property. If there are several items of property, the deduction may be allocated among the items up to the limit. If the cost exceeds the limit, the balance

Limits for Section 179 Expensing

Taxable Year Beginning In	Maximum Expensing
1999	19,000
2000	20,000
2001	24,000
2002	24,000
2003 and thereafter	25,000

Fig. 12–14. The limits for section 179 expensing will gradually rise over the next several years.

must be depreciated in the normal manner. *Depreciation may begin the same year the section 179 deduction is taken.*

For example, in 2001, a breeding farm with taxable income in excess of $24,000 purchases a stallion for $40,000 and immediately uses this horse for breeding mares. Of the stallion's purchase price, $24,000 qualifies for the section 179 deduction. Subtracting this amount from the stallion's $40,000 cost leaves a $16,000 adjusted basis to be depreciated beginning that year. If the farm's income in the first year was only $13,000, the owner could only deduct up to $13,000. If the stallion's purchase price had been $8,500, the section 179 deduction would be limited to that amount (unless there was another item to expense that year).

When the cost of the section 179 property is more than $200,000, special limits are imposed to discourage abuse of the expensing privilege. The maximum limit is reduced by one dollar (but not below zero) for each dollar of section 179 property placed in service that year in excess of $200,000. For example, if in 2001 a horse operation were to purchase a racehorse for $210,000, the maximum section 179 deduction would be reduced to $14,000. Therefore, the majority of the cost would still have to be depreciated in the normal manner.

Section 179 Deduction Limitations

Deductions are limited:

- **to qualifying property:**
  - **a. personal (not real) property put to use in a trade or business.**
  - **b. purchased property (not property taken in trade).**
  - **c. property placed in service during the current tax year.**
- **to the amount of taxable income. Businesses with no taxable income are ineligible.**
- **to the current limit, even if taxable income exceeds this amount.**
- **when the cost of qualifying property exceeds $200,000. (The current limit is reduced by $1 for each dollar of section 179 property placed in service that year in excess of $200,000.) This restriction is meant to discourage abuse of the expensing privilege.**

Fig. 12–15. Section 179 deductions, properly taken, can significantly reduce taxable income.

If a business owner elects to expense the cost of section 179 property, depreciation may not be taken to the extent of that election. In other words, the same cost may not be recovered twice. By the same token, when a section 179 deduction is used for the full cost of the property, the owner no longer has a cost basis in the property; if the property is sold, all of the section 179 deduction must be "recaptured," or reported as ordinary income.

When electing a section 179 deduction, IRS Form 4562 should be attached to the original tax return for the tax year the property was placed in service.

How to Correct Errors in Depreciation

There may be errors made on depreciation schedules, including those relating to cost basis, useful life, allowable methods, and conventions. The IRS has created a method whereby errors can be corrected. This revenue procedure provides an automatic consent that permits a taxpayer who has claimed less than the depreciation allowable to change the taxpayer's method of accounting to claim the omitted or understated depreciation.

For example, in 1997, Norman Wortman paid $35,000 for a broodmare for use in his breeding business. He properly claimed an $18,000 expense deduction but erroneously used the percentage for seven-year property to depreciate the remaining $17,000. He used the percentage for seven-year property to depreciate the broodmare again in 1998. Since the broodmare was 13 years old when Norman placed her in service in 1997, she would qualify as three-year property. In 1998, Norman also paid $28,500 for a pickup truck for use in his horse operation. He again properly claimed a $18,500 expense deduction under section 179 but erroneously used the percentage for seven-year property, instead of the correct percentage rate for five-year property. The depreciation Norman claimed and the proper depreciation for 1997 and 1998 are shown in Figure 12–16.

These erroneous amounts of depreciation were reported on 1997 and 1998 tax returns, but were not noticed until time to prepare the 1999 tax return. How does Norman correct the amount of depreciation taken to reflect the correct amounts for 1997 and 1998? First, he corrects his depreciation schedule to the proper amounts, and deducts that amount for 1999 on his tax return. Then he calculates the omitted depreciation. The amount of this "catch-up" depreciation is $5,978. This amount is also deducted on the 1999 tax return. In addition Norman attaches IRS Form 3115 (Application for Change in Accounting Method) to his tax return for 1999. He must also mail a copy of the Form 3115 to the IRS National Office.

It is somewhat more involved and complicated when the amount of depreciation taken is more than amount that should have been claimed. When you discover errors in depreciation, it is wise to seek the counsel of a certified public accountant or qualified tax accountant for help with the necessary calculations and forms.

GAINS & LOSSES

When a horse or other business property is sold, there is generally a gain or loss reported on the owner's tax return. This gain or loss is the difference between the basis of the property and the money received. (While the words gain and profit are often used interchangeably, gain indicates the result of the sale of an asset, whereas profit implies total income remaining after all expenses have been taken.)

Gain from the sale of horses and other property can vary depending on the property's basis and whether depreciation has been taken. If the entire investment in a raised horse (feed, maintenance, etc.) has already been deducted as an operating expense, the basis of the horse is zero. Subtracting the basis (zero) from the sales price leaves all the money received from the sale to be considered gain.

For the sale of a purchased horse held primarily for resale, the basis is the original cost of purchasing the animal instead of zero. Gain is then figured by subtracting the animal's original cost from the selling price. Gain from the sale of a purchased horse held for breeding or sport is figured using its adjusted cost, or tax basis. Because this horse has been depreciated, its basis is no longer its original cost. Thus, gain must be calculated by subtracting the tax basis of the animal from the selling price.

Asset & Year	Section 179 Deduction	Depreciation Basis	Depreciation Claimed	Proper Depreciation	Difference
Broodmare					
1997	$18,000	$17,000	$1,822	$4,250	$2,428
1998	$0	$17,000	$3,253	$6,375	$3,122
Pickup Truck					
1998	$18,500	$10,000	$1,072	$1,500	$428

Fig. 12–16. An example of erroneous depreciation.

290

Gain and Loss

• *If selling price is greater than basis:*

Selling Price – Basis = Gain

• *If basis is greater than selling price:*

Basis – Selling Price = Loss

Fig. 12–17. Formulas for calculating gain and loss.

Capital Gains and Losses

Section 1231 of the Internal Revenue Code allows special treatment for certain types of business property—such as horses or farm equipment—that qualify as long-term capital gains and losses. Capital gains treatment means having income from the sales of this type of property taxed at a different rate than ordinary income. Gains from sales of horses held at least 24 months for racing, breeding, or draft purposes are taxed at the 20% capital gains rate (10% for those in the 15% bracket). For taxable years beginning after December 31, 2000, the maximum capital gains rates for assets that are held more than 5 years become 18% and 8%, respectively. The fact that the capital gains rate of tax is less than the rate of tax for ordinary income is a benefit for the taxpayer.

When there is a capital loss, it is generally deducted first, against any capital gains. Then if there is still a loss, up to $3,000 can be deducted against ordinary income in one year. Any loss in excess of $3,000 can be carried forward to subsequent tax years (and deducted against capital gains in the same manner) until the balance is recovered.

Criteria for Capital Gains Treatment

Horses and other property that are used in a trade or business may qualify for capital gains treatment when sold or exchanged.

In order to qualify for capital gains treatment, the horse or other property cannot be inventory, or held primarily for sale. (This income is instead taxed at the ordinary income rate.) Because most horses are for sale if the price is right, it may not be easy to determine just when a horse is held primarily for sale.

Horses that were originally purchased for breeding, showing, or racing but are later sold would not be considered held primarily for sale. However, horses that were originally purchased for training and reselling are considered held primarily for sale, and do not qualify for capital gains treatment. The purpose for which the horse is held can usually be determined by the owner's use of the animal, and the written records of that use.

Horses held in a business for breeding, draft, or sport (racing is considered sport) must be held for at least 24 months, and other business property must be held for at least 18 months to qualify for capital gains treatment. If sold before this time, then all of the gain would be considered ordinary income and subject to the ordinary income tax rate. Whenever this type of property is sold, detailed records must be kept to determine the amount of gain or loss from the sale.

Occasionally, profits from horses held for investment (such as the appreciation and resale of stallion syndicate shares) would qualify for capital gains treatment.

Installment Sales

Selling horses using the installment method is a common practice in the horse industry, especially when dealing with high-priced animals. Because many owners find themselves either on the buying or selling end of an installment sale in the course of business, it is important that they have a general understanding of how the payments are treated.

When payments from the sale of business property are distributed over more than one year, they may be considered "installment sale income." Each payment represents a portion of the horse's sales price. Tax on this income (for the seller) may fall due in the year received, or may fall due in the year of the sale, depending on the amount of profit the seller made and whether the horse had been depreciated. (This circumstance is discussed in part 2 of the following section.)

Conditions of Installment Sale Treatment

It should be noted that most sales of horses in the business of farming will qualify for installment sale treatment. One exception might be where the farmer is using the accrual method of accounting. Because all business property is considered inventory under the accrual method (see the section entitled "Methods of Accounting"), and inventory does not qualify for installment sale treatment, the farmer's sales could not be treated as installment sales. *Note: Property sold at a loss cannot qualify for installment sale treatment.*

The Internal Revenue Code imposes some limitations on installment sales. To be eligible for installment sale treatment, the following conditions must be met:

1. A minimum rate of interest must be charged when property is sold using an installment or deferred payment plan. While there is no interest charged on the down payment, interest is charged on all subsequent payments, and must be reported separately as ordinary income. The IRS establishes an "Applicable Federal Rate (AFR)" of interest to be charged on installment sales. These rates are redetermined every month and are published by the IRS in the Internal Revenue Bulletin. Most interest charged on installment sales is higher than the AFR, so meeting the federal standard for interest usually is not a problem. Once a rate of interest has been determined, it should remain the same for the duration of the contract. This is called a *fixed rate* of interest.

If no interest is charged, or if the interest charged is less than the AFR, the IRS will impute interest. *(See Figure 12–18.)* This means that a part of each payment is treated as though it is interest income (for the buyer, interest expense) instead of part of the property's price. In effect, the price is reduced, which means the seller has less gain. When the sale involves a capital gain, charging inadequate interest forces the seller to report less income at the capital gains rate and more at the ordinary rate. (Remember, for taxpayers in higher income brackets, the capital gains rate is more favorable than the ordinary income rate.) Thus, it is beneficial to charge the correct amount of interest from the beginning.

2. When depreciated property is sold using the installment method, all depreciation recapture must be reported in the year of sale. Recapture of depreciation is simply adding back into ordinary income that amount previously deducted as a depreciation expense. If the amount of gain equals or is less than the recaptured depreciation, there can be no installment sale. Any gain in excess of the recaptured depreciation can be reported on the installment method. Although payments may not be received in an amount to cover the profit, that profit will be taxed in the year of sale to the extent that it represents recapture of depreciation.

For example, if a horse was purchased for $8,000, and depreciation was taken in previous years in the amount of $5,000, this leaves a tax basis of $3,000. If the horse was sold for $9,000 there is a gain of $6,000. If payment of the $9,000 were spread over three years at $3,000 (plus interest) per year, it is an installment sale.

The year of sale payment ($3,000) represents $3,000 of the depreciation to be recaptured as ordinary income. In addition, another $2,000 of the income is recognized (reported on the tax return as income) in the year of sale to total the $5,000 depreciation recapture. The remaining $1,000 of gain is treated as installment sale income and is recognized upon receipt of each of the three payments.

How to Calculate Interest for an Installment Sale

1. Selling price of horse	$9,000.00
2. Minus 1st installment (collected at time of sale)	– $3,000.00
3. Balance	$6,000.00
4. Times fixed rate of interest (example: 7%)	x .07
5. Equals interest charged in 2nd year	$420.00
6. Plus 2nd year installment	+ $3,000.00
7. Equals total collected in 2nd year	$3,420.00
8. Balance due in 3rd year	$3,000.00
9. Times fixed rate of interest (example: 7%)	x .07
10. Equals interest charged in 3rd year	$210.00
11. Plus 3rd year installment	+ $3,000.00
12. Equals total collected in 3rd year	$3,210.00

13. Total interest collected (add number 5 and number 10)	$630.00
14. Plus total payments collected (may be eligible for capital gains treatment)	+ $9,000.00
15. Equals total payments and interest collected	$9,630.00

WHAT HAPPENS WHEN INADEQUATE INTEREST IS CHARGED?

1. Total (inadequate) interest collected	$300.00
2. Plus total payments collected	+ $9,000.00
3. Total (including payments and interest)	$9,300.00
4. Minus interest that should have been collected (this amount still taxed at ordinary income rate)	– $630.00
5. Equals total payments collected (reduced income which may be eligible for capital gains treatment)	$8,670.00

Fig. 12–18. An example of how interest applies to installment sales.

Taxable Gain From Installments

When looking at installment sales, think of each payment as being made up of three parts:

1. Interest

2. Return of the investment (property's basis)

3. Gain from the sale

Interest has already been discussed in part one of the previous section, so let's look at return of the investment and how to calculate gain from the sale.

The amount of gain from an installment sale is calculated by subtracting the property's basis (along with any sales expense such as commission) from the selling price. When depreciation recapture is involved, as in the previous example, the amount of the recapture is added back to the basis for this calculation. The amount of gain (gross profit) is then divided by the contract price (gross sales price) to find the gross profit percentage. This percentage is applied to each principal payment (payment before interest) to determine the amount of gain to be taxed.

If the horse in the previous example had not been depreciated, the cost basis would be $8,000. If the same sale for $9,000 had been made there would be a gain of $1,000 to be recognized. Dividing the $1,000 gain by the $9,000 sales price would mean 11.11% or $333.33 of each yearly payment of $3,000 would be taxable gain to the seller. Thus, the taxable gain is spread equally over the three years as the payments are received. *(See Figure 12–20.)*

Gain from an installment sale in which the horse was depreciated is eligible for capital gains treatment. However, the interest received from such a sale would be taxed at the rate for ordinary income. When a horse that has not been depreciated receives installment sale treatment, all gain and interest received are taxed at the ordinary income rate.

Installment Sale (horse that was depreciated)	
1. Purchase price of horse	$8,000.00
2. Minus total depreciation	– $5,000.00
3. Equals tax basis	$3,000.00
4. Selling price (or gain)	$9,000.00
5. Minus tax basis	– $3,000.00
6. Equals gross profit	$6,000.00
7. Year of sale payment (amount of each installment)	$3,000.00
8. Plus difference between total depreciation and first installment	+ $2,000.00
9. Equals recaptured depreciation/taxable gain in year of sale	$5,000.00
10. Gross profit (from above)	$6,000.00
11. Minus depreciation recapture taxable in year of sale	– $5,000.00
12. Equals seller's installment sale income/taxable gain over 3 years	$1,000.00

Fig. 12–19. A detailed example of calculating taxable gain from an installment sale. The yearly installment does not include interest in this example.

Installment sales rules apply automatically when a sale qualifies for this treatment. To use this installment sale provision, the taxpayer simply reports the sale on IRS Form 6252. This form shows the computation of gross profit from the installment sale, and is attached to the regular tax return. If an individual does not want installment sale treatment for qualifying sales, an election must be made to opt other treatment. To make this election, the taxpayer would report the sale on Form 4797 or Schedule D rather than Form 6252.

(See Chapter 5 for more information on installment sales. See Appendix A for an example of an installment purchase and security agreement, a UCC-1 Form, and a promissory note, all of which are needed for installment sales.)

Exchanges of Property

Often, people in the horse business trade horses or exchange them for other farm property. Gain or loss is generally not reported when business property is exchanged for like-kind property (property comparable in description and function, such as two broodmares). In exchanges of this type, the basis of the old property becomes the basis of the new property.

Suppose a stallion with a basis of $30,000 is traded for a stallion with a basis of $35,000. Instead of a $5,000 gain, the basis of the new stallion would be reduced to $30,000. This is what is known as a tax-free exchange of like-kind property. (When exchanging horses, like-kind means the animals must be of the same sex.) Horses held in inventory that are primarily for sale are not eligible for like-kind exchanges.

Gain or loss from exchanges is only reported when the property involved in the exchange is non like-kind (not comparable in description or function) and there is a difference in value. When there is an exchange of this type, the gain or loss is generally the difference between the value of the property exchanged and the

Installment Sale (horse that was not depreciated)	
1. Purchase price of horse	$8,000.00
2. Minus total depreciation	− 00.00
3. Equals cost basis	$8,000.00
4. Selling price (or gain)	$9,000.00
5. Minus cost basis	− $8,000.00
6. Equals gross profit	$1,000.00
7. Gross profit (from above)	$1,000.00
8. Divided by selling price (gross sales price)	÷ $9,000.00
9. Equals gross profit percentage	11.11%
10. Yearly installment	$3,000.00
11. Multiplied by gross profit percentage	x .1111
12. Equals seller's installment sale income/taxable gain in each of the 3 years	$333.33

Fig. 12–20. A detailed example of calculating taxable gain from an installment sale. The yearly installment does not include interest in this example.

value of the property taken in trade, plus any money or services received.

For example, if a horse with a basis of $15,000 is traded for a horse trailer with a fair market value of $20,000, the person receiving the trailer must report a taxable gain of $5,000. If the trade had included the horse plus $2,000 cash, the person receiving the trailer would have to report a $3,000 taxable gain. If both the horse and the trailer were worth $20,000, however, no gain or loss would be reported.

Insurance Proceeds

When insurance proceeds are received upon the death of a horse or the loss or damage to other business property, no gain is reported for tax purposes provided the proceeds are reinvested in like or similar property. This is true even if the proceeds exceed the basis of the horse or other property. If the insurance proceeds are less than the animal's basis, the difference between the insured amount and the basis of the horse at the time of loss determines the amount of loss to be reported.

If insurance proceeds are not reinvested in similar property, the difference between the insured amount and either the tax basis or the fair market value of the horse at the time of the loss determines the amount of gain or loss to be reported.

Loss of Uninsured Property
Casualty Losses

A casualty loss is deductible for income tax purposes if the horse has been purchased, and the loss is sudden, unexpected, and unusual. For example, a 21-year-old mare was purchased for breeding at a cost of $10,000. She was not insured. Two years later, she was struck by lightning in the pasture and died. This was a sudden, unexpected, and unusual loss, and was therefore treated as a casualty loss. The mare's tax basis at the time of death was $3,750 ($10,000 minus $6,250 in depreciation.) Although the fair market value of the mare at the time of death was only $2,500, a full casualty loss of $3,750 was allowed because the property was destroyed. If a raised horse was lost this way, the loss would not be deductible because the horse has no cost basis.

Involuntary Conversions

A horse held for at least 24 months that is lost through theft or disease is considered an involuntary conversion, and the loss is deductible as a capital loss. If the 21-year-old mare in the previous example had died from colic, it would be considered an involuntary conversion rather than a casualty loss. For this involuntary conversion, the same amount (the $3,750 tax basis) would also be deductible, but as a capital loss rather than an ordinary expense.

Net Operating Losses

When there is an excess of permissible deductions over gross earnings for the tax year (after certain adjustments are made) a net operating loss (NOL) is incurred.

When the NOL is from house business, or from any other business which is run as a sole proprietorship, partnership, or an S corporation, the owner's share of these losses can be deducted against any income from other sources (except to the extent that such losses are limited by the passive loss limitation)

The foremost component of a NOL is operating losses, but losses from casualty and theft of both business and non-business property will also be included in computing a net operating loss for the tax year.

The first step is to determine whether there is a NOL for tax year. This can be quite complicated at times, and can involve modifications. After it is concluded that there is a net operating loss, then it is carried back, and carried forward if necessary. These losses can be carried back two years to receive a refund of taxes paid earlier or carried forward twenty years as an offset against income in future years when a profit is made.

Carrying a NOL back to a prior year and therefore reducing the income on which taxes have already been paid, will entitle the taxpayer to a refund of taxes. To receive this refund a claim must be filed on the appropriate form in a timely manner.

When the net operating loss is carried forward, the loss will usually lessen the taxable earnings in the future years and lessen the tax liability before the tax is actually paid. This means that the income for the year to which the NOL is carried must also be recalculated to take into consideration any modifications necessary.

Since the computation of the amount of a net operating loss and the adjustments which are required when a loss is carried to another tax year can be rather complicated, it is suggested that the help of a tax accountant be secured.

DONATING HORSES

There may be circumstances where giving a horse to charity is an appealing alternative to selling the horse. Donating a horse to a charitable organization may solve the problem of what to do with a horse if it is injured and no longer meets the needs of its owner. Or it may be that the owner's operation has changed and the otherwise talented horse is put out of work. Conformation faults or temperamental traits can lessen the horse's desirability on the open market. Whatever the reason, in most cases it is possible to deduct part or all of the donated horse's value from taxable income. This way, the charity gets the horse as a gift, and the taxpayer benefits by having a lower tax bill. It is almost like "selling" the horse to Uncle Sam.

All charitable donations are subject to limitation and must meet certain requirements. So it is not just a matter of giving away the horse and writing off the price set by the taxpayer on the next tax return. There may be times when the advantages of donating the horse could be outweighed by the hassle of accommodating the IRS tax code. Here are some questions to help decide if donating is the wisest and most beneficial way to dispose of a horse that is no longer of value to the business.

Who is eligible for an equine donation?

A list of qualified organizations which is updated annually, can be obtained from the IRS. Included are:

- educational institutions

- charitable organizations

- churches

- hospitals

- governments

- humane organizations

- private foundations

- public parks

For the donation of a horse to be deemed deductible, the charity must use it in a manner that is compatible with their purpose. Donating a horse to a riding program at a church camp would meet this criteria. However, one could not just expect to donate the same horse to the local school or the Goodwill and expect that to count as a legitimate donation.

Can the owner be sure of how the charitable organization uses the horse?

The best thing to do is get a letter from the charitable organization certifying that the use of the horse is in accordance with their mission. If the IRS were to disallow the deduction at a later date, the horse would still belong to the charity.

How much is the horse worth?

To determine the fair market value (what the horse would bring in a sale between a willing seller and a willing buyer on the open market) will require an appraisal by a qualified equine appraiser. As for as the IRS is concerned, a person who routinely does horse appraisals is eligible to make an evaluation of the horse's worth. Many things may be included in the appraisal of the horse. This could include show or race records, pedigree, health history and for breeding stock could include progeny and reproductive records.

The appraiser must be willing and able to substantiate the stated value in a court of law, and must not be involved in the donation personally. Having the horse appraised by a qualified equine appraiser will cost somewhere between $100 and $300 and this cost is not a tax-deductible expense.

What part of the horse's worth can be deducted?

Just because $30,000 was paid for the horse doesn't mean that this would be the amount of the taxable deduction. It is possible that horse's value may have decreased or even increased in the time lapsed since its purchase. The "fair market value" of horses used for breeding, racing or showing and held for 24 months is generally the amount of the donation. The 24 month ownership requirement imposed by the IRS is meant to curtail the donation of horses bought inexpensively and immediately upgraded.

Even though the fair market value of the horse donated to a charitable organization is usually the deductible amount, there are occasions where the amount needs to be reduced.

When the donation of a horse to a charitable organization involves a horse that is eligible for capital gain treatment has been depreciated, the amount of the gift is the fair market value of the horse less the recapture of depreciation. For instance, a racing operation has owned a stallion for five years and decides to donate him to the Ohio State University Animal Husbandry Department. The stallion has a fair market value of $17,000. His purchase price was $12,000 and his tax basis is zero because he has been fully depreciated. This would make the amount of the donation $5,000 ($17,000 less $12,000). If the racing operation had sold the stallion rather than donating him to the University the $12,000 would have been treated as ordinary income because of recapture of depreciation, thus affecting the amount of the gift.

As in every other donation to charity, when the taxpayer receives some goods or services in return for their contribution, the amount of the deduction will be reduced by the value of the goods or services. It is possible that an owner might be rewarded for the donation of the horse by the offer of a number of free tickets to some kind of performance. If the value of the tickets is $300 and the fair market value of the horse is $3,000, the amount of the charitable contribution would be $2,700.

Is there a limit on how much can be donated/deducted?

The total annual charitable contributions can reach 20% of gross adjusted income before the IRS begins to limit donations. Up to that point, the fair market value of the donated horse determines what must be done to comply with the tax code. Donations of horses valued under $250 require minimal documentation. As the value of non-cash charitable contributions increase through three levels ($250 – $500, $501 – $5,000, and over $5,000), so, too, does scrutiny of the IRS. The $5,000 ceiling, instituted in 1994, has the practical effect of marking down the marginally more valuable horses simply because donors find it easier to avoid the added paperwork and IRS attention associated with high-end contributions.

What kind of documentation does the IRS require?

Any taxpayer needs to have proof of non-cash deductions, and it is no different for the donation of horses. Records should include the name and address of the charity, the date and location of the contribution, a description of the horse along with its fair market value, and the understanding of the use of the horse. For amounts between $250 and $5,000, the IRS requires the donor have a written acknowledgment from the charitable organization which includes a description of the property received, statement of any goods and services received and the value of such.

If the deduction is more than $500, IRS Form 8283 "Noncash Charitable Contributions," Section A needs to be filled out. In addition to the information above, this section wants to know how the taxpayer acquired the horse, date of acquisition, cost or basis of the horse, and method of valuation. When the value of the horse exceeds $5,000, section B of this form must be filled out, and an appraisal performed within 60 days prior to the donation. A copy of the appraisal must be attached to the tax return.

The donation of horses to charity can be a complicated matter and the IRS has made it that way because it is an area that could easily be abused. It is best for the horse owner who wants to donate a horse to charity to first seek advice from a qualified CPA.

EQUESTRIAN RETIREMENT PLANS

For a profitable horse operation, a significant tax-cutting opportunity is a pension plan. What plan is best for the operation depends on the form of doing business. A Keogh plan or an IRA is appropriate if operating as a sole proprietorship or partnership; a pension plan is appropriate for a corporation.

Because of the nature of the horse industry, many horsepeople may find they are less than well prepared financially for retirement. However, there is at least one equine foundation that has developed a retirement plan for the horse business. This plan offers a long-term, tax-deferred savings plan for the professional horseperson.

This plan is available to anyone who makes a living working with horses. This includes farriers, grooms, trainers, instructors, store employees and such. It is possible for employers to enroll all of their employees and pay the plan's cost, or individuals can enroll on their own. The annual enrollment fees are usually less than $100.

Both independent contractors and those who have W2 wages can invest as much as 15% of their annual net income in this plan. This can be done via a paycheck deduction or anytime during the year.

Those who enroll in the plan have a variety of options for investment with diverse risks and rates of return. When the participant reaches $59^1/2$ the funds are available for withdrawal.

SUMMARY

While this chapter cannot anticipate or offer solutions to every financial circumstance, it can help owners to get a financial handle on their operations and enable them to communicate more effectively with their accountants. Because every business is unique, all business owners are advised to seek the assistance of an accountant or tax attorney to help them determine the best financial route for their business.

With the information provided in this book and an accountant's sound advice, owners can take advantage of every possible break the IRS allows. Then, they can ease their minds and focus their attentions on the more pleasant aspects of owning a successful horse business.

APPENDIX A

AGREEMENTS
&
CONTRACTS

Partnership Agreement
(Example)

This Partnership Agreement is made _____ (date), by and between _____, and _____.

The parties desire to enter into the business of _____ _____.
The parties therefore desire to join together in a general partnership under and pursuant to any applicable state code.

In consideration of their mutual promises, covenants, and agreements, the parties hereto do hereby promise, covenant, and agree as follows:

1. Name: The name of the Partnership will be _____ _____. This name will be registered in the office of the Secretary of State as a fictitious name of the Partnership. This name will also be published as a fictitious name of the Partnership in a newspaper of general circulation.

2. Principal Place of Business: The principal place of business of the Partnership (the "Office") will be located at _____ _____ and any other place or places that may be mutually agreed on by the parties.

3. Business and Purpose: The business and purposes of the Partnership are to _____ _____.

The Partnership may also do and engage in any and all other things and activities and have all powers incident to the said acquisition, holding, management, sale, and leasing of the Property, or any part or parts thereof.

4. Term: The Partnership commences upon execution of this Agreement, and terminates pursuant to the further provisions of this Agreement.

5. Capital: The original capital contributions to the Partnership of each of the Partners will be made concurrently with their respective executions of this Agreement in the following dollar amounts set forth after their respective names:

_____ $_____

_____ $_____

An individual capital account will be maintained for each Partner. The capital account of each Partner will consist of his/her original capital contribution, increased by additional capital contributions made by him/her, and his/her share of Partnership profits. The capital account will be decreased by distributions of such profits and capital to him/her, and his/her share of Partnership losses.

Except as specifically provided in this Agreement, or as otherwise provided by and in accordance with law to the extent such law is not inconsistent with this Agreement, no Partner will have the right to withdraw or reduce his/her contributions to the capital of the Partnership.

6. Profit and Loss: The percentages of Partnership Rights and Partnership Interest of each of the Partners will be as follows:

_____   _____%

_____   _____%

The determination of each Partner's distributive share of all items of income, gain, loss, deduction, credit, or allowance of the Partnership for any period or year will be made in accordance with, and in proportion to, such Partner's percentage of Partnership Interest as it may then exist.

7. Distribution of Profits: The net cash from operations of the Partnership will be distributed at such times as may be determined by the Partners in accordance with Paragraph 8 of this Agreement among the Partners in proportion to their respective percentages of Partnership Interest.

8. Management of the Partnership Business: All decisions respecting management, operation, and control of the Partnership business and determinations made in accordance with the provisions of this Agreement will be made only by the unanimous vote or consent of all Partners.

The Partners agree to devote to the conduct of the Partnership business as much of their respective time as may be reasonably necessary for the efficient operation of the Partnership business.

9. Salaries: Unless otherwise agreed by the Partners in accordance with Paragraph 8 of this Agreement, no partner will receive any salary for services rendered to or for the Partnership.

10. Legal Title to Partnership Property: Legal title to the property of the Partnership will be held in the name of _____ _____ or in such other name or manner as the Partners determine to be in the best interest of the Partnership.

11. Banking: All revenue of the Partnership will be deposited regularly in the Partnership savings and checking accounts at such bank or banks as are selected by the Partners.

12. Accounting: Accurate and complete books of account will be kept by the Partners and entries promptly made therein of all of the transactions of the Partnership, and such books of account will be open at all times to the inspection and examination of the Partners.

13. Transfer of Partnership Interest and Partnership Rights: Except as otherwise provided in Paragraphs 14, 15, and 16, no Partner (hereinafter referred to as the "Offering Partner") will, during the term of the Partnership, sell, hypothecate, pledge, assign, or otherwise transfer with or without consideration (hereinafter collectively referred to as the "Offer") that portion of his/her Partnership Interest and Partnership Rights in the Partnership subject to the contemplated transfer (hereinafter referred to as the "Offered Interest") first to the Partnership, and, secondly, to the other Partners at a purchase price (hereinafter referred to as the "Transfer Purchase Price") and in a manner as agreed.

14. Purchase Upon Death: Upon the death of any Partner (the "Decedent") the Partnership will neither be terminated nor wound up, but instead, the business of the Partnership will continue as if such death had not occurred. Each Partner will have the right of testamentary disposition to bequeath all or any portion of his/her Partnership Interest and Partnership Rights in the Partnership to a member of his/her immediate family or to any trust in which any one or more members of his/her immediate family retain the full beneficial interests.

The aggregate dollar amount of the Decedent Purchase Price will be payable in cash on the closing date, unless the Partnership elects prior to or on the closing date to purchase the Decedent Interest in installments as provided in Paragraph 19.

15. Purchase Upon Bankruptcy or Retirement: Upon the bankruptcy or retirement from the Partnership of any Partner (the "Withdrawing Partner"), the Partnership will neither be terminated nor wound up, but, instead, the business of the Partnership will continue as if such bankruptcy or retirement, as the case may be, had not occurred. The Partnership will purchase and the Withdrawing Partner will sell all of the Partnership Interest and Partnership Rights (the "Withdrawing Partner's Interest") owned by the Withdrawing Partner in the Partnership on the date of such bankruptcy or retirement (the "Withdrawal Date").

16. Notices: Any and all notices, offers, acceptances, requests, certifications, and consents provided for in this Agreement will be in writing and will be given and be deemed to have been given when personally delivered against a signed receipt or mailed by registered or certified U.S. mail, return receipt requested, to the last address which the addressee has given to the Partnership.

17. Dissolution: On dissolution of the Partnership other than as provided in Paragraphs 13, 14, and 15 of this Agreement, the affairs of the Partnership will be wound up, the assets liquidated, the debts paid, and the surplus divided among the Partners according to their respective Partnership Interests at that time.

18. Governing Law: This Agreement, and the rights, duties, obligations, and liabilities of the parties will be determined in accordance with the laws of the State of _____.

19. Miscellaneous Provisions: This Agreement will be binding upon and inure to the benefit of all Partners, their personal and legal representatives, guardians, successors, and their assigns to the extent, but only to the extent, that assignment is provided for in accordance with, and permitted by, the provisions of this Agreement.

Nothing herein contained is to be construed to limit in any manner the parties, or their respective agents, servants, and employees, in carrying on their own respective business or activities.

The Partners agree that they and each of them will take whatever actions as are deemed by counsel to the Partnership to be reasonably necessary or desirable from time to time to effectuate the provisions or intent of this Agreement.

This Agreement and exhibits attached hereto set forth all (and are intended by all parties hereto to be an integration of all) of the promises, agreements, conditions, understandings, warranties, and representations among the parties hereto with respect to the Partnership, the business of the Partnership, and the property of the Partnership, and there are no promises, agreements, conditions, understandings, warranties, or representations, oral or written, express or implied, among them other than as set forth in this Agreement.

In Witness Whereof, the parties have set their hands and acknowledged this Agreement as of the date first above written.

_____

Signature of Partner

_____

Address

_____

Percentage of Partnership Interest and Partnership Rights

_____

Signature of Partner

_____

Address

_____

Percentage of Partnership Interest and Partnership Rights

In Witness Whereof, I have set my hand and seal as of the date first above written.

_____

Signature of Witness

The Articles of Incorporation
(Example)

First: I, _____, being at least eighteen (18) years of age, hereby form a corporation under and by virtue of the general laws of the State of _____.

Second: The name of the corporation (hereinafter referred to as the "Corporation") is _____.

Third: The purpose for which the Corporation is formed is:

(a) _____.

(b) to do anything permitted by the appropriate laws of the state.

Fourth: The address of the principal office of the Corporation in this state is _____.
The name and address of the Resident Agent of the Corporation are _____.
Said Resident Agent resides in this state.

Fifth: The total number of shares of capital stock which the Corporation has authority to issue is _____ (_____) shares of common stock, without par value.

Sixth: The number of Directors of the Corporation shall be increased or decreased pursuant to the Bylaws of the Corporation, but shall not be fewer than three (3) unless:

(a) there is no stock held but then no fewer than one (1); or

(b) if no fewer than the number of stockholders.

Seventh: The names of the Directors who shall act until the first meeting are _____
_____.

Eighth: The following provisions define, limit, and regulate the powers of the Corporation, the Directors, and stockholders:

(a) The Board of Directors of the Corporation may issue stock.

(b) The Board of Directors may classify or reclassify any unissued stock.

(c) The Corporation may amend its Charter to alter contract rights of any outstanding stock.

(d) _____.

Any enumeration of rights is not meant to limit any powers conferred upon the Board of Directors under state statute now in force or in force in the future.

Ninth: Unless the Board of Directors states otherwise, no shareholder has special rights to buy, convert, or in any other way acquire stocks.

I sign these Articles of Incorporation on _____ _____ (date).

_____
Signature

_____
Address

Syndicate Agreement
(Example)

This Agreement is made _____ (date), between the persons whose names and addresses are set out in the Schedule attached and who have subscribed for the number of units set forth opposite their names ("Owners").

Owners desire to form a Syndicate to purchase the horse described below:

Name: _____

Age: _____ Sex: _____

Breed: _____

Color/Markings: _____

Height: _____

Reg./Tattoo No.: _____

Owners will pay the sum of _____ dollars ($_____) per unit. There will be _____ (_____) units in this Syndicate. _____ _____, acting for this Syndicate, will purchase the horse for the sum of _____ dollars ($_____) and will accept delivery of the horse.

Upon purchase of said horse, the Syndicate shall be in existence for the ownership and management of the horse upon the following terms and conditions.

1. Ownership: The ownership of the horse will be divided into _____ (_____) units, to be insured at a price of _____ dollars ($_____) per unit. Each of the units will be on an equal basis with the others, and only a full unit shall have any rights.

2. Location: The horse will be stabled at _____ _____ subject to change by consensus, and will be under the personal supervision of _____, as Syndicate Manager.

3. Manager's Duties: Subject to the approval of Owners, Syndicate Manager has full charge of and control over the management of the horse and of all training matters arising out of this enterprise. He/she will keep accurate account of all show/race records. He/she will exercise his/her best judgment in all training decisions.

4. Resignation, Incapacity, or Death of Syndicate Manager: Upon the resignation, incapacity, or death of Syndicate Manager, _____ will serve as the successor Syndicate Manager, or if refused, then any individual or entity approved by Owners.

5. Expenses and Income: Each Owner will pay his/her proper share of the expenses of the Syndicate, including organizational, legal, accounting, advertising, board, veterinary, farrier, etc., proportionate to the number of units which he/she holds. Invoices will be sent out monthly and are payable within fifteen (15) days.

For administrative convenience, Owners agree that all income is to be paid to and collected by Syndicate Manager, and they hereby irrevocably appoint said Manager their agent to receive and collect such income.

6. Insurance: Syndicate Manager agrees to insure the horse for liability, with the Syndicate named beneficiary. The expense of the insurance will be shared by Owners as set forth in Paragraph 5 of this Agreement.

7. Accounting: In January of each year, Syndicate Manager will furnish each Owner with an annual statement of the previous year's activities, and distribute any income at that time. Said statement will show all expenditures and income, the results of racing or showing the horse, and such other information as he/she may deem pertinent.

8. Liability of Manager: Syndicate Manager will not be held personally liable for any act or omission committed by him/her except for willful misconduct or gross negligence.

9. Special Meetings: A special meeting of the Owners may be called by any Owner at any time of mutual convenience with reasonable notice.

10. Active Participation: Notwithstanding Syndicate Manager's duties, each Owner agrees to materially and substantially participate in the day-to-day decisions affecting and relating to this joint venture and all management decisions relating to said horse.

11. Transferability: Units may be transferred subject to the terms of this Agreement; provided, however, that each Owner is given the first refusal to purchase any unit or units which an Owner may desire to sell. The transferring party will notify the other Owners in writing of his/her intention to sell. The Owners will have thirty (30) days to accept the offer to sell.

12. Notices: All required notices will be effective and binding if sent by prepaid registered mail, telegram, cable, or delivered in person to the address of the respective Owners set out in the Schedule attached. Such address changes will be designated in writing to the Syndicate Manager, addressed to: _____

_____.

13. Miscellaneous: This Agreement, when executed by Owners, constitutes the complete agreement between the parties, and will be binding upon Owners, their executors, heirs, and assigns.

14. Liability: This Agreement will not be deemed to create any relationship by reason of which any party might be held liable for the omission or commission of any other party, unless otherwise provided.

15. Termination: This Syndicate terminates upon the sale of the horse, at which time the Syndicate Manager will furnish each Owner with an accounting statement. All income and expenses will be shared in accordance with the proportionate ownership of units as set forth in Paragraphs 5 and 7 of this Agreement.

In Witness Whereof, we have executed this Agreement the day and date first above written.

_____

Signature

_____

Units Purchased

_____

Signature

_____

Units Purchased

Bill of Sale
(Example)

I, _____ (Seller),
whose address is _____
in consideration of _____ dollars ($_____), hereby
paid by _____,
whose address is _____
do sell the following horse:

Description: Name: _____

                Age: _____   Sex: _____

                Breed: _____

                Color/Markings: _____

                Height: _____

                Reg./Tattoo No.: _____

I hereby represent that I am the owner of the horse and that I have the right to sell the horse, and that I will guarantee and defend said horse against any and all lawful claims and demands made by all persons.

Signed on _____ (date).

_____
Signature of Seller

Purchase Agreement
(Example)

This Agreement is made between _____ (Purchaser), and _____ (Seller), for the horse described below:

Name: _____

Age: _____   Sex: _____

Breed: _____

Color/Markings: _____

Height: _____

Reg./Tattoo No.: _____

1. Price: Seller agrees to sell and Purchaser agrees to buy the above described horse for the total sum of _____ dollars ($_____), based on the following terms.

2. Terms: Purchaser agrees to pay $_____ as of this date as a deposit. The balance due of $_____ shall be paid on _____ (date).

3. Warranties: Seller guarantees that he/she is the owner of the horse and that he/she has the right to sell said horse and he/she will defend the horse against any and all lawful claims and demands made by all persons. Seller makes no other guarantee, express or implied, including warranty of fitness for a particular purpose.

4. Transfer of Ownership: Seller shall transfer all ownership and registration papers to Purchaser once payment has been received in full.

5. Risk of Loss: Seller assumes all risk of loss until Purchaser takes delivery of the horse, or Purchaser starts transfer of the horse, whichever comes first.

6. Breach: This Agreement is terminated upon a breach of any material term and the wronged party has the right to collect all reasonable fees and costs from the breaching party.

7. Laws: The laws of the State of _____ shall govern this Agreement.

In Witness Thereof, the parties hereto have signed and sealed this Agreement as of _____ (date).

Seller:

_____

Signature

_____

Address

Purchaser:

_____

Signature

_____

Address

Consignment Agreement
(Example)

This Agreement is made between _____, (Consignor), and _____, (Consignee).

Consignor desires to sell the following horse. Consignee agrees to make his/her best effort to sell said horse on behalf of Consignor.

1. Description:

Name: _____

Age: _____   Sex: _____

Breed: _____

Color/Markings: _____

Height: _____

Reg./Tattoo No.: _____

2. Terms of Sale:

Minimum Selling Price: _____

Commission: _____

Terms: _____

Consignor shall receive the balance of all funds within fifteen (15) days of receipt of said funds by Consignee. A late charge of 1.5% per month shall be applied to any late payment from Consignee to Consignor.

3. Board: In consideration of $_____ per month paid by Consignor on the first day of each month, Consignee agrees to board said horse until sold or this Agreement is terminated.

4. Care of Horse: Consignee agrees to provide normal and reasonable care to maintain the health and well-being of said horse. This care includes:

_____

_____

_____

_____

Routine veterinary and farrier care are authorized with direct billing to Consignor. Any extraordinary care requires the consent of Consignor unless on an emergency basis.

5. Emergency Care: If medical treatment is needed, Consignee will attempt to contact Consignor but, in the event Consignor is not reached, Consignee has the authority to secure emergency veterinary and/or farrier care. Consignor is responsible to pay all costs relating to this care. Consignee is authorized as Consignor's agent to arrange billing to Consignor.

6. Exercise: Said horse shall be ridden or lunged by Consignee or a competent rider employed by Consignee at least _____ (____) days per week for _____ (____) hours per day.

7. Assumption of Risk at Sale: Purchaser may take possession only upon transfer of full consideration to Consignee. The risk of loss passes to Purchaser at Consignee's facility upon delivery of any relevant registration papers and a bill of sale. Purchaser assumes all cost at the point of said transfer and prior to the horse's release from Consignee's premises.

8. Lien: Consignee agrees to keep horse free and clear of all liens and encumbrances.

9. Power of Attorney: Consignor hereby makes, constitutes, and appoints Consignee as his/her true and lawful Attorney with exclusive rights to sell Consignor's horse under the terms and conditions of this Agreement and for the express purpose of effecting the sale of said horse. These terms are further evidenced by a separate document, assigning Limited Power of Attorney to Consignee specifically for the sale of said horse, executed this date.

10. Attorneys' Fees: This Agreement is terminated upon a breach of any material term and the wronged party has the right to collect all reasonable attorneys' fees and court costs from the breaching party.

11. Termination: This Agreement may be terminated by either party prior to the sale of said horse upon _____ (____) days' written notice to the other party, provided that all expenses for board of said horse are paid prior to removal of said horse from Consignee's property.

12. Applicable Law: This Agreement will be governed by the laws of the State of _____.

_____

Signature of Consignor   Date

_____

Address

_____

Signature of Consignee   Date

_____

Address

Buyer's Authorized Agent
(Example)

_____ (Date)

To: _____ (Sale Owner)

I have this day appointed

_____

Name

_____

Street Address

_____

City, State, Zip

to act for me until further notice, or for such shorter period as may be indicated below. Said appointee, as my duly appointed and authorized agent, shall have full power and authority to act for me in any and all matters in connection with or arising out of the purchase of horses at _____ (Sale Owner) during the time period which may be set forth below. Said agent is further authorized to execute any and all documents in connection with the purchase of horses, including granting _____ (Sale Owner) a security interest in all horses purchased. I authorize said agent to do all things incidental to and in furtherance of the purchase of horses, and I agree to pay for all horses purchased by said agent on my behalf in accordance with _____'s (Sale Owner's) conditions of sale. This agency is revocable only in writing.

Duration of Agency: _____

Other Instruction: _____

Signature: _____

Print Name: _____

Address: _____

_____

State of _____

County of _____

The foregoing instrument was acknowledged before me on

_____ (Date)

by _____
(Name)

as _____
(Title)

for and on behalf of _____
(Firm Name)

My Commission expires: _____

_____
Notary Public

Limited Power of Attorney
(Example)

Know All Men By These Presents That, I, _____ _____ (Seller), do make, constitute, and appoint _____ true and lawful Attorney for me in my name to act on my behalf in any and all matters concerning the sale of the horse described below, with full power to execute and transact matters and documents relating to said horse, and to act in my behalf concerning all financial matters relating to said horse.

Description:

Name: _____

Age: _____   Sex: _____

Breed: _____

Color/Markings: _____

Height: _____

Reg./Tattoo No.: _____

In Witness Whereof, I hereunto set my hand and seal this _____ day of _____, _____.

_____
Signature of Seller

_____
Address

This _____ day of _____, _____, personally appeared before me, _____, the above named _____, and acknowledged the foregoing Power of Attorney to be act and deed and desired the same might be recorded as such, according to law.

Witness my hand and seal the day and year last above written.

_____
Notary Public

Installment Purchase and Security Agreement
(Example)

1. Parties:

Seller: Purchaser:

_____   _____
Name   Name

_____   _____
Street or P.O. Box   Street or P.O. Box

_____   _____
City, State, Zip   City, State, Zip

_____   _____
County, Township, or Parish   County, Township, or Parish

_____   _____
Telephone Number   Telephone Number

Purchaser shall maintain the purchased horse in _____ County, Township, or Parish in the State of _____.

2. Horse Purchased: Seller agrees to sell and Purchaser agrees to buy, upon the terms and conditions set forth, the following described horse:

Name: _____

Age: _____ Sex: _____

Breed: _____

Color/Markings: _____

Height: _____

Reg./Tattoo No.: _____

With foal at side by: _____

In foal to: _____

With breeding right to: _____

3. Price: The total price shall be _____ dollars ($_____), payable according to the following terms:

$_____ Down Payment due _____. The unpaid balance of $_____ shall be paid by Purchaser over _____ (____) months with _____ percent (____%) fixed interest on the unpaid balance. The first payment shall be due _____ and all payments shall be due and owing on or prior to _____ of each year thereafter. A late fee of _____ dollars ($____) shall be paid by Purchaser for cash installment obligations over _____ (____) days late. The terms in this paragraph are further evidenced by a Promissory Note executed this date.

4. Prepayment Privilege: Purchaser may prepay any portion of the unpaid principal balance at any time. Prepayments shall apply to the last principal installments falling due.

5. Registration and Ownership Transfers: Upon payment in full, Seller agrees to execute all necessary papers and to take all steps necessary to transfer ownership and registration of said horse to Purchaser at the expense of Seller.

6. Seller's Warranties: Seller warrants that he/she is the owner of the horse and that he/she has the right to sell said horse and he/she will defend the horse against any and all lawful claims and demands of all persons. Seller warrants the horse's description as stated in Paragraph 2 above; this express warranty is exclusive of all others. Purchaser accepts the horse as is and subject to any and all faults or defects that may now exist or subsequently appear. Any implied warranty of fitness, merchantability, or otherwise is excluded.

7. Acceptance, Notice of Claims, and Limitation of Remedies: Purchaser accepts the horse by signing this Agreement, and risk of loss passes immediately from Seller to Purchaser. Purchaser is responsible for all board, veterinary, farrier, and transportation expenses after the date hereof. Purchaser shall make no claim for any breach of this Agreement, for rescission or revocation, nor for any warranty, misrepresentation, mistake, or other tort, unless Purchaser first notifies Seller in writing of the basis and nature of the claim within thirty (30) days of the date of this Agreement. Purchaser's remedies in Agreement, tort, or otherwise are limited to refund of all amounts paid, upon return of the horse to Seller. All incidental and consequential damages are excluded, to the full extent permitted by law.

8. Purchaser's Warranties: Purchaser agrees to provide adequate feed, water, shelter, deworming, vaccinations, veterinary care, and farrier care. Purchaser shall keep the horse free of all liens and encumbrances and pay all taxes levied with respect to the horse when due. Purchaser shall be responsible for all sales, transactions privilege, and other taxes that may be imposed as a result of this transaction. Purchaser warrants that this purchase is for business or commercial purposes rather than for personal use. Purchaser shall not remove the horse from the County, Township, or Parish identified in paragraph 1 for longer than three (3) months, unless Seller is given advance written notice of the new location.

9. Insurance and Indemnification: Purchaser shall promptly obtain and maintain "full mortality" insurance in an amount not less than any unpaid balance on this Agreement, naming Seller as additional beneficiary to the extent of Seller's interest. Purchaser shall provide Seller proof of such insurance, from a company acceptable to Seller, upon execution of this Agreement and upon each renewal. Purchaser shall indemnify Seller against any claims arising out of this Agreement or related in any way to the horse, including the expenses of defending any such claim.

10. Security Interest: To secure performance of all obligations of this Agreement, Purchaser grants Seller a security interest in the horse and all its offspring, produce, and proceeds, including all foals born or in utero on or after the date hereof. Purchaser will execute such documents and perform such acts as may be required for Seller to perfect a security interest and insure its validity and enforceability, including but not limited to execution of UCC-1 Financing Statement(s). Seller is also authorized to file or record a photocopy of this Agreement as a financing statement.

11. Purchaser's Default and Cure: Should Purchaser default in the timely payment of any installment of principal or interest, or fail to fulfill any other obligation of this Agreement, the entire unpaid balance will, upon written notice to Purchaser of late payment or other default, automatically become due and payable together with interest on all amounts due at the fixed rate of _____ percent (____%) per annum, or the highest legal rate, whichever is less, from the date of such default until paid. Purchaser may cure the default and reinstate the installment payment schedule within thirty (30) days of the mailing of the first notice of late payment or other default.

12. Seller's Remedies on Default: Upon any default by Purchaser that is not timely cured following proper notice, Seller shall have all rights and remedies provided by law, cumulatively, successively or concurrently, including but not limited to the following. Seller may take possession of the horse without further notice to Purchaser and without legal process, to the extent permitted by law. Seller may require Purchaser, and Purchaser hereby agrees, to make the horse available to Seller at the location of this sale or other place convenient to both parties. To protect the collateral, Seller may pay any taxes or liens levied on the horses and may provide insurance, feed, water, shelter, exercise, deworming, vaccinations, veterinary care, or farrier care on Purchaser's behalf and add such costs and expenses to the principal amount due under this Agreement. Seller may resell by public or private sale; if a private sale, Seller's customary methods of attracting potential buyers without public advertising will be deemed reasonable. Ten

(10) days' notice will be deemed reasonable notice of resale. No delay or omission by Seller in exercising any right or remedy will operate as a waiver of that or any other right or remedy, and no waiver of any Purchaser's breach or Seller's right or remedy will be deemed a waiver of any other or future breach, right, or remedy.

13. Non-Assignability and Due on Sale: Purchaser's interest in the horse, foal(s), breeding right(s) and other rights or obligations under this Agreement may not be assigned or sold without Seller's prior written consent, which may not be unreasonably withheld. All amounts due will become immediately due and payable without notice if Purchaser sells or assigns Purchaser's interest in the horse, foal(s), breeding right(s), or obligations under this Agreement, or purports to do so, without Seller's prior written consent.

14. Notices: All notices, requests, and consents required or permitted by paragraphs 7, 8, 11, and 13 of this Agreement shall be in writing, signed, and personally delivered or mailed by registered or certified U.S. Mail to the address specified in paragraph 1 above, or such other address of which the sender has been given written notice.

15. Applicable Law, Jurisdiction, and Attorneys' Fees: This contract shall be construed and governed by the laws of the State of _____. At the option of Seller, jurisdiction and venue for any dispute arising under or in relation to this Agreement shall lie only in the county and state identified below the signature lines. In the event lawsuit is brought with respect to this Agreement, or Seller engages an attorney to repossess the horse or collect amounts due, the prevailing party shall be entitled to reasonable attorneys' fees.

16. Entire Agreement and Severability: This Agreement contains the entire understanding of the parties concerning its subject matter; there are no oral or written promises or representations upon which Purchaser is relying except as expressly set forth herein. This Agreement may be modified only in writing executed by both Purchaser and Seller. The invalidity or unenforceability of any terms or clauses of this Agreement shall not affect the validity and enforceability of any other terms or clauses, but otherwise this Agreement is indivisible notwithstanding any allocation of prices the parties may agree upon for tax, insurance, or other reasons.

17. Signature and Date: Purchaser has read and accepts all terms appearing on each of the six pages of this Agreement.

In Witness Thereof, the parties have signed and sealed this Agreement as of _____ (date).

Seller:

_____
Signature

Purchaser:

_____
Signature

This instrument was recorded at the request of:

⌐   ¬

∟   ⌐

The recording official is directed to return this
instrument or a copy to the above person.

Space Reserved for Recording Information

UNIFORM
COMMERCIAL CODE
FINANCING STATEMENT—For UCC-1

Effective Date	County and State of Transaction
DEBTOR (Name, Address, and Zip Code)	SECURED PARTY (Name, Address, and Zip Code)
Assignee of Secured Party (Name, Address, and Zip Code)	Record Owner of Real Property, If Not Debtor (Name, Address, and Zip Code)
Counties Where Collateral Is Located	☐ Products of Collateral are also covered. ☐ Proceeds of Collateral are also covered.

Financing Statement covers the following types or items of property:

If collateral is lumber to be cut, crops growing or to be grown, or minerals or the like, accounts to
be financed at the wellhead or minehead of the well or mine, or goods which are or are to become
fixtures, the real property to which these are affixed or concerned is legally described:

☐   This financing statement is to be filed in the office where a mortgage on the real property
would be recorded.

This Financing Statement is filed without Debtor's signature to perfect a security interest in collateral which:

☐   Is already subject to a security interest in another jurisdiction when it was brought into the
    state, or which Debtor changed location to this State;
    Are proceeds of the original collateral described above in which a security interest was perfected;
☐   Is no longer effective due to lapse of the original filing;
☐   Was acquired four months or less after Debtor has changed its name, identity, or
☐   corporate structure.

_____   _____

_____   _____

Signatures of Debtor or Assignor   Signatures of Secured Party or Assignee

Promissory Note
(Example)

$_____   _____
Principal Sum   Date

For value received, _____ (Maker) does hereby promise to pay to the order of _____ (Payee) the sum of _____ dollars ($_____), together with interest on the unpaid principal balance at the fixed rate of _____ percent (____%) per annum from the date hereof in installments beginning on _____ until the entire principal balance is paid in full or unless sooner paid, as follows:

Due Date	Principal	Interest	Total Payment

This Note may be prepaid in whole or in part at any time without penalty. Any partial prepayment shall be applied to the last principal installments, and Maker shall remain obligated to pay the remaining principal installment according to the above schedule. In the event of partial or whole prepayment, the interest shall be recomputed to give effect to the prepayments of principal so that interest shall be paid only on the principal balance outstanding at any time.

This is the Note referred to in the Installment Purchase and Security Agreement between the same parties of even date herewith, and is secured according to the Security Agreement contained therein.

In the event Maker defaults in the timely payments of principal or interest due hereunder, or in any other obligation of the Installment Purchase and Security Agreement referred to, the entire then remaining unpaid balance of principal and interest shall automatically become due and payable, without any right of set-off or hold-back, upon written notice to Maker of such late payment or other default, unless the default is cured within fifteen (15) days of the mailing or delivery of the first notice of late payment or other default.

Such accelerated amount due shall bear interest at the rate of _____ (____%) per annum or at the highest legal rate, whichever is less, from the date of such default until all sums due hereunder are paid. No delay, omission, extension, or non-exercise by Payee of any rights or remedies hereunder shall constitute a waiver of that or any other right or remedy.

Maker and any endorsers of this Note agree to be jointly and severally bound and severally hereby waive presentment, protest, and demand and notice of protest, demand, dishonor, and non-payment of this Note and any defense by reason of extension of time or other indulgences granted by Payee, and bind themselves as principals and not as sureties, and promise that, in the event this Note is forwarded to an attorney for collection, Maker agrees to pay reasonable attorneys' fees.

This Note is issued in the County, Township, or Parish of _____, State of _____ and the execution, delivery, and performance hereof are governed by the laws of the State of _____ unless otherwise provided in the above referred to Installment Purchase and Security Agreement.

_____
Signature of Maker

_____
Address

Purchase Agreement—Unborn Foal
(Example)

This Agreement is made between _____ (Purchaser), and _____(Seller).

Whereas, Seller is the sole owner of _____ (Mare), and Mare is in foal to _____ and Seller expects a foal to be born on or about _____ (date), and both Purchaser and Seller agree to affect an immediate sale of said unborn foal.

Therefore, in consideration of the terms of this Agreement, Purchaser agrees to buy and Seller agrees to sell the unborn foal upon the following terms and conditions.

1. Term: The term of this Agreement as to Mare and foal shall begin on _____ and shall terminate when all conditions have been fulfilled and Purchaser has taken physical possession of the foal.

2. Location of Mare and Foal: Seller agrees, according to the terms of this Agreement, to keep and maintain Mare and her unborn foal at _____ Farm at no cost to Purchaser until such time as the foal is weaned and possession of the foal is transferred to Purchaser. Seller agrees that neither Seller nor anyone acting on Seller's behalf will remove either Mare or her foal from _____ Farm unless and until Purchaser gives written consent to the move.

Seller agrees to give Purchaser thirty (30) days' written notice of any such proposed move, during which time Purchaser will make all appropriate filings or recordings necessary to fully protect his/her security interest in the foal. In no event shall Mare or foal be moved outside of the United States of America or within any jurisdiction within the United States of America which has not adopted the Uniform Commercial Code.

3. Care of Mare and Foal: Seller agrees to provide and maintain a suitable environment for Mare and foal with all utilities, housing, proper feed, water, deworming, veterinary and farrier care, and all other reasonable and necessary goods and services for Mare and foal until the foal has been weaned and Purchaser has taken physical possession of the foal.

4. Provisions for Purchaser's Interest: Seller shall and hereby does retain full title to Mare; however, so long as the foal is in utero, Seller recognizes Purchaser's interest in said foal and agrees that until the foal is weaned, Seller will not sell or in any way transfer or hypothecate Seller's interest in Mare to any other person unless and until arrangements have been made for the care of the foal which are satisfactory to Purchaser. Whether any proposed arrangements are satisfactory will be at the sole discretion of Purchaser, and unless and until Purchaser has expressed his/her satisfaction in writing to Seller, no change will be made.

5. Other Assignment: Neither party may assign this Agreement or his/her interest hereunder without prior written consent of the other party.

6. Consideration: Purchaser agrees to pay Seller _____ dollars ($_____) as follows:

A Down Payment of _____ dollars ($_____), payable upon signing of this Agreement.

On or before _____, Purchaser will deposit in an attorney's trust account the balance of the agreed upon consideration. The balance will be paid out of the attorney's trust account to Seller upon fulfillment of the following terms and conditions:

(a) Mare foals.

(b) A veterinarian pronounces the foal live, healthy, and insurable.

(c) Purchaser or Purchaser's attorney receives written conformation, by a reputable insurance company, of full all risk of mortality and accident insurance on said foal in the full amount of the purchase price, naming Purchaser as beneficiary. The statement for the premium of said insurance policy will be sent to Purchaser for payment.

7. Live Foal Guarantee: Mare must give birth to a live foal by _____, on or about _____, but in no event before _____ (dates). Said foal must remain alive and in good health for at least _____ (_____) hours, be sound and be both insurable and in fact insured for the full purchase price against all risks.

8. Veterinary Certificate: Seller agrees to obtain, at Purchaser's expense, a certificate of the foal's soundness and good health, signed by a veterinarian and delivered to Purchaser or Purchaser's attorney.

9. Registration of Foal: All documents which are required by the _____ Horse Registry to effect transfer of the foal from Seller to Purchaser will be executed by Seller and delivered to Purchaser or Purchaser's attorney. It is understood that should the _____ Horse Registry or any other entity or body require any other forms or certificates signed by Seller, Seller agrees to, within five (5) days of receipt, properly complete, execute, and return all documents sent to Seller by Purchaser.

10. Approval: No approval, consent, or withholding of objection is required from any governmental authority with respect to the entering into or performance by Seller of this Agreement or the documents to be executed by Seller, or if any such approval is required, it has been obtained.

11. Third Party Interests: The entering into and performance of this Agreement and the documents to be executed by Seller will not violate any judgment, order, law, or regulation applicable to Seller or result in any breach or constitute a default under, or result in the creation of any lien, charge, security interest, or other encumbrance upon a foal pursuant to any indenture, mortgage, deed or trust, bank loan, or credit arrangement or other instrument to which Seller is a party or by which Seller or Seller's assets may be bound.

There are no suits or proceedings pending, or to the knowledge of Seller, threatened, in any court or before any regulatory commission, board, or other governmental authority against or affecting Seller, which will have a material adverse effect on the ability of Seller to fulfill his/her obligations under this Agreement.

The unborn foal has not in any way been sold to or hypothecated to anyone other than Purchaser.

There exists no defect or impediment on the registration of Mare, with the _____ Horse Registry, and the _____ Horse Registry will issue a certificate for the foal when it is born, showing that its sire is _____ and its dam is _____, and that foal is a duly qualified and registered _____ foal.

12. Identification of Purchaser: Seller will, from the date of the signing of these documents, to the date that physical possession of the foal is delivered to Purchaser, clearly identify—by markings or other indications—in any conversations that the foal is owned by Purchaser and Seller will expressly advise anyone who inquires or indicates any interest in either Mare or foal that Seller no longer has any interest in the foal, and the fact that the foal is owned by Purchaser.

13. Taxes: Seller agrees to pay, and indemnify and hold Purchaser harmless from all license and registration fees and all taxes, including, without limitation, income, franchise, sales, use, personal property stamp, or other taxes, levies, and post duties, charges, or withholdings of any nature, together with any penalties, fines, or interest thereon, imposed against Seller by any federal, state, or local government or a taxing authority with respect to the purchase, ownership, delivery, possession, use, or transfer with respect to the foal. All amounts payable by Seller pursuant to this section shall be payable to the extent not already paid upon written demand of Purchaser.

14. Notice: Any notice required or permitted to be given by either party hereto shall be deemed to have been given when deposited in the U.S. certified mail, postage prepaid, and addressed to the other party at the address indicated in this Agreement, or addressed to either party at such other address as such party shall hereafter furnish to the other party in writing.

15. Termination by Purchaser: If any obligation of Seller has not been met or fulfilled, or if any of the conditions set forth above have not been fulfilled by Seller, Purchaser shall have the right to terminate this Agreement. Should Purchaser do so, Seller shall immediately refund all monies paid to Seller pursuant to this Agreement, plus interest at the rate of _____ percent (_____%) per annum, or Purchaser may sue for specific performance and demand strict compliance by Seller with the terms of this Agreement, or any combination of remedies pursued by Purchaser. Seller agrees to pay as additional damages all court costs, expenses, and reasonable attorneys' fees of Purchaser necessary to collect said monies from Seller or enforce his/her rights as set forth in this Agreement.

16. Liquidated Damages: It is understood by both parties that, in the event of Seller's default in any of the terms of this Agreement, Purchaser's damages could vary widely and would be very difficult to ascertain. Therefore, Purchaser and Seller agree that should Seller default, Purchaser has the option of demanding the sum of _____ dollars, ($_____) from Seller as liquidated damages for any of Purchaser's claims hereunder. This provision is not provided as a penalty, and it is specifically agreed that should this remedy be selected by Purchaser, and suit be brought to enforce the terms of this Agreement, that Seller, in addition to said liquidated damages, will also pay all court costs, expenses, and reasonable attorneys' fees incurred by Purchaser in enforcing this provision.

17. Governing Law: This Agreement shall be governed by the laws of the State of _____.

The parties have executed this Agreement on _____ _____ (date).

Seller:

_____
Signature

_____
Address

_____
Telephone Number

Purchaser:

_____
Signature

_____
Address

_____
Telephone Number

Boarding Agreement
(Example)

This Agreement is made between _____ (Stable), and _____ (Owner), owner of the horse(s) described in Paragraph 3.

1. Fee:

(a) In consideration of $_____ per horse per month paid by Owner in advance on the first day of each month, Stable agrees to board said horse beginning _____ on a month-to-month basis.

(b) Options to the basic fees paid in a timely fashion are available as listed below. Each additional requested service must be circled and initialed by Owner. These options can be changed at any time Stable receives written notice from Owner. The fees are subject to change given _____ (_____) days' written notice by Stable.

(1) _____ $_____

(2) _____ $_____

(3) _____ $_____

(4) _____ $_____

2. Right of Lien: Stable has the right of lien as set forth in the law of the State of _____ for the amount due for board and additional agreed upon services and shall have the right, without process of law, to retain said horse until the indebtedness is satisfactorily paid in full.

This Agreement is subject to the laws of the State of _____. The parties have executed this Agreement on _____ _____ (date).

3. Description of Horse:

Name: _____

Age: _____ Sex: _____

Breed: _____

Color/Markings: _____

Height: _____

Reg./Tattoo No.: _____

4. Standard of Care: All care is provided by Owner **OR** Stable agrees to provide normal and reasonable care to maintain the health and well-being of said horse. This care shall include:

Hay: _____

Grain: _____

Stall: _____

Paddock/Pasture: _____

Special Instructions:

(a)_____

(b)_____

(c)_____

5. Shoeing and Deworming: Stable agrees to implement a shoeing and deworming program, consistent with recognized standards. Owner is obligated to pay the expenses of such services, including a reasonable stable charge. Such bill shall be paid within fifteen (15) days from the date it is submitted to Owner.

6. Ownership/Coggins Test: Owner warrants that he/she owns the horse and will provide, prior to delivery, proof of a negative Coggins test to Stable.

7. Emergency Care: If emergency treatment is needed, Stable will attempt to contact Owner but, in the event Owner is not reached, Stable has the authority to secure emergency veterinary and/or farrier care. Owner is responsible to pay all costs relating to this care. Stable is authorized as Owner's agent to arrange billing to Owner.

8. Risk of Loss: While the horse is boarded at Stable, Stable shall not be liable for any injury, sickness, death, or theft suffered by the horse or any other cause of action arising from or connecting to the boarding of the horse. Owner fully understands that Stable does not carry any insurance for any horses not owned by it for boarding or for any other purposes, for which the horses are covered under any public liability, accidental injury, theft, or equine mortality insurance; all risks are assumed by Owner. Owner agrees to hold Stable harmless from any loss or injury to said horse. All costs, no matter how catastrophic, connected with boarding or for any other reason for which the horse is on the premises of Stable, are to be borne by Owner.

9. Hold Harmless: Owner agrees to hold Stable harmless from any claim resulting from damage or injury caused by said horse and agrees to pay legal fees incurred by Stable in defense of a claim resulting from damage by said horse.

10. Termination: Either party may terminate this Agreement given thirty (30) days notice to the other. In the event of a default, the wronged party has the right to recover reasonable attorneys' fees and court costs resulting from this failure of either party to meet a material term of this Agreement. Owner cannot assign this Agreement unless Stable agrees in writing.

Stable:

_____

Signature

_____

Address

_____

Telephone Number

Owner:

_____

Signature

_____

Address

_____

Telephone Number

Lease Agreement
(Example)

This Agreement is entered into between _____ (Lessor), and _____, (Lessee).

1. Term of Lease: This Lease shall commence _____ and terminate _____ and covers the horse described in paragraph 2.

2. Description:

Name: _____

Age: _____   Sex: _____

Breed: _____

Color/Markings: _____

Height: _____

Reg./Tattoo No.: _____

3. Fees: In consideration of this Agreement, Lessee agrees to pay Lessor a fee of $_____ payable as follows:

Date	Amount
_____	_____
_____	_____
_____	_____

4. Option to Renew/Buy: Lessee has the option to renew this lease for an additional _____ (____) months by advising Lessor in writing at any time prior to sixty (60) days prior to the expiration of this Lease. At expiration of said Lease, and up to _____ (____) months thereafter, if Lessor places the horse up for sale, Lessee shall have the first option to purchase the horse for _____ dollars ($_____).

5. Purpose: Lessee covenants not to use the horse for any purpose other than _____, and Lessor warrants that said horse is capable and suited for said purpose.

6. Instructions for Care: Lessee will follow all practices consistent with quality care at Lessee's own expense. Lessee shall provide all necessary veterinarian and farrier needs at Lessee's own expense. In addition, said horse requires:

_____

_____

_____

7. Risk of Loss: Lessee hereby assumes risk of loss or injury to said horse except where caused by negligence of Lessor. Lessee agrees to purchase full horse mortality insurance on said horse in the amount of $_____ covering the terms of this Agreement and naming Lessor as sole beneficiary.

8. Hold Harmless: Lessee hereby agrees to hold Lessor harmless from any claim resulting from damage or injury caused by said horse for the term of the Lease. Lessee agrees to carry liability insurance in the amount of $_____, naming Lessor additional insured. Lessee must provide to Lessor a certificate of insurance prior to having right to possession of said horse.

9. Ownership: Lessor warrants that he/she has good clear title to said horse, free from any liens or encumbrances, and has the right to execute this Lease.

10. Default: Upon material breach of this Agreement by one party the other party may terminate this Lease. On any breach, the wronged party shall have the right to recover from the breaching party all reasonable court costs and attorneys' fees.

This Agreement is subject to the laws of the State of _____.

Executed on _____ (date), at

_____.

City   County   State

Lessor:

_____

Signature

_____

Address

_____

Telephone Number

Lessee:

_____

Signature

_____

Address

_____

Telephone Number

Breeding Agreement
(Example)

This Agreement is made on _____ (date), by and between _____ (Stallion Owner), and _____ (Mare Owner).

1. Consideration: In consideration of _____ dollars ($_____), Stallion Owner hereby agrees to breed the stallion _____ to Mare Owner's mare _____.

2. Payment: Mare Owner agrees to pay said $ _____ on the dates indicated below:

Date	Amount
_____	$_____
_____	$_____

3. Live Foal Guarantee: In the event that Mare Owner's mare does not take and become in foal, Stallion Owner agrees to breed that mare again for $ _____ additional consideration at any time before _____ (date). "Live Foal" means able to stand and nurse for at least 24 hours after birth.

In the event that said mare does not deliver a live foal, Stallion Owner agrees to give Mare Owner the right to an additional service to said mare at any time within _____ (___) months from the last date of breeding said mare under this Agreement. Stallion Owner shall have no further liability hereunder for servicing said mare.

4. Veterinarian Certificates: Mare Owner warrants that said mare is free from disease or infection that could be transmitted to said stallion, and agrees to pay for and provide, upon arrival, a veterinarian certificate, showing freedom from disease or infection.

Stallion Owner warrants that said stallion is free from disease or infection that could be transmitted to said mare, and agrees to pay for and provide a veterinarian certificate, showing such freedom from disease or infection.

5. Care and Feeding of Mare: In addition to the above breeding charge, Mare Owner agrees to pay the following:

$_____ per day for feed and board.
Feeding Instructions: _____
Stall Instructions: _____
Turnout/Pasture Instructions: _____
$_____ per day for exercise.
Exercise Instructions: _____

6. Veterinarian and Farrier Care: Stallion Owner agrees to use reasonable care and caution for said mare while in his/her possession or control, pursuant to this Agreement, and is authorized to obtain any necessary reasonable veterinarian or farrier care as required, but only after taking steps to contact Mare Owner without success.

7. Risk of Loss and Hold Harmless: Mare Owner agrees to assume the risk of loss due to injury, sickness, or death of said mare except where caused by negligence of Stallion Owner, or his/her agent or employee.

Mare Owner agrees to indemnify and hold Stallion Owner harmless for any loss or injury due to acts of said mare while on premises or under control of Stallion Owner except where caused by negligence of Stallion Owner. To protect against said loss or injury, Mare Owner agrees to secure liability insurance in the amount of $_____ for personal injury per accident, $_____ per injury, and $_____ property damage and to provide a certificate of insurance having Stallion Owner named as additional insured. Mares that are not halter broken or cannot be hobbled will not be accepted.

8. Registration: Stallion Owner agrees to execute all necessary documents of the registration of the offspring of the breeding.

9. Termination: Either party may terminate this Agreement for failure of other party to meet any material terms of this Agreement. In the case of any default by one party, the wronged party shall have the right to recover reasonable attorneys' fees and court costs incurred as a result of said default.

This Agreement is governed and shall be construed under the laws of the State of _____.

Stallion Owner:

_____
Signature

_____
Address

_____
Telephone Number

Mare Owner:

_____
Signature

_____
Address

_____
Telephone Number

Breeding Booking Contract
(Example)
Season of _____.

_____

Farm Name

_____

Address

_____

Telephone Number

1. Mare Owner:

_____

Name

_____

Address

_____

Telephone Number

2. Description of Mare:

Name: _____

Age: _____ Height:_____

Breed: _____

Color/Markings: _____

Reg./Tattoo No.: _____

Sire: _____

Dam: _____

In Foal to: _____

Date Due to Foal: _____

To be Bred to: _____

Service Fee: _____

Each mare sent to the farm must have an identification tag on her halter and be accompanied by a completed Identification Form.

3. Transfer of Booking: Mare is booked specifically by name; the booking may not be transferred to another mare without the prior written consent of Stallion Owner.

4. Hold Harmless: Stallion Owner, his/her agents, and employees shall not be held liable for injury, sickness, or death suffered by any animal from any cause whatsoever, while in his/her custody. Mare Owner specifically asserts to such condition and waives each and every claim for damages resulting from any such injury, death, or disability.

5. Terms: The service fee is due and payable when Mare gives birth to a live foal or ownership of Mare changes, whichever comes first. A 1% service charge will be added to any balance over 30 days. For the purpose of this Agreement, "live foal" means able to stand and nurse for at least 24 hours after birth. If Mare fails to produce a live foal, a service fee paid in advance shall be refunded upon receipt of a certificate from a veterinarian stating specifically that Mare has been pronounced barren after leaving the farm or has slipped her foal, or has given birth to a dead foal, in which event the certificate must be presented to Stallion Owner no later than 30 days after foaling. In the event of a slipped foal, a service fee will be refunded only if Mare had at least two vaccinations during pregnancy for Equine Rhinopneumonitis. Unless such vaccinations were given by Stallion Owner, a veterinarian's statement giving the date of such vaccinations must accompany the claim for refund. In the event that Mare is sold, the service fee, if unpaid, shall immediately become due and payable and no refund shall be due from Stallion Owner unless such refund is guaranteed by it in writing prior to her sale.

6. Veterinarian Certificate: Mare must have proof of a negative Coggins test for Equine Infectious Anemia (Swamp Fever). A veterinarian's certificate that Mare was tested within 30 days prior to her arrival at the farm must accompany Mare.

7. Death of Mare or Stallion: In the event that Stallion dies, is relocated, or in any way becomes unfit for service prior to servicing Mare, or if Mare dies or otherwise becomes unfit to be bred, then this Booking Contract becomes null and void.

8. Right of Stallion Owner to Reject Mare: Stallion Owner reserves the right to reject any mare that is in poor condition or one that is vicious or unmanageable. No mare will be accepted that is not standard and registered by _____. No barren mare, nor one that has foaled under suspicious circumstances will be serviced until she is cultured and found free of genital tract infections. After said tests are conducted, the necessary time for completion must be allowed. No blind mares will be accepted without previous written approval of Stallion Owner.

9. Dates of Breeding Season: The opening and closing dates of the farm's breeding season are determined solely by the farm.

_____

Signature of Mare Owner   Date

_____

Signature of Stallion Owner   Date

Information Form
(Example)

Being Booked to:

_____, Farm Stallion

_____
Owner's Name   Telephone Number

_____
Address

Description of Mare:

Name: _____

Age: _____   Height:_____

Breed: _____

Color/Markings: _____

Reg./Tattoo No.: _____

Anticipated Arrival Date: _____

Foal at Side: _____

Sire of Foal: _____

Date of Last Foaling: _____

Pedigree of Mare:

                                              _____
                                              Sire's Sire

                           _____
                           Sire

                                                _____
                                              Sire's Dam

  _____
Mare

                                              _____
                                              Dam's Sire

                           _____
                           Dam

                                                _____
                                              Dam's Dam

Medical History of Mare:

Colic: _____ Frequency: _____

Founder: _____ When: _____

Allergies, if known: _____

Other: _____

Tetanus Toxoid: _____ Date: _____

Influenza: _____ Date: _____

VEE: _____   Date: _____

Encephalomyelitis (sleeping sickness), Eastern & Western strains:

_____

Date of Last Deworming: _____

Dewormer Used: _____

Breeding History of Mare:

Date of Last Breeding: _____

Breeding Characteristics: _____

Breeding Problems: _____

Medications Given: _____

Hormones Used: _____

Other: _____

Is Mare to stay at farm until pregnancy is confirmed? _____

Feeding Instructions:

Type of Hay: _____   Amount: _____

Type of Grain: _____   Amount: _____

Pellets: _____   Amount: _____

Allergies: _____

Other: _____

_____

Habits of Mare:

_____

_____

Does Mare have any dangerous propensities? If yes, describe:

_____

Emergency Instructions:

If Owner cannot be reached:

_____
Name   Telephone Number

_____
Address

Insurance of Mare:

_____
Insurance Company   Telephone Number

_____
Address

_____
Amount and Type of Insurance

Stallion Lease Agreement
(Example)

This Agreement is entered into _____ (date), by and between _____ (Lessor), and _____ (Lessee).

Whereas, Lessor agrees to lease Stallion, _____ described below, to Lessee for the purpose of breeding mares owned by Lessee and/or other parties.

1. Description of Stallion:

Name: _____

Age: _____ Height: _____

Breed: _____

Color/Markings: _____

Reg./Tattoo No.: _____

2. Term: The term of this Agreement will be from _____ _____, to _____ (dates).

3. Fee: Lessee agrees to pay to Lessor the sum of _____ dollars ($_____) according to the following terms:

<u>Amount</u>   <u>Date</u>

$_____   _____

$_____   _____

4. Insurance: Lessee agrees to insure Stallion for all risk mortality purchased through a reputable insurance company in the amount of _____ dollars ($_____), with Lessor as sole beneficiary.

5. Transportation: Lessee is responsible for the expense of suitable transportation of Stallion from the stable of Lessor to the stable of Lessee and back to the stable of Lessor at the termination of this Agreement. Such transportation will be selected and designed at the Lessor's discretion.

6. Care of Stallion: Lessee will, at all times during the term of this Agreement, at his/her expense, provide adequate feed, water, vaccinations, deworming, shelter, veterinary and farrier care to Stallion in accordance to good horse care practices in the County of _____, State of _____.

7. Permission to Advertise: Lessee may, at his/her discretion, advertise Stallion as standing at _____.

8. Lessor's Portion of Stud Fees: It is understood that, during the year of _____, Lessee may, at his/her discretion, breed outside mares, charging stud fees of not less than _____ dollars ($_____), with Lessor to receive payment of _____ dollars ($_____) per outside mare bred. Lessee agrees to pay Lessor _____ dollars ($_____) within ten (10) days of each payment by mare owner of such amount. Payments not made to same within ten (10) days shall accrue interest at the fixed rate of twelve percent (12%) per year.

9. Number of Mares to be Bred: Lessee may also breed _____ (_____) mares belonging to him/herself and others designated by Lessee on the Schedule attached to this Agreement, at no cost to Lessee. However, the book must be closed at not more than _____ (_____) mares for the lease period. Lessee will provide Lessor with a written report of all breedings performed by Stallion at least every sixty (60) days.

10. Stallion Report/Breeding Certificates: Lessor agrees to execute, on request of Lessee and on presentation of evidence that such breedings were made, the Stallion Report for the year _____ on Stallion which is required by the _____ Horse Registry by _____ (date), and further, to sign all breeding certificates duly executed as stated in paragraphs 8 and 9 above. Lessor only has the right to sign such documents, unless otherwise agreed by Lessor in writing.

11. Live Foal Guarantee: Lessor will assume only the following responsibility for re-breeding a mare upon Stallion's return to Lessor, and Lessee agrees to have only the following foal guarantee terms in Lessee's breeding contracts.

(a) Should a mare not be declared in foal by the end of forty-five (45) days from the last breeding of said mare, Lessee agrees to re-breed said mare at any time during the _____ (year) breeding season. Should the mare not become in foal after re-breeding, neither Lessor or Lessee has any further re-breeding obligation.

(b) Should a mare be declared in foal and not have a live foal, then the Lessee agrees to re-breed the mare during the _____ (year) breeding season. "Live foal" means standing and nursing for at least 24 hours after birth. The mare owner shall have no further rights of breeding or re-breeding, nor further rights to a live foal after such breeding.

12. Lessor's Breedings: Lessee agrees that Lessor will retain the privilege of having _____ (_____) mares bred to Stallion during the term of this Agreement, with Lessee receiving no fee for such breedings except customary cost of board at the rate of _____ dollars ($_____) per mare per day for the care of such mares while at Lessee's farm.

13. Renewal of Lease: Lessor agrees that Lessee will have the option to lease Stallion, for the year, _____, on the same terms and conditions as this Agreement, with additional _____ dollars ($_____) paid by _____ (date). It is further agreed that Lessee must give Lessor at least sixty (60) days prior written notice of his/her intent to exercise said option. Failure to meet the timely notice necessary to exercise said option, the requirements thereof, or the payment of the additional fee gives Lessor the right to terminate this Lease as of _____ (date).

366

14. Termination: This Agreement may be terminated upon ten (10) days' written notice by mutual agreement of Lessor and Lessee, or for any of the following reasons:

(a) by Lessor, for failure of Lessee to pay the consideration as set forth in Paragraph 3 within ten (10) days when due.

(b) by Lessor, if, in his/her opinion, Stallion was not receiving proper care.

(c) by Lessee, if upon presentation of evidence from a veterinarian, Stallion was found to be impotent or unable to perform breeding because of any physical condition. If such occurs, Lessee will have no right to a refund of any monies paid and the $_____ must be paid by Lessee irrespective of any such conditions occurring to Stallion.

(d) by either party for a material breech of this Agreement. In the event of a breach, the wronged party has the right to collect reasonable attorneys' fees and court costs from the breaching party.

This Agreement will be enforced and construed in accordance with the laws of the State of _____.

In Witness Whereof, the parties have executed this Agreement as of the day and year first above written.

Lessor:

_____
Signature

_____
Address

_____
Telephone Number

Lessee:

_____
Signature

_____
Address

_____
Telephone Number

Broodmare Lease Agreement
(Example)

    This Agreement is entered into between _____ (Lessor), and _____ (Lessee).

    Lessor hereby leases to Lessee, who is engaged in the business of breeding _____ horses, the following mare for the purpose of breeding:

1. Description of Mare:

        Name: _____

        Age: _____   Height:_____

        Breed: _____

        Color/Markings: _____

        Reg./Tattoo No.: _____

    2. Term: This Lease commences on _____, and ends when the foal to be received by Lessee under the terms of this Agreement has been weaned. Should Lessor leave Mare with Lessee beyond the term of this Lease, Lessor will pay Lessee $_____ per day for board, care, and feed of Mare, plus necessary veterinary and farrier fees, after at least five (5) days' written notice from Lessee that Mare is ready to be returned to Lessor.

    3. Consideration: In consideration of the rights and benefits received, Lessee agrees to pay Lessor the following:

    $_____ to be paid when Mare is pronounced in foal.

    $_____ on or before_____ (date). If the mare does not come into foal by_____ (date), Lessee, at his/her option, may continue the Lease on the same basis in _____ (year) with no additional payment over and above those noted above. Or, he/she may terminate this Lease and return Mare to Lessor and Lessee will assume the costs of maintenance to date of termination according to the terms set forth in Paragraph 4.

If Mare is pronounced in foal, but a live foal is not born to Mare for any reason, Lessee may, at his/her option, renew this Lease on the same terms in _____ (year), without additional payments. Or, Lessee may terminate this Lease and all monies paid will be refunded to Lessee. However, in either case, Lessee will assume the cost of maintenance to date as provided in Paragraph 4. "Live foal" means able to stand and nurse for at least 24 hours after birth.

4. Care and Maintenance: As further consideration to Lessor, Lessee agrees that he/she will assume the full care and maintenance of Mare during the term of this Lease and agrees to provide reasonable breeding conditions and facilities, proper feed, water, shelter, exercise, veterinary and farrier care as required, in a manner consistent with good breeding practices in the State of _____ at Lessee's own expense as determined by Lessee. However, after Lessee has received the five (5) days' notice described in Paragraph 2, Lessor will assume all costs related to Mare.

5. Permission to Inspect: Lessee will permit Lessor to inspect Mare at any and all reasonable times after reasonable notice of Lessor's intent to do so.

6. Use of Mare: Lessee is authorized to use Mare for breeding purposes only.

7. Sublease/Assignment: Lessee agrees not to assign this Lease, or any interest herein, nor sublet any mare or filly, nor in any manner permit the use of Lessor's mare for any purpose other than as set forth in this Agreement.

8. Risk of Loss: Lessor will bear all risk of loss from the injury, sickness, or death of any of his/her horses unless such loss is caused by the gross negligence of Lessee, his/her agents or employees, in which case Lessee will bear such loss. Lessee has no responsibility to maintain mortality insurance on Mare during the term of this Agreement.

9. Insurance: Lessee shall, at his/her own expense, at all times during the term of this Lease, maintain insurance for injury to or death of persons or loss or damages to their property occurring in or about the premises on which Lessor's horse shall be used in the amount of $_____ per injury, $_____ per accident, and $_____ property damage.

10. Indemnity: Lessee agrees that he/she will indemnify Lessor against, and hold Lessor and Lessor's horses free and harmless from all liens, encumbrances, charges, and claims whether contractual or imposed by operation of law.

11. Default: If either party defaults with respect to any term of this Lease, the other party may, but need not, declare this Agreement to be terminated. The breaching party will be responsible to the wronged party for reasonable attorneys' fees and court costs related to any breach.

12. Waiver: No delay or omission to exercise any right, power, or remedy accruing to either party on any breach or default of this Lease will impair any such right, power, or remedy, nor will it be construed to be a waiver of any such breach or default, or an acquiescence therein, or in any similar breach or default; nor will any waiver of any single breach or default theretofore or thereafter occurring. Any waiver, permit, or approval of any kind or character on the part of either party of any breach or default under this Lease, or any waiver on part of the other party of any provision or condition of this Lease, must be in writing and should be effective only to the extent specifically set forth in such writing. All remedies, either under this Lease or by law, or otherwise afforded to Lessor, are cumulative and not alternative.

13. Effect of Lease: The provisions of this Lease will be binding on the heirs, administrators, executors, and assigns of Lessor and Lessee in like manner as on the original parties, unless modified by mutual agreement.

This Lease Agreement is to be governed by the laws of the State of _____.

Executed on _____ (date), at

_____.

City   County   State

Lessor:

_____

Signature

_____

Address

_____

Telephone Number

Lessee:

_____

Signature

_____

Address

_____

Telephone Number

Breeding Agreement—Every-Other-Foal
(Example)

This Agreement is made between _____, owner of both Mare and Stallion (Owner), and _____ _____ (Lessee).

1. Description of Mare:

Name: _____

Age: _____ Height:_____

Breed: _____

Color/Markings: _____

Reg./Tattoo No.: _____

2. Description of Stallion:

Name: _____

Age: _____ Height:_____

Breed: _____

Color/Markings: _____

Reg./Tattoo No.: _____

Whereas, Owner and Lessee agree to breed said Mare to said Stallion and to each receive a foal, based on the following terms and conditions:

3. First Breeding: Owner agrees to breed Stallion to Mare, in the _____ (year) breeding season, prior to _____ (date). When a duly licensed veterinarian declares Mare to be in foal, Owner agrees to advise Lessee thereof. Upon being advised that Mare is in foal, Lessee agrees to secure Mare from Owner and to thereafter maintain her.

4. Boarding Fee: Should Lessee fail to secure Mare from Owner within five (5) days after notice, then Lessee will pay Owner $_____ per day for the boarding care, and feeding of Mare.

5. Care of Mare by Lessee: Lessee agrees to furnish proper feed, water, shelter, and exercise, and to obtain all veterinary and farrier care required for Mare (during the term of this Agreement) at Lessee's expense. All care is to be provided in a manner consistent with good horse breeding practices in the State of _____.

6. Failure to Conceive at First Breeding: Should Stallion not place Mare in foal during the _____ breeding season, Lessee at his/her option may terminate this Agreement or select another mare belonging to Owner for use herein.

7. Failure to Receive a Live Foal: Should Mare not produce a live foal, Lessee may terminate this Agreement or continue on the same terms and conditions as set forth herein, until a live foal is received. For this Agreement, "Live Foal" means able to stand and nurse for at least 24 hours after birth.

8. Risk of Loss: Title and risk of loss passes to Owner 24 hours after the moment of birth of the first foal.

9. Second Breeding: When Mare has foaled, or when earlier directed by Owner, Lessee will return Mare and foal to Owner for a second breeding by Stallion. Mare may be returned to Lessee again when pronounced in foal or at such time as directed by Owner, but no later than when the first foal is weaned. Owner will inform Lessee as to when to secure Mare. If Lessee fails to secure Mare from Owner within five (5) days after notice, then Lessee shall pay Owner for the boarding, care, and feeding of Mare as set forth in Paragraph 4.

10. Failure to Conceive at Second Breeding: After Owner has received the first foal, should for any reason Stallion not bring Mare in foal or be unavailable for breeding for reasons beyond the control of Owner, Lessee, at his/her option, may request any other stallion owned by Owner be used for breeding Mare. Should Mare not be available for whatever reason, Lessee may use any other mare belonging to Owner provided Owner consents. Owner's consent is not to be unreasonably withheld.

11. Veterinary Fees Related to the First Foal: All veterinary fees and charges related to the first foal (i.e. Owner's foal) will be assumed by Owner from time of birth. Birth is defined as the time the foal has completely left Mare's body and the umbilical cord has broken. Veterinary care of Mare related to this foaling will be Mare veterinary expenses and will be assumed by Lessee.

12. Care of First Foal: Lessee will provide reasonable care and maintenance of Owner's foal while in his/her care at no cost to Owner.

13. Veterinary Fees Related to the Second Foal: All veterinary fees and charges related to the second foal (i.e. Lessee's foal) will be assumed by Lessee.

14. Insurance: Lessee will maintain an insurance policy with reasonable limits to cover liability for injury to persons or damage to property caused by Mare during the term of this Agreement.

15. Default: If either party defaults with respect to any term of this Agreement, the other party may, but need not, declare this Agreement to be terminated. The breaching party shall be responsible to the wronged party for reasonable attorneys' fees and court costs related to any breach.

No delay or omission to exercise any right, power, or remedy accruing to either party on any breach or default of this Agreement shall impair any such right, power, or remedy of said party, nor shall it be construed as a waiver of any such breach or default, or an acquiescence therein, or in any similar breach or default.

Any waiver, permit, or approval of any kind or character on the part of either party of any breach or default under this Agreement, or any waiver on the part of the other party of any provision or condition of this Agreement, must be in writing and should be effective only to the extent as specifically set forth in such writing. All remedies, either under this Agreement or by law, or otherwise afforded to either party, shall be cumulative and not alternative.

16. Assignment: The provisions of this Agreement shall be binding on the heirs, executors, administrators, and assigns of Lessee and Owner in like manner as on the original parties, unless modified by mutual agreement.

This Agreement shall be governed by the laws of the State of _____.

Executed on _____ (date), at _____.

City   County   State

Lessee:

_____

Signature

_____

Address

_____

Telephone Number

Owner:

_____

Signature

_____

Address

_____

Telephone Number

Breeding Certificate
(Example)

I, _____ owner of the stallion
named _____, and described as follows:

_____
Name   Color/Markings   Foaled   Breed   Reg. No.

hereby certify and warrant that said stallion bred the mare named
_____, owned by _____
_____, and described as follows:

_____
Name   Color/Markings   Foaled   Breed   Reg. No.

on the following dates and times:

<u>Date</u>   <u>Time</u>

_____   _____

_____   _____

_____   _____

_____   _____

I hereby agree to execute all necessary registration papers for
any foal(s) of said described breedings.

Executed on _____ (date),
at _____.
City   County   State

_____

Signature of Stallion Owner

_____

Address

_____

Telephone

Show Horse Training Agreement
(Example)

This Agreement is entered into _____ (date), by and between _____ (Owner), and _____ Training Stable (Trainer).

Witnesseth that Owner owns the below described horse(s) and covenants with Trainer to train said horse(s) for the purpose and under the terms hereto agreed as follows:

1. Description and Delivery of Horse(s): Owner agrees to deliver, on or about _____ (date), the following described horse(s) to Trainer:

Name	Age	Color	Sex	Breed	Reg. No.

2. Terms of Payment: Owner agrees to pay Trainer the sum of $_____ per day per horse, payable as follows:

(a) Each payment is due and payable by the first of each month.

(b) Any payment not received by the seventh (7th) of each month shall incur interest at twelve percent (12%) per annum for the number of days past the first of each month.

(c) Any payment not received by the fifteenth (15th) of each month is subject to a twenty dollar ($20) penalty charge over and above the monthly bill.

3. Duties of Trainer: Trainer shall fulfill these duties in a manner consistent with good training practices in the County, Township, or Parish of _____ in the State of _____.

a. _____

b. _____

c. _____

4. Expenses: Owner shall bear all cost of all transportation incidental to the purposes of this Agreement, including, but not limited to, veterinary and farrier costs, entry fees, and special equipment. Owner will not be responsible for additional expenses exceeding _____ dollars ($_____) per month without prior written approval. All expenses are due and payable on the first of the month as provided.

5. Care and Feed: Trainer will provide the following care and feed:

_____

_____

_____

6. Authority to Obtain Veterinary and Farrier Care: Owner hereby authorizes Trainer to obtain all necessary emergency veterinary and non-emergency farrier care to maintain said horse(s) in good health. All other non-emergency care needs shall be first approved by Owner unless otherwise authorized hereunder. Owner shall pay all such veterinarian and farrier services in accordance with this Agreement.

7. Horses Out of Training: If said horse(s) is (are) out of training for over _____ (_____) consecutive days, Owner shall pay Trainer the cost of board at _____ dollars ($_____) per day plus incidental expenses as required. Owner must be notified within _____ (_____) days if said horse is taken out of training.

8. Terms and Termination: The term of this Agreement shall be on a _____ basis. Either party may terminate Agreement given _____ (_____) days' written notice, provided a final accounting by Trainer is presented and all payments have been made by Owner prior to taking possession of said horse(s).

9. Insurance: Owner shall bear all risk of loss from the injury, sickness, or death of said horse(s) unless such loss is caused by gross negligence of Trainer, his/her agents or employees, in which case Trainer shall bear such loss.

Trainer agrees/does not agree to carry insurance protecting Owner against any losses caused by negligence of Trainer, his/her agents and employees. Owner agrees to reimburse Trainer _____% of the premium for said insurance. Trainer agrees/does not agree to maintain liability insurance: $_____ per person, $_____ per accident, $_____ property damage. If insurance is so provided, Trainer will make a copy of the policy available to Owner.

10. Indemnification: Owner agrees to indemnify Trainer unless otherwise provided by insurance against all liability or claims, demands, and cost for or arising out of this Agreement unless such are caused by the gross negligence of Trainer, his/her agent or employees.

11. Showing Name: Owner's horses shall be shown in the name of _____, Owner, and _____, Trainer.

12. Binding Effect: The parties agree that this Agreement shall be binding on their respective heirs, successors, executors, and assigns.

Failure of either party to abide by and perform any and all other terms, covenants, conditions, and obligations of this Agreement shall constitute a default and shall, in addition to any other remedies provided by or in equity, entitle the wronged party to reasonable attorneys' fees and court costs related to such breach.

In all respects, this Agreement shall be construed in accordance with, and governed by the laws of the State of _____. This Agreement contains the final and entire Agreement between parties and neither they nor their agents will be bound by any terms, conditions, or representatives unless amended to this Agreement and initialed by both parties.

In Witness Whereof, the parties have executed this Agreement on the day and year first above written.

Owner:

_____
Signature

_____
Address

_____
Telephone Number

Trainer:

_____
Signature

_____
Address

_____
Telephone Number

Racehorse Training Agreement
(Example)

This Agreement is made _____ (date), by and between _____ (Owner), and _____ (Trainer).

Whereas, Owner is the legal owner of certain Thoroughbred horses described in Paragraph 1 bred for racing and desires to have these horses trained and raced. Trainer is a Thoroughbred racehorse Trainer and agrees to train and race said horses.

In consideration of the covenants and agreements herein set forth, the parties agree to the following terms:

1. Description and Delivery of Horses: Owner agrees to deliver the following horses to Trainer, to be trained and raced at race-tracks throughout the State of _____.

Name	Age	Color	Sex	Reg. No.

2. Payment for Training: Owner agrees to pay Trainer _____ dollars ($_____) per day per horse trained and/or raced, subject to the provisions in Paragraph 7. This daily charge shall be payable on or before the seventh (7th) day of each month.

3. Trainer's Duties: Trainer shall train and race the horses and feed and care for them, subject to Paragraph 4 of this Agreement, in a manner consistent with accepted racehorse training practices in the State of _____. Trainer, at his sole discretion, shall decide when any of Owner's horses are sufficiently trained to be entered in a race, and Trainer has sole discretion to decide what type of race any horse may be entered in and how often each horse should be raced, except that:

(a) Trainer shall not enter any of Owner's horses in any claiming race for the sum of _____ dollars ($_____) or less without prior consent of Owner.

(b) Trainer shall not enter any of Owner's horses in any race which Trainer has another horse in his/her barn that is to be entered in the same race, without prior written consent from Owner.

4. Expenses: Owner shall bear the cost of transporting the horses from one track to another or otherwise, veterinary and farrier fees, costs of preparation of racing silks, jockey fees, pony leads, and/or any costs of equipment that Trainer deems necessary to the proper training and racing of any of Owner's horses, in addition to insurance costs as set forth in Paragraph 8 below.

5. Accounting and Billing: Trainer shall pay all expenses referred to in Paragraph 4, keep an accurate account of said expenses, and bill Owner for the same at the end of each month. If Owner fails to reimburse Trainer for such expenses when payable, Trainer is authorized to deduct an amount equal to such expenses from Owner's account from the Horsemen's Bookkeeper at the racetrack where Owner's horses are being trained and raced, pursuant to the Limited Power of Attorney set forth in connection with this Agreement and incorporated herein by reference.

6. Other Compensation to Trainer and Jockey: In the event that any of Owner's horses win a race, Owner shall cause to be deducted from Owner's share of the purse money ten percent (10%), to be paid to Trainer over and above any other compensation provided for under this Agreement. In addition, Owner shall deduct ten percent (10%) from such purse money and cause the same to be paid to the jockey riding Owner's horse in the winning race, in addition to regular jockey fees. No deductions from any other money awarded to Owner for any other finishing position of Owner's horses shall be deducted from such purses and paid as additional compensation to Trainer or jockey other than the regular jockey mount fees.

7. Horses Out of Training: If, during this Agreement, any of Owner's horses are taken out of training after being put into training, Owner shall pay the cost of boarding, feeding, veterinary services and medicine, and transportation in maintaining any such horse, but shall not pay Trainer compensation for training as set forth in Paragraph 2. Trainer shall notify Owner as soon as it is known that Owner's horse is or has been removed from training, and Owner shall pay thereafter _____ dollars ($_____) per day until the horse can be returned to race training or can no longer remain at the racetrack.

8. Insurance: Upon receipt of the horses herein described, Trainer shall procure Thoroughbred racehorse insurance protecting Owner against all losses due to fire, theft, death, or other disability arising from any injuries or accidents to said horses. Such insurance is to provide coverage in an amount not less than _____ dollars ($_____). Owner agrees to reimburse Trainer for such insurance costs in the manner set forth in Paragraph 5.

9. Indemnification: Trainer agrees to indemnify Owner from all liability or claims, demands, damages, ad costs, for or arising out of training and racing Owner's horses, whether it be caused by the negligence of Trainer, his agents or employees, or otherwise.

10. Amendment of Agreement: This Agreement may be amended at any time by writing into the provisions herein set forth, the description of any additional racing stock desired by both parties to be placed within the terms of this Agreement, and the amendment must be initialed by both parties.

11. Duration and Termination of Agreement: The term of this Agreement shall be for _____, commencing _____, and terminating _____. Either party may cancel this Agreement upon ten (10) days' written notice to the other party, provided all funds owed to Trainer are paid before Owner takes possession of said horses. Both parties may renew this Agreement for the term hereof on written agreement by the other party hereto.

12. Racing Name: Owner's horses shall be raced in the name of _____, Owner, and _____, Trainer.

Owner:

_____
Signature

_____
Address

_____
Telephone Number

Trainer:

_____
Signature

_____
Address

_____
Telephone Number

APPENDIX B

Bibliography

Adams, Eric J. Super Software. *Independent Business* 3(4):20–27, 1992.

Anthony, Christine. Retirement Plan for Equestrians. *Equus* 209:76–77, 1995.

Battersby, Mark E. Taxes: Making the Most of Losses. *The Quarter Racing Journal*, Apr. 1995:44–45.

Bielski, Mark. Where Did All That Money Go?. *Equus* 9:44–49, 70, 1978.

Bock, C. Allen. *1997 Farm Income Tax School Workbook*. Urbana: University of Illinois, 1997.

Branam, Judson. Liability reform rolls on. *Equus* 191:94, 96, 1993.

Brega, Julie. *The Horse Equestrian Business*. London: J.A. Allen & Company, 1994.

Brewer, Jim. Riding the Information Superhighway. *Modern Horse Breeding*, Dec. 1994:32–35.

Brockhoff, Timothy C. Computerizing Your Farm or Clinic. *The Horse*, Dec. 1977:87–90.

Clarke, Elizabeth. The True Value of Written Contracts. *Trail Blazer*, May/June 1997:35.

Close, Pat. Conference Highlights. *Western Horseman*, May 1996:170–172.

Cohan, John Alan. Trying to Avoid Taxing Headaches. *Hoof Beats*, Apr. 1997:????.

Cohan, John Alan. Valuation of Property. *The Backstretch*, Feb./Mar. 1995:13.

Craigo, Richard W. Handling a Hobby Loss Audit: Part One. *The Blood-Horse*, Jan. 7, 1995:40–42.

Craigo, Richard W. How To Avoid a Hobby-Loss Audit. *Western Horseman*, Mar. 1997:143–149.

Craigo, Richard W. Business or Hobby?. *Equus* 246:108–115, 1998.

Davis, Thomas A. *Horse Owners and Breeders Tax Manual*. American Horse Council, Washington D.C., 1997.

Del Castillo, Janet with Lois Schwartz. *Backyard Race Horse: The Training Manual*. Florida: Prediction Publications & Productions, 1992.

DeMartini, Tom. A guide to insuring your stock. *Thoroughbred Times,* Mar. 15, 1997:54–55.

Desjardins, Doug. Independent Contractor or Employee? *Price Club,* Mar. 1990.

Donald, Douglas I. Taxes. *The Backstetch,* Mar./Apr. 1998:134.

Du Teil, Karen Kopp. Insurance Trends. *Equus* 160:37–40, 85–87, 1991.

Du Teil, Karen Kopp. The Frugal Horseman. *Equus* 167:38–44, 114–116, 1991.

Editorial Staff. Trends at a Glance. *Equus* 217:28–31, 1995.

Editorial Staff. Into the Future. *Equus* 229:33–49, 1996.

Editorial Staff. Fix Up Your Farm and send the Feds the bill. *Practical Horseman* 19(4):50–64, 1991.

Editorial Staff. *Tax Bulletins.* Vols. 203, 208, 219, 223, 227. Washington, D.C.: American Horse Council, 1988–1990.

Editorial Staff. *Tax Court Reported and Memorandum Decisions.* New Jersey: Prentice Hall, Inc., 1988.

Ehringer, Gavin. Brand Inspections: A Safeguard for Horse Owners. *Western Horseman,* Sept. 1996:156–158.

Ehringer, Gavin. False Registration Papers, *Western Horseman,* Oct. 1996:68–71.

Evans, Keith. Sales Calls Sell Horses. *The Quarter Horse Journal,* Oct. 1994:8.

Evans, Keith. Be Well Known. *The Quarter Horse Journal,* Jan. 1995:8.

Evans, Keith. Elements of an Effective Ad. *The Quarter Horse Journal,* Mar. 1995:8.

Evans, Keith. Satisfied Customers. *The Quarter Horse Journal,* Apr. 1995:8.

Evans, Keith. What does your ad sell?. *The Quarter Horse Journal,* May 1995:8.

Evans, Keith. If You Tell Them, They Will Come. *The Quarter Horse Journal,* July 1995:8.

Evans, Keith. Building Ads. *The Quarter Horse Journal,* Feb. 1996:8.

Evans, Keith. Illustration. *The Quarter Horse Journal,* Mar. 1996:12.

Evans, Keith. The Headline. *The Quarter Horse Journal,* May 1996:8.

Evans, Keith. Write Right. *The Quarter Horse Journal,* June 1996:8.

Evans, Keith. Logos. *The Quarter Horse Journal,* July 1996:8.

Evans, Keith. Distinction. *The Quarter Horse Journal,* Aug. 1996:8.

Evans, Keith. Non–Traditional Approaches. *The Quarter Horse Journal,* June 1997:8.

Evans, Keith. The Real Deal. *The Quarter Horse Journal,* July 1997:8.

Evans, Keith. Business Cards. *The Quarter Horse Journal,* Dec. 1997:8.

Evans, Keith. Be Attractive. *The Quarter Horse Journal,* Jan. 1998:8.

Evans, Keith. Get Noticed. *The Quarter Horse Journal,* Mar. 1998:8.

Fankhauser, Tara. When Horses Become Your Business: Accounting Tips for Turning Your Hobby Into a Viable Business. *The Quarter Horse Journal,* Oct. 1994:42–44.

Fankhauser, Tara. When Horses Become Your Business: Accounting and Bookkeeping for the Non-accountant Horseperson. *The Quarter Horse Journal,* Nov. 1994:45–49.

Fankhauser, Tara. When Horses Become Your Business: Hey! Why Don't We Just Write It Off? *The Quarter Horse Journal,* Dec. 1994:54–57.

Feit, Lisa. Push-Button Horse Management. *Equus* 134:26–29, 53–54, 1988.

Fershtman, Julie I. *Equine Law and Horse Sense.* Michigan: Horses & The Law Publishing, 1996.

Fershtman, Julie I. Equine Contracts, Part 3, *The Backstretch,* Mar./ Apr. 1998:22–26.

Fershtman, Julie I. 15 Common Myths about Equine Insurance, *Horse Illustrated,* 21(7):64–73, 1997.

Finke, Marilyn A. Gateway Equine Medical Center. *The Gateway Equine Digest,* Feb. 1995:23–25.

Geske, Alvin J. and Thomas A. Davis. *Tax Tips for Horse Owners.* Washington, D.C.: American Horse Council, 1989.

Gillman, Stanley. Farms and the "Nanny Tax." *Thoroughbred Times,* Jan. 14, 1995:55.

Gillman, Stanley A. It's a gift! It's wages paid! It's sharecropping! *Thoroughbred Times,* June 10, 1995:40.

Gillman, Stanley A. A Yankee Doodle Kind of Ruling. *Thoroughbred Times,* Apr. 12, 1997:58.

Gilmore, Jodie. Which computer program is best for my stable?

Equus 225, July 1996:124–128.

Green, Leonard C., and Jonathan Green. Dispelling myths in the Thoroughbred industry. *Thoroughbred Times,* Apr. 22, 1995:36.

Green, Leonard C., and Jonathan Green. A new breed of owner. *Thoroughbred Times,* May 27, 1995:43.

Green, Leonard C., and Jonathan Green. The business of breeding. *Thoroughbred Times,* June 24, 1995:43.

Green, Leonard C., and Jonathan Green. Protecting the Buyer's Interests. *Thoroughbred Times,* June 28, 1997:53.

Green, Leonard C., and Jonathan Green. Knowing when to hold and when to fold. *Thoroughbred Times,* Apr. 26, 1997:87.

Hall, Tim. Foal Sharing. *The Horse,* Feb. 1998:77–80.

The Hawkins Guide Staff. *1994 Hawkins Guide: Horse Trailering On the Road.* North Carolina: Blue Green Publishing, Inc., 1993.

Hayes, Sophia F. Cadwalader. A Pony for Uncle Sam. *Practical Horseman* 19(1):20–24, 101–104, 1991.

Hayes, Sophia F. Cadwalader. Depreciation—What's It All About? *Practical Horseman* 19(1):105, 1991.

Hayes, Sophia F. Cadwalader. Selling Your Horse in a Down Market. *Practical Horseman* 19(6):25–32, 1991.

Hayes, Sophia F. Cadwalader. Staking Yourself to Your Horse Business. *Practical Horseman* 19(4):26–45, 1991.

Haywood, LaDonna. Insurance—How to Protect Your Assets and Keep Horses, Too. *Horseplay,* Feb. 1995:26–28.

Hess, Vernon. Horse Property. *Horse Illustrated,* Nov. 1994:67–69.

Hillenbrand, Laura. Risky Business. *Equus* 246:43–61, 1998.

Hillenbrand, Laura. When Horse Insurance Makes Sense. *Equus* 212:77–90, 1995.

Immigration and Naturalization Service. *Handbook for Employers.* U.S. Department of Justice, Washington, D.C., 1991.

Internal Revenue Service. U.S. Department of Treasury. *Farmer's Tax Guide* Pub. 225. Washington, D.C., 1993.

Internal Revenue Service. U.S. Department of Treasury. *Depreciation* Pub. 534. Washington, D.C., 1993.

Internal Revenue Service. U.S. Department of Treasury. *Employ-*

ment Taxes Pub. 539. Washington, D.C., 1993.

Internal Revenue Service. U.S. Department of Treasury. *Circular A Agricultural Employer's Tax Guide.* Washington, D.C., 1994.

Internal Revenue Service. U.S. Department of Treasury. *Instructions for Form 1040 and Schedules A, B, C, D, E, F, and SE.* Washington, D.C., 1994.

Ivers, Tom. *The Racehorse Owner's Survival Manual.* New Jersey: Prober, Inc., 1989.

Ivers, Tom. Buying a used racehorse. *Thoroughbred Times,* Jan. 21, 1995:76.

Johnson, George G. Jr. Equine Liability Statutes. *Western Horseman,* Apr. 1997:183–187.

Katz, Gary R. *The Equine Legal Handbook.* Maryland: Half Halt Press, Inc., 1993.

Kilby, Emily with John Leech MS. Start Your Engines. *Equus* 211:45–56, 1995.

Kuhne, Cecil. When Keeping Horses Becomes a Legal Nuisance. *Horseman,* Sept. 1989:30–31.

Kuhne, Cecil. The Legal Responsibilities of Horse Care. *Horse Illustrated* 15(11):22–25, 1991.

Lee, Virginia. Should you use a shipping company?. *Equus* 208:68–71, 1995.

Levinsky, H. R. Think Stalls, Not Horses. *Racing Northeast,* May 1995:40–42.

Levinsky, H.R. Helping Owners Succeed. *Racing Northeast,* May 1995:26–31.

Lohman, Jack, and Arnold Kirkpatrick. *Successful Thoroughbred Investment in a Changing Market.* Kentucky: Thoroughbred Publishers, Inc., 1984.

Lynch, Betsy. Horse Insurance. *Western Horseman,* Dec. 1995:62–74.

Macdonald, Janet W. *Running a Stable as a Business.* London: J.A. Allen, 1980.

Marder, Sue Ellen. *Legal Forms, Contracts, and Advice for Horse Owners.* New York: Breakthrough Publications, Inc., 1991.

Marder, Sue Ellen, and Leslie Winter. *Tax Planning and Prepara-*

tion For Horse Owners 1994. New York: Breakthrough Publications, Inc., 1994.

Marder, Sue Ellen, and Leslie Winter. *Bookkeeping For Horse Owners 1994.* New York: Breakthrough Publications, Inc., 1994.

Minimizing Risk In Volatile Investments. *The Blood-Horse,* July 5, 1997:3606–3610.

Moore, Jack. Should I Donate My Horse? *Equus* 219:68–71, 1996.

Mutchler, Marvin. Horse Cents: A Guide to Financing Your Horse Operation. *Western Horseman,* Dec. 1993:112–113.

O'Kelley, Barbara Ann. *Developing a Business Plan for an Equine Operation.* Michigan: O'Kelley's Arabians, 1991.

Patrick, Marge. Audit Survival Tips. *The Quarter Horse Journal,* Sept. 1996:70–73.

Parise, Joy. Giving Lessons. *The Quarter Horse Journal,* Aug., 1996:59–61.

Perrault, Bonnie J. Private to Public. *Horseplay,* Dec. 1994:16–17.

Phillips, Lyda. The Tax Man Cometh. *Equus* 147:17–19, 1990.

Pontius, Donald H. Are You Considering Leasing A Horse? *Hoof Beats,* Aug. 1994:?????.

Rogers, Allison. HMOs for horses. *Equus* 231:66–67, 1997.

Rudmann, Jeanne M. Buying The Farm. *Horse Illustrated,* Sept. 1997:60–69.

Scheve, Neva & Tom. Trailering Tips. In *1994 Hawkins Guide: Horse Trailering On the Road.* North Carolina: Blue Green Publishing, Inc., 1993.

Szuwalski, Cary L. Have Horse—Will Travel. *Horse Illustrated* 20(9):34–42, 1996.

Texas Racing Commission. *Laws and Rules Governing Pari-Mutuel Racing in Texas.* Texas: Texas Racing Commission, 1994.

Thorson, Juli S. Stable Start-Ups. *Horse & Rider,* Apr. 1997:67–104.

Toby, Milton C., J.D. Lien On Me. *The Horse,* Mar. 1997:71–73.

Toby, Milton C., J.D. Are You Liable? *The Horse,* Nov. 1995:32–34.

Van Court, Laurie. A Guide to Buying Your Own Horse Property. *Western Horseman* 61(5):110–120, 1996.

Wagoner, D.M. ed. *Breeding Management and Foal Development.* Texas: Equine Research, Inc., 1982.

Wilcke, Richard W. Finding and Keeping Employees? *The Back-*

stretch, July 1996:26, 82.

Wood, Kenneth A. *Horse Operations Business Plan.* Arizona: Farnam Companies, Inc., 1993.

Wood, Kenneth A. *How to Avoid Legal Hassles as a Result of Owning Horses.* Nebraska: Farnam Companies, Inc., 1979.

Wood, Kenneth A. *Law for the Horse Breeder.* California: Wood Publications, Inc., 1983.

Figure Credits

All Figures courtesy of
Scholargy Custom Publishing

Glossary

150% declining balance method Regular method of depreciating farm property under MACRS, where more of the property's cost is recovered over a shorter period.

accrual method Method of accounting where income is reported when earned and expenses are reported when incurred.

advisor Anyone who gives a business owner advice, e.g. bloodstock agent, trainer, farm operator, lawyer, or accountant.

A.M. Best Company that rates insurance companies based on quality of service.

appreciation Increase in property's value over time.

arbitration Settlement of a dispute by a person or persons chosen to hear both sides and come to a decision.

assets Property that has sale or exchange value; economic resources.

assigns People who have been designated, or given an interest or full ownership in a property by the owner through a will or trust, or as a gift.

basis The original cost, or other value of property.

business entity A separate entity, distinct from its owner(s) and from every other business.

capital Money (or some other resource) used in a business for investment.

capital expenditure Amount spent in the purchase of certain business property.

capital gain Gain from the sale or exchange of certain business property.

capital loss Loss from the sale or exchange of certain business property.

cash method Method of accounting where income is reported when received and expenses reported when paid.

casualty loss Loss of purchased property that is sudden, unexpected, and unusual; may be deductible from ordinary income.

claim To request something that is rightfully yours, e.g. insurance proceeds or a racehorse claimed in a claiming race.

Coggins test Blood test for Equine Infectious Anemia (EIA), also called swamp fever.

conformation Size, shape, and symmetry of the horse's body parts.

consideration Fee for a product or service; payment.

consignment Selling a horse through an outside facility or agent.

covenant To promise in a legally binding document.

conversion Unlawful appropriation and use of another's property.

deduction Amount taken as expense (subtracted from taxable income) for tax purposes.

default To breach or fail to fulfill an agreement.

depreciation A means of recovering the cost of business property that has a useful life of more than one year.

disbursement The act of disbursing; money paid out, expense.

disposition Selling or giving away of property.

diversify To make diverse; give variety to, e.g. to divide investments into several companies or to increase the variety of products or services offered.

elective surgery Surgery that is not necessary to save a horse's life, but is cosmetic or for the convenience of the owner, e.g. castration.

employee Person who performs services for another, where the employer dictates what the job is and how it should be done.

encumbrance Lien or legal claim on property that might interfere with the sale of the property.

endoscopic examination To view by endoscope, a small camera that can be inserted into a body cavity, hollow organ, blood vessel, etc.

escrow To put in the care of a third party until certain agreed-upon conditions are met.

expenses Amounts spent on ordinary and necessary items used in the operation of the business.

fair market value Estimated value, or amount of money the property may bring on the open market; usually determined by an appraiser.

farmer An individual, partnership, or corporation that cultivates, operates, or manages a farm for profit.

gain The difference between the basis and selling price of an asset.

gestation The period of development of the young from fertilization of the egg to birth; pregnancy.

gross income The total amount of income before expenses are deducted.

hold harmless and release statement See **release.**

income Money taken in for products or services as a part of normal business activities.

independent contractor A business person who offers a service to the general public and is not under the control or direction of another.

installment sale When payments from the sale of purchased property are distributed over more than one year and interest is charged on the balance.

insurance proceeds Compensation received from insurance policies for property which has been lost or stolen.

investment Amount of time, effort, or money devoted to the business.

invoice A written statement of amounts owed.

involuntary conversion When business property is condemned, destroyed, or lost by theft, casualty, or other event (such as disease).

IRA Individual Retirement Account.

ISP Internet service provider; a business that, for a fee, allows access to the internet, e-mail accounts, and/or space on their server for a web site.

lessee Person to whom property is leased.

lessor Person who owns property, and for a fee, is allowing another person to use it.

liability Having legal responsibility.

lien See **stableman's lien.**

like-kind property Property of the same quality or character.

litigation Settlement of a dispute in a court of law.

MACRS Modified Accelerated Cost Recovery System. The mandatory system for depreciating most business property.

marketing Anticipating and satisfying the wants and needs of a potential customer group.

material participation participation in a business on a regular, continuous, and substantial basis. The IRS has seven tests for material participation. See also **passive activity.**

nerving Cutting a nerve to eliminate the sensation of pain, usually one or both posterior digital nerves serving the heel area of the foot.

net income See **profit.**

notice Formal announcement or warning of intent to change or end an agreement, relation, or contract by a certain time.

owner A person who has possession of and title to property.

passive activity Any business activity in which the owner does not materially participate, or is not involved to a sufficient extent in the workings of the business.

perfecting To take some action that brings the lien or security interest to completion.

premium, insurance Amount paid or charged on a regular basis for insurance coverage.

premium, incentive Reward or prize given to induce a customer to buy or do something.

profit Amount of income after expenses are deducted. Also called net income.

profit motive Intention to make a profit in a business.

projections Forecasts of estimated financial conditions.

property Any item a person or business has a right to posses, use, and dispose of; may or may not have sale or exchange value.

pursuant Following upon; in accordance, or compliance with.

release Statement signed by a participant affirming that he or she is aware of the risks involved in an activity and will not hold the facility responsible for damage or injury.

rider Addition or amendment to a contract or policy.

season, stallion Right to breed a specific stallion to a mare.

section 179 deduction Electing to treat all or part of the cost of certain qualifying business property as an ordinary expense rather than a capital expenditure.

signalment form Form showing the outline of a horse from different viewpoints, on which any horse's individual markings may be filled in for identification.

stableman's lien A right to the property of someone else as security toward the payment of a legitimate indebtedness.

statutory agent Attorney who is the legal representation of a corporation.

straight line method An elected method of depreciation under MACRS, providing equal yearly deductions throughout the recovery period.

tax basis The cost of business property, plus additions or improvements, less depreciation.

title Right to ownership; evidence of right of ownership; a deed.

tort A civil wrong against the person or property of another, for which legal action for damages may be brought.

ultrasound examination To view with ultrasound, an imaging technique in which deep structures of the body are visualized by recording the reflections (echoes) of ultrasonic waves directed into the tissues.

URL Web site address.

uterine biopsy Removal and examination of a small piece of the lining of the uterus to test its health.

variable Factors that can change or vary depending on circumstance or on each other.

venue Locality in which an event takes place or cause of action occurs.

waiver Voluntarily relinquishing a right, claim, or privilege; a formal, written statement of such relinquishment.

warranty Guarantee or assurance, express or implied, of one or more factors to be considered a condition of sale, especially a seller's assurance to a buyer that a horse is as it is represented.

zoning To divide a city into areas based on specific restrictions on types of construction, as into agricultural, residential, and commercial zones.

Index